Robert Nozick

Robert Nozick is one of the most creative philosophical voices of the last thirty years. His most famous book, *Anarchy, State, and Utopia* (1974), presents the classic defense of the libertarian view that only a minimal state is just. That book has ignited debate and controversy among political theorists since its first appearance. However, Nozick also has made significant contributions in later publications to areas such as rational choice theory, ethics, epistemology, and philosophy of mind.

This volume contains contributions by a distinguished roster of philosophers who treat the full range of Nozick's work. Outside philosophy the book will be of particular interest to professionals and students in political science, law, economics, sociology, and psychology.

David Schmidtz is Professor of Philosophy and Economics at the University of Arizona.

Contemporary Philosophy in Focus

Contemporary Philosophy in Focus will offer a series of introductory volumes to many of the dominant philosophical thinkers of the current age. Each volume will consist of newly commissioned essays that cover major contributions of a preeminent philosopher in a systematic and accessible manner. Comparable in scope and rationale to the highly successful series **Cambridge Companions to Philosophy**, the volumes will not presuppose that readers are already intimately familiar with the details of each philosopher's work. They will thus combine exposition and critical analysis in a manner that will appeal both to students of philosophy as well as to professionals and students across the humanities and social sciences.

FORTHCOMING VOLUMES:

Stanley Cavell edited by Richard Eldridge
Donald Davidson edited by Kirk Ludwig
Daniel Dennett edited by Andrew Brook and Don Ross
Ronald Dworkin edited by Arthur Ripstein
Jerry Fodor edited by Tim Crane
Thomas Kuhn edited by Thomas Nickles
Alasdair MacIntyre edited by Mark C. Murphy
Hilary Putnam edited by Yemina Ben-Menahem
Richard Rorty edited by Charles Guignon and David Hiley
John Searle edited by Barry Smith
Charles Taylor edited by Ruth Abbey
Bernard Williams edited by Alan Thomas

Robert Nozick

Edited by

DAVID SCHMIDTZ
University of Arizona

CAMBRIDGE
UNIVERSITY PRESS

PUBLISHED BY THE PRESS SYNDICATE OF THE UNIVERSITY OF CAMBRIDGE
The Pitt Building, Trumpington Street, Cambridge, United Kingdom

CAMBRIDGE UNIVERSITY PRESS
The Edinburgh Building, Cambridge CB2 2RU, UK
40 West 20th Street, New York, NY 10011-4211, USA
10 Stamford Road, Oakleigh, VIC 3166, Australia
Ruiz de Alarcón 13, 28014 Madrid, Spain
Dock House, The Waterfront, Cape Town 8001, South Africa

http://www.cambridge.org

© Cambridge University Press 2002

First published 2002

Printed in the United States of America

Typefaces Janson Text 10/13 pt. and ITC Officina Sans   *System* LaTeX 2$_\varepsilon$ [TB]

A catalog record for this book is available from the British Library.

Library of Congress Cataloging in Publication Data
Robert Nozick / edited by David Schmidtz.
    p.   cm. – (Contemporary philosophy in focus)
    Includes bibliographical references and index.
    ISBN 0-521-78226-0 – ISBN 0-521-00671-6 (pbk.)
1. Nozick, Robert.   I. Schmidtz, David.   II. Series.
B945.N684 R63   2001
191–dc21   2001035263

ISBN 0 521 78226 0 hardback
ISBN 0 521 00671 6 paperback

40497

Contents

Abbreviations

ASU	*Anarchy, State, and Utopia*
EL	*The Examined Life*
NR	*The Nature of Rationality*
PE	*Philosophical Explanations*
SP	*Socratic Puzzles*

Contributors

MICHAEL E. BRATMAN is Durfee Professor in the School of Humanities and Sciences and Professor of Philosophy at Stanford University. He is author of *Intention, Plans, and Practical Reason* (Harvard, 1987; reissued by CSLI Publications, 1999), *Faces of Intention: Selected Essays on Intention and Agency* (Cambridge, 1999), and various articles in the philosophy of action and related fields.

GERALD F. GAUS is Professor of Philosophy at Tulane University and member of The Murphy Institute of Political Economy. He is author of *Political Concepts and Political Theories* (Westview, 2000), *Social Philosophy* (M. E. Sharpe, 1999), *Justificatory Liberalism: An Essay On Epistemology and Political Theory* (Oxford, 1996), *Value and Justification: The Foundations of Liberal Theory* (Cambridge, 1990), and *The Modern Liberal Theory of Man* (St. Martin's Press, 1983). He and Chandran Kukathas are editing the *Handbook of Political Theory* (Sage, forthcoming).

LOREN E. LOMASKY is Professor of Philosophy at Bowling Green State University. He is author of *Persons, Rights, and the Moral Community* (Oxford, 1987) and, with Geoffrey Berman, *Democracy and Decision: The Pure Theory of Electoral Preference* (Cambridge, 1993).

DAVID MILLER is Official Fellow in Social and Political Theory, Nuffield College, Oxford. Recent publications include *On Nationality* (Clarendon, 1995), *Pluralism, Justice and Equality* (coeditor, with Michael Walzer, Oxford, 1995), *Principles of Social Justice* (Harvard, 1999), *Citizenship and National Identity* (Polity, 2000), and *Boundaries and Justice* (coeditor, with Sohail Hashmi, Princeton, 2001).

ELIJAH MILLGRAM is Associate Professor and E. E. Ericksen Professor of Philosophy at the University of Utah. He is the author of *Practical Induction* (Harvard, 1997) and editor of *Varieties of Practical Reasoning* (MIT, in press).

PHILIP PETTIT is Professor of Social and Political Theory at the Research School of Social Sciences, Australian National University, and a regular Visiting Professor of Philosophy at Columbia University. He is author of several books, including *Republicanism: A Theory of Freedom and Government* (Oxford, 1997), *Three Methods of Ethics* (Routledge, 1977, with M. Baron and M. Slote), *The Common Mind: An Essay on Psychology, Society, and Politics* (Oxford, 1993), and *Theory of Freedom* (Oxford, 2001).

JOHN T. SANDERS is Professor of Philosophy at the Rochester Institute of Technology. He is the author of *The Ethical Argument Against Government* (University Press of America, 1980), coeditor of volumes 1–5 of *The Philosopher's Annual*, of *For and Against the State: New Philosophical Readings* (Rowman and Littlefield, 1996), and of *Debating the State of Philosophy: Habermas, Rorty, and Kolakowski* (Praeger, 1996).

DAVID SCHMIDTZ is Professor of Philosophy and joint Professor of Economics at the University of Arizona. He is coauthor (with Robert Goodin) of *Social Welfare and Individual Responsibility* (Cambridge, 1998), author of *Rational Choice and Moral Agency* (Princeton, 1995), and coeditor (with Elizabeth Willott) of *Environmental Ethics: What Really Matters, What Really Works* (Oxford, 2002). He currently is working on a book on *The Elements of Justice*.

MICHAEL WILLIAMS is Professor of Philosophy at the Johns Hopkins University. He has also taught at Northwestern, the University of Maryland, and Yale. He is the author of *Groundless Belief* (Blackwell, 1977), *Unnatural Doubts* (Blackwell, 1991), and *Problems of Knowledge* (Oxford, 2001).

1 | Introductions

DAVID SCHMIDTZ

Robert Nozick's brilliance is nowhere more apparent than in the way he introduces his books. One theme runs through his introductory essays: a plea for noncoercive, contemplative, conversational, yet analytical, philosophy. In his first book, Nozick writes,

> One view about how to write a philosophy book holds that an author should think through all of the details of the view he presents, and its problems, polishing and refining his view to present to the world a finished, complete, and elegant whole. This is not my view. . . . There is room for words on subjects other than last words. Indeed, the usual manner of presenting philosophical work puzzles me. Works of philosophy are written as though their authors believe them to be the absolutely final word on their subject. (ASU, xii)

What disturbs Nozick is an unarticulated consensus that the only way to do good philosophy is to present our work in a way that fundamentally distorts it. In truth, "Having thought long and hard about the view he proposes, a philosopher has a reasonably good idea about its weak points; the places where great intellectual weight is placed upon something perhaps too fragile to bear it, the places where the unraveling of the view might begin, the unprobed assumptions he feels uneasy about" (ASU, xii). When the time arrives to present our work, however, it comes out like this:

> One form of philosophical activity feels like pushing and shoving things into some fixed perimeter of specified shape. All those things are lying out there, and they must be fit in. You push and shove the material into the rigid area getting it into the boundary on one side, and it bulges out on another. You run around and press in the protruding bulge, producing yet another in another place. So you push and shove and clip off corners from the things so they'll fit and you press in until finally almost everything sits unstably more or less in there; what doesn't gets heaved *far* away so that it won't be noticed. (ASU, xiii)

1

Why would we do such a thing? Nozick is not sure. "The reticence of philosophers about the weaknesses they perceive in their own views is not, I think, simply a question of philosophical honesty and integrity, though it is that or at least becomes that when brought to consciousness. The reticence is connected with philosophers' purposes in formulating views. Why do they strive to force everything to fit into that one fixed perimeter?" (ASU, xiii). Perhaps there is no reason. We are that sort of creature, so we do that sort of philosophy. Nozick, though, aspires to transcend that way of doing things.

> Philosophers often seek to deduce their total view from a few basic prin-
> ciples . . . one brick is piled upon another to produce a tall philosophical
> tower, one brick wide. . . . Instead of the tottering tower, I suggest that our
> model be the Parthenon. First we emplace our separate philosophical in-
> sights, column by column; afterwards, we unite and unify them under an
> overarching roof of general principles or themes. When the philosophical
> structure crumbles somewhat, as we should expect on inductive grounds,
> something of interest and beauty remains standing. Still preserved are some
> insights, the separate columns, some balanced relations, and the wistful look
> of a grander unity eroded by misfortunes or natural processes. (PE, 3)

Nozick would like to see philosophical work, especially his own, as a stage in an ongoing process of maturation. "The goal is getting to a place worth being, even though the investigation may change and deepen the idea of worth" (PE, 2). Note: the investigation *may* deepen our idea of worth. How sad if it does not. How sad if it remains true even of mature professional philosophers that, with only minor adjustments, "we are directed through life by the not fully mature picture of the world we formed in adolescence or young adulthood" (EL, 11).

NONCOERCIVE PHILOSOPHY

We might even wonder whether academic training limits rather than enhances our ability to avoid having our later thoughts be deformed and trun-
cated by earlier ones. Nozick says, "Philosophical training molds arguers:
it trains people to produce arguments and (this is part of the arguing) to
criticize and evaluate them. . . . Children think an argument involves raised
voices, anger, negative emotion. To argue with someone is to attempt to
push him around verbally. But a philosophical argument isn't like that – is
it?" (PE, 4). Nozick answers his own question by saying that, often enough,
it is very much like that.

A philosophical argument is an attempt to get someone to believe something, whether he wants to believe it or not. A successful philosophical argument, a strong argument, *forces* someone to a belief. Though philosophy is carried on as a coercive activity, the penalty philosophers wield is, after all, rather weak. If the other person is willing to bear the label of "irrational" or "having the worse arguments," he can skip away happily maintaining his previous belief. ... Wouldn't it be better if philosophical arguments left the person no possible answer at all, reducing him to impotent silence? Even then, he might sit there silently, smiling, Buddhalike. Perhaps philosophers need arguments so powerful they set up reverberations in the brain: if the person refuses to accept the conclusion, he *dies*. (PE, 4)

There is a grain of truth in the caricature, and Nozick probably has done more than anyone to draw our attention to it. We are taught to have a rather odd picture of what good philosophy must look like. Perhaps because of this, as Nozick says in his next book, "There are very few books that set out what a mature person can believe" (EL, 15).

What then should we expect from Nozick? What is his alternative? Will he demonstrate a different way of doing philosophy, such that his demonstration convinces us, making us say, "Yes! That's how you do it!" Probably not. As Nozick says, "My thoughts do not aim for your assent – just place them alongside your own reflections for a while" (EL, 15).

To understand Nozick, we need to understand that when he says he is not aiming for your assent, he really means it. Such passages are charming. They are, in a word, disarming. But they are more than that. They are not merely an argumentative ploy. Nozickian disarmament is a genuine methodological shift.

Are we supposed to be converted to Nozick's nonadversarial approach? Probably not. Again, when Nozick says his thoughts do not aim for our assent, *he really means it*, even when his thoughts concern philosophical method. Probably the most adult way of responding to Nozick's method would be simply to mull it over, to judge it to be worth considering, worth setting alongside our own for a while. Better to come away from the exercise with a more mature version of our own approach than to try to adopt Nozick's. It would be more serious – more adult – for us to reflect for a while on the idea of what a mature person can believe, and to reflect on what it would be like to read or to write a book like that.

Nozick stresses that, "it is not quite *positions* I wish to present here" (EL, 17). So, what is the alternative? One gathers that Nozick is, to some degree, simply trying to explain how life looks to him, as one rational mind to another. Nozick wishes he could avoid presenting us with conclusions frozen in time, detached from the intellectual journey that leads to and from those provisional conclusions. And if that cannot be avoided when publishing a book, he at least can ask readers to be mindful of the relation between thought and printed page. It is a bit like the relation between a moving object and a photograph thereof.

Nozick wants us to see the "finished" product as a process – or part of a process – of mulling. He wants us to be aware of the scurrying around he did, trying to hide the leaks and bulges. Beyond that, Nozick wants to scurry a bit less. He does not want us to see his work as sloppy, but he does not want us to see it *merely* as a polished final product, either. He wants us to see it as an invitation to keep him company for a while in an ongoing journey. He wants us to accept this invitation, and to accept it in a certain spirit. His purpose is not to show us he is already at *the* destination. He is a fellow traveler, not a mentor. When we finish reading him, Nozick wants us to have ideas we did not have when we first sat down with him. The ideas will be our ideas, though, not Nozick's, and that is how Nozick wants it. He is not trying to force us to choose between adopting his ideas and having a brain hemorrhage.

THE PROBLEM WITH BEING INFLUENTIAL

As Elijah Millgram suggests (in this volume), Nozick seems never to have wanted to cultivate disciples. Nozick is sufficiently concerned about the more subtle coercion latent in philosophical mentorship and scholarship to raise the topic again in *Socratic Puzzles*. There, he says,

> [w]hen you approach a topic through the route of someone's theories, that person's mode of structuring the issues limits how far you can stray and how much you can discover. You think within their "problematic." Psychologists have investigated a phenomenon they call "anchoring and adjustment." For example, a subject is asked to estimate a person's height by estimating how far that height deviates from a fixed benchmark – from, say, five feet tall. If he thinks the person is five foot seven, he says "plus seven inches." The interesting fact is that the expressed estimates of a person's height will differ, depending on the fixed benchmark. In theory, that particular benchmark should make no difference. If it is six feet instead of five feet, then the height of someone who is five foot seven can be said to deviate by "minus five inches" from that taller benchmark. Nevertheless, the estimate of a

given person's height by a group of judges who start with the five-foot benchmark will be less than the estimate by a group of judges who start with the benchmark of six feet. . . . It is similar, I think, when you approach a topic through the thought of another. Even when your own conclusions do deviate, they are "gravitationally" pulled toward those of your source. (SP, 8–9)

Nozick's remark explicitly concerns working on historical figures, but of course we also are subject to the undue influence of people around us: classmates, teachers, and so on. Less obviously, teachers who become gurus are reciprocally subject to the undue influence of their disciples. As disciples compete for admission to the teacher's innermost circle by becoming ever more adept at treating the teacher's work as sacred text, the teacher becomes incapacitated, losing touch with the habit of assessing and reassessing earlier thoughts in a thoroughly critical way. Part of the problem with being unduly influenced by disciples, then, is that it makes us prone to undue influence by our own earlier selves. Potentially, philosophical argument is not merely coercive, but self-coercive. It is not only other people who exert gravitational pull on us. We pull ourselves as well.

In his first book, Nozick admits, "I do not welcome the fact that most people I know and respect disagree with me" (ASU, x). Nozick says (in SP), however, his reason for not defending the earlier work against the sometimes vicious commentary it generated was that he did not want defensiveness to define and constrain his future thought. He wanted to be more than an arguer. We may conjecture that "gravitational pull" is worse in political theory than in other areas. We do not simply *judge* Nozick's political views; instead, we judge them by judging how they deviate from our benchmark. And if we are unduly influenced by benchmarks even when judging something as simple as a person's height, how much worse must it be when we judge matters political? How much worse is the distortion when judging views like Nozick's, so very distant from the benchmarks of the academic mainstream?

So, we may worry about the influence particular philosophers have on us. We also may worry about being unduly constrained by our own earlier thinking. A further thought: Perhaps these worries connect. Worrying about the influence of our earlier thinking presumably is bound up with worrying that our earlier thinking was too much a product of those we studied, and studied with.

What about our students? Will they be themselves?

THE WORK AT HAND

Especially given Nozick's wish to have his work regarded as part of an ongoing journey rather than as his final word, it is easy to see why he would find it "disconcerting to be known primarily for an early work" (SP, 1). But he is, after all, known primarily for that work, and several of this volume's authors accordingly choose to focus on it. David Miller ponders Anarchy, John T. Sanders confronts the State, and Loren Lomasky explores Utopia. Miller explains what we can (and what we cannot) learn from the exercise of imagining a state spontaneously emerging from a hypothetical starting point. Sanders and Lomasky each consider the understated but crucial role that personal projects play in making life meaningful. To Lomasky, this role underscores the role that toleration must play in any utopia worthy of our aspiration. To Sanders, this role helps to explain why we have reason to respect property rights. Philip Pettit likewise sees meaningful personal projects as crucial but comes to different conclusions about the upshot for Nozick's theory of rights.

Gerald Gaus, like Sanders, Lomasky, and Pettit in their own ways, explores the relation between principles, goals, and (symbolic) meanings. Gaus sees that relation as pivotal to the theory of rationality presented in Nozick's later work, and wonders how well the later theory of rationality fits with the earlier theory of justice.

In the remaining essays, Michael Williams and Michael Bratman reflect on two of the most enduring contributions of Nozick's second book – his theories of knowledge and of free will, respectively. (Bratman also relates his discussion of free will's importance to Nozick's "closest continuer" theory of personal identity.) Elijah Millgram offers a radical alternative to interpreting Nozick's third book as the presentation of a theory. My essay on the meaning of life is a self-conscious tribute to Nozick, not only in terms of its topic but in terms of its method as well.

I will say no more, for these essays speak for themselves better than I could speak on their behalf. Perfunctory summary paragraphs cannot do them justice. Instead, this essay focuses on the larger picture. I use these pages to frame the essays within a general reflection on Nozick's philosophical method, hoping readers will find that this serves not only the immediate goal of understanding this volume but also the larger goal of understanding Nozick.

Regarding the approach of these essays, Nozick himself says he believes philosophers of the past would have preferred having their writing mined for insights rather than "having their views meticulously and sympathetically stated in all parts and relations. The respect *they* paid their predecessors was philosophy, not scholarship" (PE, 8). The essays collected here take that thought seriously. We intend them to help readers understand Nozick but, to a large degree, the homage we pay is via philosophical engagement rather than meticulous reconstruction.

LATER WORKS

Do Nozick's later books continue the same project of distancing himself from coercive philosophy? I am tempted to push and shove the leaks and bulges into a shape such that the result appears to support a resounding Yes. The truth: while the theme is still there, it is more implicit. Perhaps Nozick felt he had already said enough about his methodological aspirations.

Nozick says rationality "is a crucial component of the self-image of the human species" (NR, xii). However,

> Evolutionary theory makes it possible to see rationality as one among other animal traits, an evolutionary adaptation with a delimited purpose and function. This perspective can yield important consequences for philosophy.... If rationality is an evolutionary adaptation with a delimited purpose and function, designed to work in conjunction with other stable facts that it takes for granted and builds upon, but if philosophy is an attempt of unlimited scope to apply reason and to justify rationally every belief and assumption, then we can understand why many of philosophy's traditional problems have turned out to be intractable and resistant to rational resolution. These problems may result from attempts to extend rationality beyond its delimited evolutionary function. (NR, xii)

This discussion seems in keeping with Nozick's earlier explorations of the prospects for a more humanly engaging philosophical method. Nozick remains a firm believer in the power of reason for all that, however, and appears in more combative mode when he goes on to say,

> In recent years, rationality has been an object of particular criticism. The claim has been put forth that rationality is *biased* because it is a class-based or male or Western or whatever notion. Yet it is part of rationality to be intent on noticing biases, including its own, and controlling and correcting these. (Might the attempt to correct for biases itself be a bias? But if that is a *criticism*, from what quarter does it come? Is there a view that holds that bias is bad but that correcting it is bad too? ...) Charging a bias in existing standards does not show that one exists.... It is not sufficient merely to say

that we (all) see the world through our conceptual schemes. The question is: in what specific ways, and by what exact mechanisms, do our particular conceptual schemes and standards distort? (NR, xii–xiii)

Another possibly discordant note appears in *Socratic Puzzles*, when Nozick declares that he thinks of Socrates as "the philosopher" (SP, 2). Why would this note be discordant? My thought: Is not Socrates more or less the patriarch of coercive philosophy? Is it not from Socrates, first and above all, that we learn how admirable it is, how much fun it is, to beat up our interlocutors, proving they are our intellectual inferiors? Is this not precisely the style that Nozick has so eloquently rejected as a model for his own work?

Of course, this is not at all what Nozick had in mind. In the title essay of *Socratic Puzzles*, Nozick indicates that what impresses him is Socrates' unflinching willingness to admit what he does not know and to embrace philosophy all the same, confident there is something worthwhile to be learned, even while suspecting that what we learn will never be the final word. Nozick admires Socrates because, unique among philosophers, Nozick says, Socrates teaches with his *person*. We learn what beauty of soul is, "not by being presented with an explicit theory but by encountering Socrates" (SP, 155). See Millgram's essay for a discussion of philosophy as the presentation of a persona.

CONCLUSIONS

Throughout all of his work, Nozick's objective is to produce more literally an examined life than a debate-tested proposition. In all of his introductions, observe the probing, tentative quality of the thoughts expressed. Nozick does not try to win debates. Instead of trying to stop the conversation, Nozick tries to raise the level of the conversation. Those who read him as an adversary are already misreading him before we even begin to interpret the content. Nozick does not write for adversaries.

> Philosophy without arguments, in one mode, would guide someone to a view. . . . At no point is the person forced to accept anything. He moves along gently, exploring his own and the author's thoughts. He explores together with the author, moving only where he is ready to; then he stops. Perhaps, at a later time mulling it over or in a second reading, he will move further. . . . Such a book could not convince everybody of what it says – it wouldn't try. (PE, 7)

With characteristically reflective humility, though, Nozick cautions that his own work does not live up to this ideal, "even though I would like to present a philosophical view in this way, author and reader traveling together, each continually spurting in front of the other. Not only do I lack the art to do this, I do not yet have a philosophical view that flows so deeply and naturally" (PE, 7). Perhaps. Yet, Nozick's introductions undeniably provide a glimpse of what attaining this ideal would be like. They are, simply, works of art.

2 | The Justification of Political Authority[1]

DAVID MILLER

Robert Nozick's *Anarchy, State, and Utopia* (ASU) is a bold and imaginative attempt to show that the minimal state, and nothing beyond the minimal state, can be morally justified. An institution is a state if it claims, and to a large extent enjoys, a monopoly on the use of force in a given geographical territory; it is a minimal state if it restricts its activities to protecting the rights of people living in that territory and punishing those who violate them, the rights in question being the traditional Lockean rights to life, liberty, and property. Nozick develops his argument in three stages, corresponding to the three parts of ASU. In the first, he sets out to show that the minimal state is justified, by demonstrating that it could arise by morally legitimate means from a state of nature in which no form of political authority existed. In the second part, he argues that states that do more than the minimal state does – for instance, redistribute resources between their citizens, supply public goods by means of compulsory taxation, or force citizens to contribute to schemes of social security – are not justified. And in the third part, which is as it were a pendant to the other two, he paints a picture of life under the minimal state as constituting a kind of utopia, unlike other utopias by virtue of the fact that it can encompass a huge variety of different ways of life.

Not surprisingly, most of the critical attention lavished on Nozick since the publication of ASU in 1974 has been directed against the book's second part. For here Nozick directly confronts the received wisdom of the age on the proper functions of the state, as well as almost the entire corpus of twentieth-century political thought, which has sought to defend some version of the regulatory or welfare state, if not positions well to the left of this.[2] Nozick's central argument is that state activities beyond the minimum must necessarily violate the fundamental rights of their citizens. A central point of contention has been whether the Lockean rights defended by Nozick have either the weight or the determinacy to trump the ethical values appealed to by defenders of the more-than-minimal state, such as social justice, protection against poverty, or the public interest.

Part I, by contrast, has been much less discussed. I think there are two reasons for this. The first is that the argument of this part is directed chiefly against individualist anarchists who hold that rights can be adequately safeguarded by voluntary means, without recourse to an institution that insists that it, and it alone, is entitled to protect rights and punish offenders in the relevant geographical area. But anarchists are relatively thin on the ground; most readers will be inclined to grant Nozick's defense of the minimal state without further ado, and focus their critical gaze on his forceful arguments against Rawls and other defenders of the redistributive state. The second reason is that Nozick's reasoning is complex and at times difficult to follow. He has to show why an embryonic state (he calls it "the dominant protective agency") is justified in preventing individuals who want to defend and enforce their own rights for themselves from doing so. Showing this involves developing an argument about what it is justifiable to do by way of response to other people's risky behavior that, as we shall see later, is far from straightforward. Impatient readers head quickly toward the easier terrain of Part II.

I intend in this chapter to take the argument of Part I seriously, not because I share Nozick's intention to justify the minimal state and nothing beyond this, but because I believe there is much to learn from the failure (as I shall claim) of that argument. The justification of political authority remains a pressing concern. Although most of us have come to take the state for granted, and accept, grudgingly or willingly, the enormous impact that it has on our lives, there are siren voices telling us that we can learn to live without it – for instance, that in a global economy, we shall be able to obtain the services that the state now provides from a variety of different sources – personal protection from one supplier, healthcare insurance from another, transport facilities from a third, and so forth – thus rendering the state in its present form redundant.[3] Democratic states offer their citizens a voice in deciding who in particular shall be entrusted with the reins of government, but they do not offer any choice as far as the institution of the state itself is concerned. Individuals may emigrate but, so long as they remain in the territory of the state, they must accept its authority – its right to enforce its laws coercively, to regulate the use of property, to tax citizens for social purposes, and so forth. Clearly we need some story to explain why such an imposition is justified. Nozick's account rests on the slenderest basis: 'individuals have rights, and there are things no person or group may do to them (without violating their rights)' (ASU, ix). From this simple premise, he endeavors to demonstrate the legitimacy of the minimal state. I shall show that at key points in the argument Nozick is forced to appeal to considerations that are excluded by his own parsimonious moral framework. His failure in this respect helps us to see how a better justification of political authority can be developed.

A SKETCH OF NOZICK'S ARGUMENT

Following a time-honored tradition, Nozick's argument begins by imagining people placed in a state of nature, without political authority.[4] They are equipped with rights – to bodily integrity, to freedom of movement and expression, to justly acquired property, and so forth. They are justified in defending these rights against aggressors, in punishing rights-violations, and in extracting compensation from those who take or damage what is rightfully theirs. They are also permitted to exchange or transfer their rights with others who agree to the exchange or transfer. Among the rights that may be transferred is the right to enforce one's own rights and to punish those who violate them. Thus, I may empower another to act on my behalf if, say, I have been injured or some property of mine has been stolen. Groups of individuals may band together to form mutual protection associations so that they are better able to defend their rights. However, Nozick argues, because there are advantages in having a division of labor, we may expect specialized protective agencies to emerge that offer, for a fee, to provide a complete rights-enforcement service to their clients. Because rights-enforcement can be a difficult and risky business, it is reasonable to assume that most people would want to sign up with one of these protective agencies. Nozick also assumes that the agencies will by and large act rightfully: they will only pursue valid claims on behalf of their clients, they will use reasonable procedures to establish who is guilty of violating their clients' rights and who is not, they will punish only in proportion to the seriousness of the offence, and so forth. Although at first sight we may think that people would have an incentive to sign up with rogue agencies who would pursue their clients' interests regardless of such constraints, Nozick argues that there are significant disadvantages attached to being known as a client of such an agency (see ASU, 17)

Because there are advantages in being a client of a large and powerful agency, Nozick believes that market forces will operate to bring it about that, in any geographical region, there will eventually be just one dominant protective agency.[5] This agency will provide protective services to most of the people inhabiting that area. There also will be "independents," however, who insist on protecting their own rights, including taking action on occasion against the agency's clients. In order to show how a dominant agency can transform itself into a state, exercising a monopoly over rights-enforcement and punishment in the area in question, Nozick has to prove that it can justifiably prohibit the independents from taking action against its clients. He does this by arguing that people have a right not to be subjected to unreliable rights-enforcement procedures, procedures that put them at undue risk of being found at fault (and therefore punished) when they are not in fact so. The dominant agency, exercising this right on behalf of its clients, will signal which enforcement procedures it deems to be reliable, and will then prevent independents from using procedures not on the approved list against its clients. It now has a de facto monopoly on enforcement – not in the sense that it and it alone engages in the activity of enforcing rights, but in the sense that it and it alone is in a position to decide which procedures shall and shall not be used to enforce rights and impose punishment.[6]

This de facto monopoly permits us, Nozick says, to describe the dominant agency as an "ultraminimal state." It becomes a minimal state when it undertakes to provide protective services to those independents whom it has prohibited from using their own enforcement procedures, even if the independents in question are not in a position to pay its normal fee. It is morally obliged to do this by way of compensation. The independents' actions imposed risks, and may properly be prohibited, but because the prohibition is costly for the independents (who now have no way of defending their rights when these are infringed by one of the agency's clients), compensation is due. The most obvious way for the agency to provide compensation is for it to offer its own services to the independents, charging them only what it would otherwise have cost them to undertake self-help enforcement. So now the dominant agency is in the position of supplying rights-protection to *everyone* living in its domain, and this, Nozick argues, is sufficient to render it a minimal state proper.

What Nozick claims to have shown, then, is that a minimal state would arise from a prepolitical state of nature by purely voluntary means. A dominant protective agency would arise simply because individuals had pursued their interest in having the best form of rights protection available, and it would become a minimal state because it recognized that it had to compensate those would-be independents for denying them the right to use their own enforcement procedures on its clients. To cite his own summing up:

> We have discharged our task of explaining how a state would arise from a
> state of nature without anyone's rights being violated. The moral objections

of the individualist anarchist to the minimal state are overcome. It is not an unjust imposition of a monopoly; the *de facto* monopoly grows by an invisible-hand process and *by morally permissible means*, without anyone's rights being violated and without any claims being made to a special right that others do not possess. And requiring the clients of the *de facto* monopoly to pay for the protection of those they prohibit from self-help enforcement against them, far from being immoral, is morally required by the principle of compensation. . . . (ASU, 114–15)

WHAT DOES THE ARGUMENT ESTABLISH?

As the passage I have just quoted suggests, Nozick takes himself to have offered an *invisible hand* explanation of the emergence of the minimal state. An invisible hand explanation is one that explains some collective outcome in terms of the actions of many individual agents, none of whom intended to produce that outcome in particular but who interacted in such a way that the collective outcome necessarily arose. In the present case, no one in Nozick's story need *intend* to create a state in order for one to arise; one protective agency becomes dominant because individuals choose to sign up with the agency that already provides the best protection, and the transition from ultraminimal to minimal state occurs because those who control the agency act on their obligation to compensate independents, not because they want their agency to qualify as a minimal state. Nozick regards it as a point in favor of his explanation that it takes this form (he says of invisible hand explanations generally that they have a "specially satisfying quality" [p. 18]). But here we need to draw a distinction between invisible hand stories that are *purely explanatory*, and those that are *justificatory* as well.

An invisible hand explanation might simply aim to explain how a certain patterned outcome arose, without in any way trying to justify that outcome. Indeed the outcome might be one that most or all of those involved in its genesis would deplore. For instance, we can explain patterns of traffic congestion by showing how individual drivers, seeking the quickest and most direct routes to their several destinations in ignorance of how other drivers will behave, converge on roads that lack the necessary carrying capacity. Or to borrow one of Nozick's own examples, we might explain (unwanted) patterns of extreme residential segregation in terms of the desire of members of ethnic groups to live in areas in which they formed a bare majority. Here, the fact that the outcome arose by an invisible hand mechanism does nothing to justify it – rather the reverse, for it shows how uncoordinated individual behavior may produce outcomes that are both unintended and unwanted.[7]

But in other cases, an invisible hand explanation can also serve as a justification, and this applies to Nozick's theory of the minimal state.[8] The story Nozick tells is meant not only to explain how a minimal state might emerge out of a state of nature but, contra the individualist anarchist, to justify the state once it has arisen.[9] So under what conditions can invisible hand explanations also serve as justifications? Two conditions are strictly necessary. The first is that the upshot of the invisible hand process should have positive value, in the sense that it represents an improvement over the preexisting state of the world (judged by some criterion). The second is that the activities coordinated by the invisible hand are themselves morally legitimate, so that by allowing it to operate no procedural injustice is perpetrated. A third condition is perhaps not strictly necessary, but it certainly adds to the justificatory force of an invisible hand story. This is that the outcome in question could either not be produced at all apart from the invisible hand process, or at least is best produced by means of it. If that same outcome could be produced more easily and directly in another way, then it is at the very least unclear what justificatory force the invisible hand explanation adds.[10]

As the quotation at the end of the last section suggests, Nozick directs almost all of his attention to the second of these conditions. He is preoccupied with the question "Could a minimal state arise out of anarchy by morally permissible means?" He devotes much less energy to showing that the emergence of the state represents an improvement on a state of nature in which individuals either defend their own rights, or contract with protective agencies to carry this out on their own behalf, with no agency achieving a position of dominance.[11] And he says very little about why a legitimate state could only arise in the way that he describes, or why its arising in that way would be superior to other possible modes of emergence, such as the social contract favored by many writers in the tradition of political philosophy with which he identifies himself. Let me take each of these points in turn.

How can Nozick show that the emergence of the state is not only something that might happen, permissibly, but that would be desirable if it did? In particular, what can he say to the anarchist who argues that the state, by exercising a de facto monopoly over the enforcement of individuals' rights, is disadvantaging all of those who would prefer to use their own (legitimate) methods of rights enforcement? Nozick, of course, claims that the minimal state by definition acts in such a way that it offers adequate compensation to those whom it prohibits from enforcing their own rights against its clients. But here what counts as adequate compensation is determined "objectively" and may not correspond to the would-be independent's own evaluation of

the relative merits of the two enforcement procedures on offer; independents may have a number of reasons for preferring to sign up with agencies
other than the dominant one. From their point of view, therefore, when one
agency becomes dominant and introduces prohibition-plus-compensation,
this represents a downward step, not an upward one. Moreover Nozick is
disbarred by his own ethical starting point from arguing that the minimal
state represents an improvement because *on balance* people are better off –
the advantages won by the clients of the dominant agency outweighing the
disadvantages suffered by the would-be independents. An argument of this
kind would directly contravene the anti-utilitarian injunction issued in the
third chapter of ASU, namely that "no moral balancing act can take place
among us; there is no moral outweighing of one of our lives by others so
as to lead to a greater overall social good. There is no justified sacrifice of
some of us for others" (p. 33).

If Nozick were to argue that even would-be independents should find
the minimal state preferable to a state of nature with competing protective
agencies – perhaps on the grounds that the state provides a more certain and
more predictable system of rights enforcement – he would have difficulty
in defending his use of the invisible hand to explain the emergence of such
a state. For it would then become unclear why the state could not arise
by mutual agreement among all the individuals in a prepolitical state of
nature. In other words, he would have to show what was wrong with the
traditional Lockean justification of a social contract, whereby individuals
expressly agree to transfer their enforcement rights to a political community
of which they all become members, and then delegate to a constitutional
government the actual task of rights enforcement.

It is curious that Nozick gives no explicit attention to a Lockean contract
as an alternative, more direct, route from the state of nature to a minimal
state. Perhaps he considers it unlikely that the diverse set of individuals
who inhabit any particular territorial area would all agree to enter such a
contract; perhaps he thinks, in other words, that there are individuals of
whom it is true that they would refuse their explicit consent when asked
to hand over their enforcement rights to the embryonic state but who
nonetheless can justifiably be incorporated into the state once it has come
into existence.[12] Alternatively, perhaps he thinks that the invisible hand
mechanism has special properties, such that a state that arose in the way
that Nozick describes would ipso facto have greater legitimacy than one
that emerged from a Lockean contract.

The second alternative appears implausible. Invisible hand mechanisms
do, in general, enjoy certain advantages: they economize on information

(no one needs to grasp the whole picture in order for the outcome to occur) and also often on moral motivation (self-interest can be turned to public advantage, as in Smith's account of the market). But their corresponding defect is precisely that individual participants cannot determine the overall shape of the outcome even if they should want to. Consider the institutional form of the minimal state – the way that it organizes its rights-protecting functions, the particular procedures that it uses to settle disputes, and so forth. Under a Lockean social contract, the institutional form of the state is decided by majority vote: according to Locke, there must be unanimous agreement to establish the political community in the first place but, once established, the community decides matters by the majority principle, including the powers and composition of the legislature and other specialized branches of government.[13] Lockean contractors, therefore, may not end up with the form of government that each of them individually prefers, but at least the majority's preference will prevail.[14] Nozick's invisible hand, in contrast, makes the outcome path-dependent, in the sense that the protective agency that ends up as dominant is likely to be the one that initially has most success in attracting clients, and this may not be the one that the majority would have preferred if it knew that it had to select one agency as an embryonic state. If agency A gets off to a flying start, either because it runs the best advertising campaign, or because it appeals to those clients who are quickest to see the advantages of a professional protective service, or for whatever reason, other clients may switch to A *not* because they like its organization or the procedures it uses but simply because of the advantages in being a client of the largest agency in town. If A eventually turns into a minimal state, its claim to legitimacy resides solely in the fact that it discharges the functions appropriate to a minimal state; it cannot claim to have been *chosen* by the people it serves, by virtue (for instance) of the superiority of its methods to those of its erstwhile rivals.[15]

The first alternative – the invisible hand beats the social contract because we cannot assume that there will be unanimous agreement to establish a state – runs straight into the problem alluded to already, namely that if the state of nature contains individuals who are hostile to the very idea of setting up a state, whether on grounds of principle or of prudence, it will not be easy to show that the minimal state adequately compensates them for their loss of enforcement rights when it offers them its services free of charge (presumably convinced anarchists would refuse to use the services of an institution that they regard as an anathema, and so they are left without a usable form of defense against the state's clients). I shall return to this question of compensation below. Let us simply conclude for now that Nozick has failed to make good his implicit claim that an invisible hand justification of the state is more satisfying than a contractual justification.

There is one last methodological point that needs to be made here. Both the invisible hand and the social contract theories of the state can be presented *either* as historical *or* as hypothetical accounts of the origin of the state: they can be proposed either as explanations of how existing states actually arose, or as explanations of how states *would* arise from a state of nature, given certain assumptions about human behavior. So we have four possible ways in which the legitimacy of a minimal state might be explained, as follows.

IH1 State S is legitimate because it *arose* from a prepolitical state of nature in morally permissible ways (without anyone intending to create a state).

IH2 State S is legitimate because it *could have arisen* from a prepolitical state of nature in morally permissible ways (without anyone intending to create a state).

SC1 State S is legitimate because it *was* brought into existence by the free agreement of individuals in a prepolitical state of nature.

SC2 State S is legitimate because it *could have been* brought into existence by the free agreement of individuals in a prepolitical state of nature.

Now if we begin by comparing SC1 and SC2 in terms of their justificatory power, we can say that whereas SC2 may be able to justify the general form of an existing minimal state, SC1 goes one better by being able to justify not only the general form but also the particular institutional structure of such a state. Suppose, to use a concrete illustration, that our minimal state takes the form of a constitutional monarchy. A successful historical argument of type SC1 would be able to provide a full justification of this state, by showing that this was the form of state that its present citizens, or perhaps their forebears, had agreed to establish. A hypothetical argument of type SC2, by contrast, would not be able to establish so much. At best, it would be able to show that our state is a member of a class of potentially legitimate states any of which might have been chosen in a prepolitical state of nature. Of course, hypothetical social contract arguments avoid some of the difficulties that attach to historical arguments – primarily perhaps the difficulty in finding *any* state that has a clean contractual origin. My point is that, when applied to existing states, their justificatory power is weaker.[16]

If we ask the same question about IH1 and IH2, then once again we find that the historical version of the invisible hand story has substantially more justificatory weight than the hypothetical version. To say of a state that it arose by voluntary and morally permissible means is not to say everything, given my earlier observations about the ethical limitations of invisible hand arguments, but it is certainly to say something of justificatory significance. But to say of a state that it *could* have arisen by such means is actually to say very little. Because of the contingency that affects invisible hand processes in cases like this – we can't assume much about what individuals' own conceptions of the good will be like, we can't assume much about the kind of protective agencies they will begin by patronizing, and so forth – the range of states that qualify is going to be quite wide. We can probably say with some confidence that tyrannical regimes could not have emerged in rights-respecting ways. But that will still leave many contenders in play, including many possible states that are not minimal in Nozick's sense (to give an invisible hand account of the more-than-minimal state, we need only suppose, for instance, that nearly all individuals are sufficiently risk-averse that they are willing to take out insurance to avoid various forms of destitution; we might imagine protective agencies that offer insurance policies of this kind alongside their rights-protection policies, and run the story forward from there . . .).

In terms of justificatory strength, then we can say that SC1 > SC2 and that IH1 > IH2. If my previous argument about the relative power of social contract and invisible hand arguments is valid, we can also say that SC1 > IH1 and that SC2 > IH2. Whatever view you take about the relative merits of SC2 and IH1 (hypothetical social contract versus historical invisible hand), it is plain that IH2 ends up at the bottom of the heap, as the least powerful (in the sense of least discriminating) of the four justifications of political authority we are considering. It can tell us only that some form of legitimate state is possible – defeating the individualist anarchist who thinks that there can be no such institution – and also perhaps that some existing states are not legitimate – defeating the Hobbesian who believes that all effective states are ipso facto legitimate. It can't achieve anything finer-toothed than this. But IH2 appears to be the form of argument that Nozick favors. His invisible hand explanation is an account of how a certain form of state *might* arise, not an account of how any existing state has actually arisen.[17]

SCRUTINIZING THE ARGUMENT

As we have seen, Nozick's argument in defense of the minimal state comes in two main stages: the emergence of a dominant protective agency in a geographical region, and the transition from dominant protective agency to minimal state, involving the prohibition of "unreliable" enforcement procedures and the provision of the agency's own enforcement procedures by way of compensation. Both stages of the argument deserve critical inspection.

About the first stage of the argument, two questions should be asked: *Would* a dominant agency arise out of the original Lockean state of nature that Nozick describes, and supposing that it did arise, would this be *welcomed* (or deplored) by those who ended up as its clients? As I noted earlier, Nozick's critics argue that the market in protective services is not such that it leads inevitably in the direction of monopoly as Nozick claims. Nozick's justification for this claim is that the value of the service being bought – rights-protection – depends on the strength of the supplying agency relative to its competitors; so it will always be rational to switch to whichever protective agency is strongest in the region you inhabit. But this seems to model rights-protection as conceived by Nozick too closely on "protection" in the protection-racket sense, where it is indeed true that if you are going to pay protection money to anybody, you should pay it to whoever has most muscle in your neighborhood. Coercive power is important to a protective agency only in situations in which interagency disputes cannot be resolved peacefully, by arbitration or negotiation. Nozick makes it clear, however, that a dominant protective agency cannot prevent other agencies from competing for its clients. All it can insist on is that one of the procedures it approves is used when one of its own clients is accused of a rights-violation.[18] Suppose, then, that you are a client of a smaller agency that prudently has decided only to use approved procedures when dealing with clients of the largest agency in its region. The largest agency cannot object if one of its clients is found to be at fault when these procedures are applied.[19] The agency's coercive power is therefore not relevant at this point. The value of its services depends on the speed and efficiency with which it is able to track down rights-violators and oblige them to make restitution or provide compensation to their victims. If your agency scores well by these criteria, what reason do you have to switch your custom to the larger one? Even if, as Nozick says, it is the only agency able to say that it, and it alone, will decide what procedures may be used against its clients, why does this give it a competitive advantage against smaller agencies who are happy to use only these procedures themselves?[20] That being so, the emergence of a single dominant agency – or, equally, the continuation of a dominant agency's dominance – appears to depend entirely on whether there are economies of scale in the provision of protective services such that a larger agency is always better placed than a smaller agency to satisfy its customers, or whether, contrariwise, bureaucratic inefficiency, corporate inertia, and so forth will give small agencies the competitive edge. This is an empirical issue, and in the absence of relevant evidence we must leave it an open question.

A different question is whether, in the event that the market in protective services is such that a dominant agency *does* emerge, this is a development that its clients (and others) would welcome. Clearly, it does not follow from the fact that people individually have reason to choose to sign up with the largest agency in their geographic region that collectively they have reason to applaud its emergence as a dominant agency. Why might they not welcome it? As Nozick himself notes, they might simply fear its power, thinking that an agency that had got itself into a monopoly position would be tempted to use that monopoly of coercive force for ends other than rights protection (ASU, 130–1). More prosaically, they might dislike monopoly for the reason that people generally dislike monopolies in market settings, namely that once the competition is eliminated there is nothing to prevent the agency from raising its prices and/or reducing its services to the detriment of its clients.[21]

If many people oppose the emergence of a single dominant protective agency for one or other of the reasons just mentioned, then they may find themselves trapped in a collective action problem. They cannot prevent their neighbors from signing up with the protective agency of their choice, at least so long as they remain bound by the set of rights that Nozick ascribes to them in the state of nature. As he makes clear, the right people have to enforce their own first-order rights can be transferred to whoever they choose; others cannot prevent the transfer on the grounds that this might lead to a situation where their own rights are put at risk (ASU, 120–30). So if there is indeed some advantage to the individual in being a client of the largest protective agency in the region (pace the considerations outlined above), it may be impossible for individuals acting alone to prevent the emergence of a dominant agency.

We might try to modify Nozick's invisible hand story to reflect this concern. Suppose that people are fearful of the dominant agency's power, and wish to exercise some degree of control over it. We might envisage that, in the state of nature, alongside protective agencies constituted in the standard way as private firms, there also would emerge protective agencies that gave voting rights to their customers in the way that mutual associations such as building societies do now. These would of course have to compete for clients in the same way as private protective agencies, but people who signed up with them would know that, in the event that their chosen agency became dominant, they would be able to influence the way that it behaved (by putting motions to its Annual General Meeting, censuring the Board of Directors and so forth). Anyone who feared the consequences of some agency's having a de facto monopoly of protective services would have reason to sign up with such a mutualized protective agency, at least so long as it offered services for fees comparable with those charged by its private rivals. So if people have the motives that Nozick readily admits they may have (it is difficult for someone with his general outlook to dismiss fear of monopoly power as an irrational aberration) then the agency that emerges as dominant might be one over which its clients collectively exercise rights of control – in other words, a *democratic* state in embryo.[22]

People placed in the state of nature might, in other words, very reasonably take the following view: if specialized protective agencies are going to be formed, then *either* there should be a genuine market in protective services, with competition between agencies ensuring that each agency responds efficiently to its customers' preferences; *or*, if there is to be a single dominant agency, this should be controlled from below by its clients to the same effect. Either of these outcomes is preferable to the one in which a single agency becomes dominant without control from below, checked neither by effective market competition nor by the combined power of its members. If people do take that view, then the particular invisible hand explanation of the state that Nozick offers fails as a justification. It leads to an outcome that is suboptimal compared to either of the two alternatives identified above. Of course, we can vary the story so that one of these better outcomes is achieved, as suggested in the last paragraph. But this merely underlines my earlier claim about the indeterminacy of (hypothetical) invisible hand explanations. There are a number of different arrangements, some involving a dominant protective agency and some not, that might plausibly arise given Nozick's starting point in the state of nature. Nozick's particular story enjoys neither explanatory nor justificatory privilege.

Now let us focus on the second stage of Nozick's argument, the stage that turns the ultraminimal state into the minimal state. Nozick has to show that a dominant protective agency may justifiably prevent independents from using their own rights-enforcement procedures against its clients, so long as it provides them with its own services by way of compensation. Let us grant him his general premise that there are circumstances in which it is justifiable to infringe a person's rights so long as that person is adequately compensated for the infringement; and let us also grant the more specific claim that *risky* behavior – behavior that threatens to violate rights but has not yet done so – may sometimes be prohibited, provided that those who would otherwise engage in it receive proper compensation. The question is whether these premises can be used to justify the incorporation of independents into the minimal state.

According to Nozick, "a person may resist, in self-defense, if others try to apply to him an unreliable or unfair procedure of justice" (ASU, 102). A procedure is unreliable when using it imposes too high a risk that people who are innocent of rights-violations will be found guilty and/or that people who are guilty of such violations will be found innocent; it is also unfair in the former case (and perhaps in the latter, too, if we hold a retributive theory of punishment). But can we assume that there is an objective fact of the matter about a procedure's reliability or unreliability? One problem is cognitive: People may disagree over the factual question whether procedure A or procedure B stands the greater chance of convicting only those who are guilty (for an example, consider the long-standing debate between supporters of adversarial systems of criminal justice and supporters of inquisitorial systems). Another problem is ethical: People may attach different relative values to the chance that an innocent person may be punished and the chance that a guilty person may go unpunished (as Nozick himself points out: see ASU, 97). Because of these problems, it seems unlikely that we can identify one particular procedure of rights-enforcement as objectively the most reliable and fair. Put another way, even if we are justified in ruling out certain procedures (such as those used in the fifteenth and sixteenth centuries to determine whether people should be put to death for witchcraft) as blatantly unfair, we will still be left with a range of procedures over which there will be reasonable disagreement: Different people will have good reasons to prefer different procedures falling within this range.

Nozick's claim about what the dominant protective agency is justified in doing vis-à-vis independents only goes through, however, if we assume that there is an objectively best procedure, and, moreover, that it is this procedure that the agency uses itself.[23] For in that case, an independent who uses a different procedure is imposing an unjustifiable risk on the agency's clients, and no wrong is done to the independent if she is prohibited from using that unreliable procedure and compensated in the way that Nozick suggests. But suppose there is no single such best procedure: the agency sincerely (and with good reason) believes that its procedure is most reliable, and the independent sincerely (and with good reason) believes that her procedure is most reliable. Because of its superior coercive power, the agency will no doubt succeed in forcing the independent to accept its offer of compensation in lieu of self-help enforcement, but why does it act permissibly in so doing? According to Nozick, "the dominant protective association may reserve for itself the right to judge any procedure of justice to be applied to its clients. It may announce, and act on the announcement, that it will punish anyone who uses on one of its clients a procedure that it finds to be unreliable or unfair" (ASU, 101). "May" here means, I take it, "is morally permitted to"; but then everything hangs on the meaning we attach to "finds" in the second quoted sentence. If "finds" means "determines on objective grounds – grounds that every reasonable person must accept," then the argument goes through; if "finds" means "determines using its own criteria of reliability and fairness – criteria that others may reasonably contest," then it does not go through. For the independent prohibited from using her own reasonable procedures is not adequately compensated by being given access to the procedures that the agency prefers. Compensation is something that has to be assessed from the perspective of the person being compensated – as Nozick puts it "something compensates X for Y's act if receiving it leaves X on at least as high an indifference curve as he would have been on, without it, had Y not so acted" (ASU, 57). Whatever the agency may think, the independent is not adequately compensated when she is offered a rights-enforcement procedure that she (reasonably) judges to be inferior to the one she would otherwise prefer to use.

A tempting response at this point is to say that, when the dominant agency imposes its own set of rights-enforcement procedures on independents who would prefer to employ different ones, it thereby brings it about that the same procedures are applied to everyone who inhabits the region it controls, and this brings with it considerable gains, in terms of stability and predictability – gains that even would-be independents will recognize, and that may therefore compensate them for being denied their own chosen procedures of rights-enforcement. Everyone knows where they stand, because they know what procedures will be followed if their rights are violated or if they are suspected of violating others' rights. But this argument – which rightly features in many general justifications of the state, including Locke's – is not available to Nozick, given his ambition to develop a justification of political authority conditional on the primacy of the prepolitical rights of individuals. For the argument points to the goods that are enjoyed collectively by everyone in a society governed by the rule of law, and Nozick cannot allow collective goods of any kind to outweigh the rights of ownership, and the secondary rights to enforce those primary rights, on which his whole political philosophy depends.

JUSTIFYING THE STATE

Nozick's ambition was to provide a justification for the state that would be compelling even to those initially most sceptical of its claims. Even hardened anarchists would be forced to admit that a statelike entity could, and very likely would, emerge by morally legitimate processes from a nonpolitical state of nature. Such an ambition is praiseworthy indeed: If we could prove to *everyone* that they had reasons to accept political authority – perhaps not the form of political authority they are currently subject to, but at least some feasible alternative form – then we would have comprehensively reconciled freedom with authority.

But the hurdle Nozick sets himself is too high. Political authority can be justified by appealing to human needs and interests that are widely shared, but it is impossible to show that everyone, regardless of their personal beliefs and ambitions, has an internal reason to accept it. Even so, we can make a case that people in this latter category can justifiably be subjected to authority, for the good of others living alongside them who do have such reason. The argument here requires two steps. First, we have to show that, in order to be effective, political authority has to be exercised inclusively across a geographical region with well-defined borders. Everyone residing inside those borders has to be subject to it – they may have the right to emigrate but, so long as they remain physically within the boundaries of the state, they may properly be compelled to accept its authority. Second, we have to show that such compulsion does not violate Nozick's Kant-derived principle that individuals may not be used merely as means to the greater social good without their consent.

Taking these steps in order, the requirement of inclusiveness is a direct corollary of the benefits that political authority in the form of the state can provide. What are these benefits? Let me focus on just two. As mentioned at the end of the last section, an effective system of political authority will create a legal regime in which laws are applied in a uniform and consistent way to every citizen, allowing each to plan his or her future in relative security. This permits a whole range of human activities, most notably economic activities, to proceed. When conflicts arise – say over the ownership of property or the interpretation of a contract – each party knows where to turn for a legal resolution, and also broadly what rules will be applied to settle their dispute. This can't happen unless a single system of authority prevails throughout the region in question.

Political authority also makes it possible to create a range of public goods, goods that benefit large numbers of people but that individuals acting alone are unable for various reasons to bring into existence. Large-scale transport systems are one example; environmental goods, such as protected areas of natural beauty, are another. Such goods can't be provided unless everyone in the relevant population is subject to political authority, which may require them to behave in certain ways (refrain from hunting wildlife in the designated areas, for instance) or to contribute resources to meet the costs of provision (pay taxes to build a rail network, for instance).

It is sometimes argued that benefits of both kinds – a uniform system of law, and public goods provision – can in principle be created by purely voluntary means and without recourse to political authority.[24] The arguments here are complex, and it would take me too far afield to address them. So let us simply assume, for present purposes, that for empirical reasons it is impossible to provide these benefits except by the exercise of political authority that embraces everyone within the boundaries of the state. The moral issue that then remains is whether people who do not sufficiently value such benefits to have reason to accept political authority themselves may nonetheless be made subject to its exercise.

Nozick would no doubt claim that such subjection is simply a case of using some people for the benefit of others, in contravention of the moral intuition that underpins his entire philosophy. But it is arguable, to say the least, whether the intuition that costs may not be imposed on individuals merely for the sake of the greater social good implies that no limitation of individuals' personal or property rights is ever permitted. Consider the following by way of analogy. Suppose ten farmers own adjoining pieces of land along the banks of a river. Because of changing meteorological conditions, there is the possibility of a disastrous flood that would wash away everything that the farmers have done to improve their land, unless all of them cooperate to raise flood barriers right along the river bank. One farmer refuses to raise barriers on his land, claiming that he has divine protection against flooding, or that he has private knowledge that the relevant weather conditions won't occur, or giving some such reason. Is it permissible for the nine other farmers to force the refusenik to raise barriers on his stretch of river? I think it clearly is permissible, and that a description of the case as one of "imposing costs on some for the greater benefit of others" misses its most salient feature, namely that the vital interests of the nine farmers – the same interests that justify their property rights in the first place – are put at risk if the tenth farmer is allowed to sabotage the cooperative solution.[25] Nozick himself recognizes that rights might have to be violated "to avoid catastrophic moral horror" (ASU, 30n), but he does not expand this to indicate what would count as a catastrophe. What is needed here is some ethical view intermediate between the utilitarian position that all policies that produce a net gain in aggregate welfare are justified and the strict deontological view that rights may never be infringed whatever the consequences. Such a view, in combination with the empirical claims about the benefits of political authority sketched above, would allow us to explain why we are sometimes justified in imposing authority on people who have neither actually given their consent to it, nor have sufficient reason (given their personal beliefs and preferences) to give consent.

Showing that political authority is justified by the vital human interests it serves does not settle the question which form of authority is to be preferred, nor does it settle the question of its geographical boundaries – the question of which state should exercise authority over the inhabitants of any given piece of territory. Nozick gives us an invisible hand answer to the second question: The agency that becomes dominant in area A is simply the agency that over time has attracted the greatest number of clients in that area. Where the boundary between this area and adjoining areas lies is merely a matter of historical accident. Nozick attaches no special weight to the possibility that people who inhabit A might share a collective identity such that it matters to them that agency 1 rather than agency 2 should be responsible for rights-enforcement among them – for instance, on the grounds that the people who staff agency 1 also share their collective identity. Of course, there is nothing in the story that he tells that excludes the possibility that people's choice of which agency to patronize might be affected by factors other than cost, effectiveness of rights-enforcement, and the like. But equally identity considerations are given no ethical status in determining where the boundaries of systems of political authority are set.

In the real world that we inhabit, such considerations count for a great deal. People care a great deal not just about how they are governed but about who governs them, to the point where they may be prepared to fight and die to escape alien rule and institute self-government (meaning government by people with whom they identify). The identities that count here are primarily *national* identities. Nozick does not mention national communities at any point in Part I of ASU,[26] although nations make a brief appearance in Part III, when Nozick is discussing why the kinds of restrictions that small face-to-face communities may legitimately impose on their members may not legitimately be imposed by the larger political communities that he there calls nations (ASU, 320–3). Is this more than a slip of the pen? Does Nozick mean by a nation simply "those people who as it happens have all chosen to acknowledge the authority of the same dominant protective agency," or is he here helping himself to the thought that viable systems of political authority require something more than such happenstance to hold their subjects together?

That people as a matter of fact care a great deal that they should be governed by those with whom they identify does not of course entail that nationality should have *ethical* significance when the boundaries of political authority are being fixed. Showing this requires an argument in defense of national self-determination, one that moves from the empirical fact that people almost everywhere desire and demand self-government to the conclusion that their demand is a legitimate one. I have attempted to make such an argument in other places,[27] and will not repeat the attempt here; for present purposes, I want merely to record my belief that no justificatory account of political authority can avoid paying attention to the boundary question, the question, that is, of how to determine the limits of the political community within and over which political authority is to be exercised. Nozick's invisible hand story treats this wholly as a matter of contingency: Individuals, one at a time, choose to sign up with agency 1, 2, or 3, agency 1 (say) attracts most customers in area A, and so, over time, becomes the dominant protective agency, and eventually the state, in A, while agency 2 does better in neighboring area B, and so on. There is no room here for the thought that the inhabitants of A might hold some collective view about how they wish to be governed, or for the thought that the appropriate line of demarcation does not fall between A and B at all, but (for instance) cuts across those two areas in a quite different way, so that $A^1 + B^1$ forms one natural unit and $A^2 + B^2$ forms another – "natural" in the sense that the people who live in $A^1 + B^1$ share a common national identity as do those who live in $A^2 + B^2$.

CONCLUSION

A successful justification of political authority would need to address the following four questions, at least. First, there is the question of general justification: Why, in general, is a system of political authority to be preferred to an anarchic state of nature in which personal protection and other essential functions are left to individual persons, or voluntary associations of persons?[28] Second, there is the question of the form that political authority should take: Who should exercise it, what institutions should be established to discharge the tasks specified in the course of the general justification? Third, there is the question of boundaries: How are we to demarcate peoples and territories so that each system of authority has its own appropriate scope? Finally, there is the question of the limits to authority: Over what matters may political authority *not* be rightfully exercised; in other words, in what areas of life must individuals be left free to act as they choose, alone or in association with others?

The justification for the minimal state that Nozick offers us in ASU, Part I comes closest to success in the answers it offers to the first and fourth of these questions. It answers the first by arguing that individuals placed in a state of nature would seek to escape from its inconveniences by contracting with protective agencies that, over time and by morally legitimate means, become minimal states. The general justification for authority lies in the rational preference of individuals for organized protection over the uncertainties of the state of nature. It answers the fourth by endowing individuals with natural rights that are not surrendered when people enter into contracts for protection. The agencies' role is restricted to the protection and enforcement of rights whose definition they cannot alter. This then sets absolute limits to justified political authority. However convincing or unconvincing one finds these answers, they plainly *are* answers to questions one and four.

If we turn to questions two and three, by contrast, we find that Nozick's approach can offer little illumination. The forms and the boundaries of states depend, in a Nozickian world, on the vagaries of the invisible hand. Here we need to refer back briefly to the distinction drawn earlier in the chapter between historical and hypothetical invisible hand explanations. An historical invisible hand explanation of the state would at least enable us to say that the institutional structure of the state reflected the choices made by individual people when deciding which protective agency to patronize, and similarly the boundaries of the state would reflect the pattern of choices people in each area had made as between the contending agencies. For reasons given earlier, these explanations don't function particularly well as justifications: There is a gap between individual rationality and collective rationality, such that people pursuing their own preferences may end up with institutional arrangements that they all regard as suboptimal. But the main point here is that a *hypothetical* invisible hand explanation can provide us with nothing at all by way of answers to questions two and three. As far as the form and boundaries of the state are concerned, there is almost nothing that *might* not have emerged historically *if* individuals had chosen to bestow their custom on protective agencies in a certain way. If we want to know whether states should be unitary or federal, whether government should be parliamentary or presidential, whether national minorities have a right to secede or no such right, telling hypothetical stories about how states might, in general, have emerged from prepolitical states of nature, will not help us at all.

I do not wish to end my discussion on a negative note. Nozick's attempt to justify political authority is provocative in the best sense. It may not give us answers to all the questions we need to ask, but in the course of grappling with its limitations, we may understand better where the answers are to be found.

Notes

[1] I am very grateful indeed to Daniel McDermott, Serena Olsaretti, David Schmidtz, and Jo Wolff for their detailed and penetrating comments on an earlier draft of this paper. Responsibility for the interpretation of Nozick that follows is mine alone.

[2] Such as theories maintaining that states may legitimately aim to achieve some substantive form of equality among their citizens – equality of income or welfare or life-chances, for instance.

[3] See J. D. Davidson and W. Rees-Mogg, *The Sovereign Individual* (New York: Simon and Schuster, 1997) for a somewhat overheated presentation of this argument.

[4] His main source is John Locke's *Second Treatise of Government*, first published in 1689. See J. Locke, *Two Treatises of Government*, ed. P. Laslett (New York: Mentor, 1965).

[5] His argument here is controversial, and has attracted criticism. See E. Mack, "Nozick's Anarchism," in J. R. Pennock and J. W. Chapman (eds.), *Nomos XIX: Anarchism* (New York: New York University Press, 1978), and H. Steiner, "Can a Social Contract be Signed by an Invisible Hand?" in P. Birnbaum, J. Lively, and G. Parry (eds.), *Democracy, Consensus and Social Contract* (London: Sage, 1978).

[6] This is a slight oversimplification, because, as Nozick points out, the dominant protective agency cannot decide which procedures will be used when one independent takes action against another. But he argues that this does not disqualify the agency from being regarded as a proto-state, because "a state, too, could abstain from disputes where all concerned parties chose to opt out of the state's apparatus" (ASU, 110).

[7] It is possible, of course, to restrict the invisible hand concept to cases in which the outcome of the hand's operation is good, compared to the prehand baseline. Jon Elster employs this restricted concept when he discusses invisible hand explanations in *Nuts and Bolts for the Social Sciences* (Cambridge: Cambridge University Press, 1989), pp. 96–7. But Nozick himself does not impose any such restriction, as a brief inspection of the examples of invisible hand explanations that he offers on ASU, pp. 20–1, will reveal.

[8] I shall treat Nozick's invisible hand account of the emergence of the minimal state as playing an essential part in his justification of that institution, though others have challenged this reading. See especially J. Wolff, *Robert Nozick: Property, Justice and the Minimal State* (Cambridge, U.K.: Polity Press, 1991), pp. 47–52, for the opposite view.

[9] This is made clear when Nozick describes his aim as one of contributing to political philosophy as well as to explanatory political theory. See especially the footnote to ASU p. 5, where he contrasts his own account with "a theory that presents a state's arising from a state of nature by a natural and inevitable process of *deterioration*, rather as medical theory presents aging or dying." Note that a theory of the latter kind might also be an invisible hand explanation.

[10] If we refer back to the original source of the invisible hand idea, Adam Smith's justification of market exchange, we see that each of these conditions is fulfilled. A free market in goods and services raises everyone's standard of living, according to Smith – so the outcome is uncontroversially valuable. Moreover, this outcome is best achieved by allowing each individual to pursue his own self-interest: "By pursuing his own interests he frequently promotes that of the society more effectually than when he really intends to promote it. I have never known much good done by those who affected to trade for the publick good" (A. Smith, *An Inquiry into the Nature and Causes of the Wealth of Nations*, ed. R. H. Campbell, A. S. Skinner, and W. B. Todd [Oxford: Clarendon Press, 1976], vol. I, p. 456). And, a point Smith takes for granted, individuals act justly when they exchange their labor and their legitimately held property for goods and services they value more highly.

[11] It has been suggested to me that Nozick need not in fact show this. His concern is to justify the minimal state by showing that it could arise by just procedures that violate no one's rights. It is unnecessary to show that the emergence of such a state is positively valuable. However, I doubt that such procedural claims alone are sufficient to justify a social institution. Consider by analogy the institution of free exchange. It might be thought that this can be justified entirely on the grounds that property owners have the right to transfer their property to whomever they choose; the right to free exchange is simply a corollary of the rights of ownership. But it is surely also of relevance that, by and large, when individuals exchange goods and services, they do so to their mutual benefit. Imagine a world in which people were such poor judges of their own welfare that when they made exchanges they nearly always ended up with items that they valued less than the items they first had. Would we want the institution of free exchange in such a world? What justifies *our* institution, in other words, is the fact that individuals have rights of disposal over their property *together* with the fact that exchanges standardly benefit both parties to them.

Nozick's primary aim, in Part I of ASU, is to defeat the individualist anarchist. But what kind of victory would he have achieved if he had to concede that the state was inferior, in terms of welfare say, to an anarchic state of nature? He would be saying to the anarchist: People might, by permissible steps, follow the downward path that leads to the state. But an anarchist, apprised of that fact, would hardly be converted. He would merely redouble his efforts to discourage people from taking that path.

[12] That he thinks this is suggested by some remarks in ASU, p. 90, top, where he claims that individuals have an interest in excluding themselves from an otherwise unanimous agreement to set up a state.

[13] Locke, *Second Treatise*, Ch. 8.

[14] I set aside here problems of social choice that may arise in case three or more alternative forms of government may be favored by members of the political community in question.

[15] This also means that people cannot be said to have consented to A's exercise of political authority, even though they may have contracted voluntarily to purchase A's protective services. As David Schmidtz has formulated the point, "The problem is that people consent to individual transactions rather than to the order that spontaneously emerges from them. In other words, that an outcome arose by consent does not entail that people consented to it" (D. Schmidtz, "Justifying the State," in J. T. Sanders and J. Narveson [eds.], *For and Against the State* [Lanham, Mass.: Rowman and Littlefield, 1996], p. 91).

[16] This point has been developed by A. J. Simmons in terms of a contrast between justification and legitimacy, where showing that a state is justified is a matter of showing that it is morally permissible and advantageous to have it, while showing that a state is legitimate is a matter of showing that it has the right to command its subjects – legitimacy, in other words, depends on the relationship between a particular state and a particular people. In Simmons's terms, hypothetical arguments, whether contractarian or invisible hand, might show that a state was justified, whereas historical arguments might in principle also show that it was legitimate – although Simmons doubts whether a successful argument of this kind could in fact be made for any existing state. See A. J. Simmons, "Justification and Legitimacy," *Ethics*, 109 (1999), 739–71.

[17] For further reflection on the relative justificatory power of hypothetical and historical invisible hand explanations of the state, see Schmidtz, "Justifying the State."

[18] I shall return shortly to the question whether the agency is *justified* in insisting that only procedures that it approves should be used.

[19] Cf. Mack, "Nozick's Anarchism," pp. 52–3.

[20] It might be said here that smaller agencies are at a disadvantage when dealing with the clients of *other* smaller agencies, since here they can give no guarantees about the procedures that will be used against their clients. But that being so, these agencies have an immediate incentive to agree to follow common procedures, to appoint arbitrators, and so on, if they are to stay in business alongside the dominant agency. So although it may be correct to say that the emergence of a dominant agency changes the market for protective services in the direction of greater predictability, this need not entail the elimination of all rival agencies.

[21] See Wolff, *Robert Nozick*, pp. 57–8, for this argument.

[22] Wolff, *Robert Nozick*, p. 58, makes a suggestion along similar lines, although it is not clear whether he thinks that a democratically controlled protective agency could emerge spontaneously from a Lockean state of nature, or whether he simply wants to point out its advantages.

[23] Strictly speaking, we should say "objectively best procedure or set of procedures," but for ease of exposition I shall use "procedure" expansively so that it can include the case where the agency in question judges all members of a set of procedures A . . . N as sufficiently reliable to be used on its clients as well as the case where just one procedure is singled out as most reliable.

[24]See, for instance, D. Schmidtz, *The Limits of Government: An Essay on the Public Goods Argument* (Boulder, Col.: Westview Press, 1991) and my discussion of Schmidtz's argument in D. Miller, "Public Goods Without the State," *Critical Review*, 7 (1993), 505–23.

[25]It should be noted that this example does not involve an appeal to the principle of fair play that Nozick discusses critically in ASU, pp. 90–5. The reason for forcing the tenth farmer to cooperate is not that he has benefited from the actions of the other nine, and must therefore reciprocate, but simply that without his cooperation the vital interests of the other nine will be put at serious risk.

[26]He does refer briefly to "nations" when discussing the issue of preemptive attack, but in a sense that is equivalent to "states."

[27]See especially D. Miller, *On Nationality* (Oxford: Clarendon Press, 1995).

[28]Not everyone agrees that this is a sensible question to ask. The contrary view would hold that political authority is such a pervasive feature of human existence that we cannot conceive of a human society without it; thus, the only questions worth asking are questions about the particular form, extent, and so on, that political authority should have. I believe that the first question does need to be asked and answered, if only as a prelude to the remaining three, and that we should ask it in a way that distributes the burden of proof as equally as possible between the anarchist and the statist. Here I follow J. Wolff, "Anarchism and Scepticism," in Sanders and Narveson (eds.), *For and Against the State*.

3 | Projects and Property[1]
JOHN T. SANDERS

"Individuals have rights." These opening words of the preface to Robert Nozick's *Anarchy, State, and Utopia* are the first indication of the boldness of his work to readers destined to become fans, and the first indication of an annoying shallowness to those destined to become critics.[2] "*Of course* people have rights," say some. "How can this be denied without abandoning morality?" Others ask: "How can a serious analysis of the political realm *begin* with a declaration that individuals have rights? This is one of the main disputed claims!"

Rights talk brings out the worst among political philosophers. How one speaks about rights draws a line in the sand, identifying the speaker as being with us or against us. Once that line has been drawn, everything else one says is likely to be viewed through the prisms devised in response by the members of one's audience.

To speak approvingly about private property rights, in particular, may be to nail down the lid on the box others construct for you. That seems to have happened to Nozick, anyway. "Individuals have rights," he said, "and there are things no person or group may do to them (without violating their rights)."[3] Among these rights, it later emerges, are private property rights.[4] Critics from all sides have decried the absence of "foundations."

It is tempting, given the likelihood of reactions of this kind, to avoid talk of private property rights altogether. Perhaps one can make progress in understanding the pros and cons of different arrangements for allocating and distributing resources without deploying rights talk.[5]

One can't avoid such talk forever, though, if for no other reason than that it is in terms of rights that most philosophical debate about property arrangements has been formulated for several centuries. Thus, the question is not so much whether to talk about rights but, rather, how to begin.

I am not one of those who had trouble with Nozick's opening lines. I thought at the time that to deny that individuals have rights would be to assert that there are no limits to what others may legitimately do to individuals. Surely there are lots of circumstances in which that's exactly how "rights" jargon gets deployed. It's this understanding of rights, I think, that makes it plausible to say that animals have rights. To say this is just to indicate that there are certain things that shouldn't be done to animals. Why not use the word "right" in this natural way? And if we accept this usage, isn't it simply uncontroversial that individuals have rights? What's wrong, then, with making that our starting point?

What is likely to be held to be wrong with this is that it deploys jargon carelessly. While it might seem harmless enough to start off by saying that individuals have rights, where one means only that there are some things that it is wrong to do to people, the implications of this way of putting things might be much more far-reaching. The history of rights talk licenses a reading of these words that makes them less harmless, since that way of talking seems to favor certain political ideologies and to rule out others.

How, then, should one begin? Unless one hopes to reduce political thought to indefeasible first foundations of some kind, a goal not widely sought in contemporary political analysis and certainly not sought by me, one has to begin with assertions that are at least to some degree fallible. Here I take it that one such assertion is that there are things that shouldn't be done to people. I don't mean by this that there is any list of things that may *never* rightly be done to anyone, in any circumstances (although neither do I mean to rule out the possibility that such a list may exist). Rather, I mean that it is possible to do things to people that it is wrong to do, and that, further, we should avoid doing these things if possible. In what follows, I hope to develop a way of talking about a certain area of moral behavior that expresses facts of this kind. I will use rights jargon in this effort, reexamining themes explored by Nozick throughout his career thus far.

I shall here try to accomplish two things. First I'll try, in a Nozickian vein, to offer some first thoughts toward a clarification of the ethical foundations of private property rights that avoids pitfalls common to more strictly Lockean theories, and is thus better prepared to address arguments posed by critics of standard private property arrangements. Second, I'll address one critical argument that has become pretty common over the years. While versions of the argument can be traced back at least to Pierre Joseph Proudhon, I'll focus on a formulation given it by Jeremy Waldron. The basic idea is that the only sound arguments for private property rights lead to the conclusion that society has an obligation to insure that every citizen possess private property. In Waldron's formulation, what is justifiable is a *general*, rather than a *special*, right to private property. I shall try to suggest that this conclusion is unwarranted.

While my own conclusions do not always agree with Robert Nozick's, the influence of his work is pervasive throughout. Furthermore, I will be discussing in passing the work of several thinkers whose works have acquired their several characteristic forms in part because of Nozick's influence. This is the case as much for those who are critical of Nozick's work as for those who agree with him. Part of the underlying message, therefore, involves the huge extent of Nozick's influence.

1. RESPECT FOR PERSONS

I begin with a principle that, as indicated above, is inevitably controversial, at least under some interpretations. But, as also indicated, one must begin somewhere. I intend its reference to "rights" to be quite broad, such that sentences like "if people don't have rights, then it is alright to do anything to them" come out true. I think it's that understanding of rights that makes the principle plausible:

> RESPECT PRINCIPLE: Even if respect for persons may not be entirely equivalent to respect for the rights of persons, the two things are very close. There can be no respect for people – or, more grandly, for humanity itself, if such a thing has any meaning at all – absent the respect for rights.

I mean to make it clear, in this formulation of the Respect Principle, that the following discussion of rights is, in the first instance, other-regarding. This is important, given a traditional inclination on the part of critics of rights theory, along with many contemporary proponents, to conceive of such theory as fundamentally egoistical and divisive. I reject that view. While there is plenty of room to criticize any particular version of human rights theory, the most fundamental motivation for all such theories involves – or at least it ought to involve – concern for fair and reasonable rules for human interaction.

Now, to say that the point of rights theory is to concoct "fair and reasonable rules for human interaction" may seem innocent at first glance. But a second glance shows that the formulation is tricky, given contemporary discussions of rights, in at least two ways.

In the first place, if rights theory is held to involve, first and foremost, rules for *human* interaction, then the idea that other animals have rights may seem to be imperiled, at least, at the outset. It seems to me, though, that this consequence may be avoided, at least for present purposes, by considering that even if a primary (or even *the* primary) role of rights theory is to produce rules for human interaction, that doesn't preclude its having other roles that might allow for talk of animal rights. If, for example, there being some things that it is wrong to do to people is sufficient to justify saying that people have rights (and that's certainly the way the Respect Principle was motivated a few paragraphs ago), then that same consideration would seem to yield the conclusion that animals too have rights. For surely there are things that can be done to animals that shouldn't be done.[6]

If, though, one has scruples about talking about animal rights because of the very different sorts of interaction that are possible among humans, on the one hand, and between humans and other animals, on the other, then perhaps one should be more careful about ascriptions of rights even if one acknowledges that there are things that morally shouldn't be done to members of those other species. Nozick, early in ASU, made an admittedly "too minimal" suggestion that he labeled "utilitarianism for animals, Kantianism for people."[7] Under this proposal, one would be obliged to maximize the total happiness of all living beings, but only humans would be understood as protected by the kind of stringent side constraints Nozick took rights to represent. Perhaps a suitably enriched version of this approach would be attractive to some.

My own view, however one resolves disputes of this kind, is that the moral and ethical reasons for not mistreating nonhuman animals do not derive from specifically human interests.[8] They derive, ultimately, from facts about those other animals and from considerations about morality that may or may not involve an appropriate deployment of rights jargon. Rights need not – and probably do not – exhaust morality, in my view.

Beyond the question of whether specifically human interaction exhausts the scope of rights theory, though, there is a second feature of my claim about the domain of rights theory that is worth examining. I claim that rights theory involves "fair and reasonable" rules for human interaction. Much recent work by more or less Hobbesian social contractarians would imply, I think, that this formulation is either redundant or wrong. Either what is fair just *is* what is reasonable, or else fairness just isn't a legitimate part of rights theory. That is, either fairness simply reduces to what is reasonable for contracting parties to agree to, or it plays no role in rights theory, since rights are thought by Hobbesians to arise out of rational agreement, whether actual or hypothetical.[9]

I don't agree with this. It seems to me that two parties might find themselves in positions where it is quite possible that what is rational for them to agree to, on a Hobbesian construal, might very well violate the rights of one of them. I have in mind first and foremost cases where the power difference between the two parties is simply overwhelming. As the weaker party, I might argue that my stronger interlocutor should consider the possibility of my later gaining power, perhaps through collusion with others, and so forth. But if the prospects of this are sufficiently slim, then it is simply not rational (on this Hobbesian construal) for the stronger party to take my arguments seriously, no matter how clever my rhetoric might be. And in those circumstances, where I as the weaker party realize that I have no genuine power, it is simply not rational for me to risk the consequences by resisting the will of the stronger party.

For Hobbes, compact by conquest was every bit as legitimate as compact by coincidence of ends, in the state of nature. For me, that's wrong. Some agreements that are rational from a Hobbesian standpoint violate rights.

Thus, again, my claim is that the most fundamental motivation for human rights theory involves concern for fair and reasonable rules for human interaction, and that "fairness" and "reasonableness" are independent (at least so long as "reasonableness" is understood in a Hobbesian way). And, finally, it seems to me to follow from the centrality of "interaction" in this formulation that all general criticism of rights theory must be prepared to address questions about where we would be left *socially* if we failed to acknowledge the rights of others.

An important upshot of this way of looking at rights is that it is not particularly isolationist or, even, individualistic. Nozick writes, "The libertarian position I once propounded now seems to me seriously inadequate, in part because it did not fully knit the humane considerations and joint cooperative activities it left room for more closely into its fabric."[10] If the problem to which he alludes is a matter of emphasis, I suspect Nozick is right. But Nozick also says that his position "neglected the symbolic importance of an official political concern with issues or problems, as a way of marking their importance or urgency, and hence of expressing, intensifying, channeling, encouraging, and validating our private actions and concerns toward them."[11] It seems to me that, while humane considerations offer all kinds of good reasons to be cautious about one's eagerness to do away with state coercion in one fell swoop, Nozick nevertheless (in EL) overestimates the importance of expressions of "official political concern" and underestimates the dangers of state power, even in the hands of democratic majorities.[12]

Whether or not I am right to worry about Nozick's more recent emphasis on the symbolic importance of official expression of political concern, though, we are certainly in agreement about the importance of knitting humane considerations more fully into the fabric of rights theory. Far from cutting us off from one another, acknowledgment of rights serves to establish our most fundamental connection with one another: Rights establish the lines of interpersonal obligation.

These general considerations about rights now set the stage for an examination of property rights, in particular. While it is in part because strict Lockean approaches to property rights do seem isolationist that they are to be rejected, there are other reasons to be suspicious of them. Indeed, Locke's work has exerted enough influence on all sides of the discussion that it deserves for that reason alone a short critical discussion before I move on to more positive considerations. The critique offered in the next section will then serve as a stepping-off point for what follows.

2. THE FAILURE OF A STRICT LOCKEAN APPROACH

In an earlier essay,[13] I argued that the grounds provided for property theory by John Locke's arguments[14] are inadequate for a number of reasons. In the first place, the famous Lockean proviso – which states that previously unowned resources may be propertized provided that enough and as good be left for others – is both conceptually incoherent and self-defeating.

Since the publication of that piece, David Schmidtz has developed the argument even further.[15] Especially noteworthy (and persuasive, it seems to me) is Schmidtz's argument that one must *save* resources from the "common" if one is to fulfill the goal of preserving them for the use of others, and that initial acquisition does precisely this.

Surely, though, this yields the conclusion that "as long as one leaves enough and as good for others" cannot function as a qualification or proviso on whatever principle is chosen as the acquisition principle. Something like it becomes, instead, (at least part of) the justification for acquisition, and the "leaving" part must be entirely dropped. Since this part is the very heart of Locke's proviso, it seems plain that the proviso should, as I have argued, simply be abandoned.

Schmidtz, by contrast, thinks that one can accommodate his argument by reinterpreting the proviso in some way. What way would that be? Something like "one may appropriate as much as one can, provided only that one leaves as little as possible unappropriated"? Erasmus Darwin once described Unitarianism as a "featherbed to catch a falling Christian."[16] Perhaps Schmidtz intends his "reinterpretation" of the Lockean Proviso to be a featherbed to catch a falling Lockean.[17]

It still seems to me that there are extremely good grounds for simply dropping the proviso from the rules for just initial acquisition of property, and these grounds are primarily other-regarding. The proviso simply doesn't protect the interests of others in the way Locke intended. In fact, it aggravates the very problems of scarcity that Locke meant to ameliorate. Nozick's discussion of various alternative versions of Lockean-like provisos shows clearly that such problems – such as Hastings Rashdall's case of the person who appropriates the only water in the desert – were very much at the forefront of his own thinking.[18]

But abandoning Locke's proviso leaves Locke's doctrine of labor-mixing; this principle, as I have insisted along with a chorus of other traditional and contemporary analysts, can lead to counterintuitive – if not downright crazy – results. Nozick has been notoriously eloquent among such analysts:

> Locke views property rights in an unowned object as originating through someone's mixing his labor with it. This gives rise to many questions. What are the boundaries of what labor is mixed with? If a private astronaut clears a place on Mars, has he mixed his labor with (so that he comes to own) the whole planet, the whole uninhabited universe, or just a particular plot? Which plot does an act bring under ownership? The minimal (possibly disconnected) area such that an act decreases entropy in that area, and not elsewhere? Can virgin land (for the purposes of ecological investigation by high-flying airplane) come under ownership by a Lockean process? Building a fence around a territory presumably would make one the owner of only the fence (and the land immediately underneath it).
>
> Why does mixing one's labor with something make one the owner of it? Perhaps because one owns one's labor, and so one comes to own a previously unowned thing that becomes permeated with what one owns. Ownership seeps over into the rest. But why isn't mixing what I own with what I don't own a way of losing what I own rather than a way of gaining what I don't? If I own a can of tomato juice and spill it in the sea so that its molecules (made radioactive, so I can check this) mingle evenly throughout the sea, do I thereby come to own the sea, or have I foolishly dissipated my tomato juice? [19]

The quest is for a principle of just acquisition of previously unowned resources that captures the benign features of labor-mixing, while getting around its apparent arbitrariness. The benign features that I have in mind include the feature that surely must have suggested it to Locke in the first place: the investment of labor almost always indicates an intent to do something or produce something that is important to the laborer. We must find a principle that hangs on to this feature without having the arbitrary and potentially destructive consequences that follow from the labor-mixing principle. It is this quest that I hope to further in the present essay. My plan is to revisit the issue of the original acquisition of previously unowned resources, and to offer an approach that avoids a variety of Lockean and non-Lockean pitfalls. In the course of this discussion, I'll address the idea that people have a "general" right to private property.

The arbitrariness of labor-mixing as a criterion for just initial acquisition of previously unowned resources is not merely theoretical. It shows up in contemporary and historical arguments that have been deployed by committed labor-mixers in ways that deprive less inveterate alterers of their rights. A glaring example is the justification occasionally offered for the European colonial expropriation of nearly the whole of North America, and large parts of other continents, on grounds involving the relative absence of tilled fields, fences, and other manifestations of labor-mixing when they got there. Other examples involve schemes that have been proposed for the reallocation of resources in countries where attempts are being made to achieve privatization of national economies. Such arguments and schemes miss an important part of the point of property rights, I hold, and reveal a serious defect in the labor-mixing criterion.

The right to acquire private property involves the centrality of personal undertakings or projects – whether conducted individually or collectively – in human life. Whether resources are altered or not by such projects, it is the projects and their importance to persons that must be respected, and for which room must be made, provided that they do not interfere with the similarly justifiable projects of others. This is vital if more than lip service is to be paid to the idea of respect for people.

3. PROJECTS AND RIGHTS

Joel Feinberg once suggested that "respect for persons . . . may simply be respect for their rights, so that there cannot be the one without the other."[20] One might well go considerably farther than this in assessing the importance to ethics of people's projects. There is an important sense in which understanding persons is impossible without understanding their projects. People are living, breathing actors, not passive things with merely static characteristics.

An interesting corollary involves questions about what makes for a desirable human life. In the course of discussing such questions with students, I have sometimes raised the following standard late-twentieth-century analytically inclined philosopher's question: if contemporary "virtual reality" technologies were improved to the extent that experiences were 100 percent convincing – a situation that has been represented in far too much recent fiction – and if one could program one's experiences in precisely the way one would like, would it be desirable to simply plug into the machine for life, instead of going through the agony and frustration of real life? Add the proviso that there is no danger whatsoever, even that life expectancy might be increased (perhaps one is laid out in a germ-free setting and nourished intravenously, thus decreasing the risk of disease – or perhaps one just agrees to become a brain in a vat, cared for by trustworthy scientists).

The machine envisioned is plainly the one Nozick has called the "experience machine."[21] It won't do to say that what is wrong with virtual reality is that it is not challenging, or that one needs frustration sometimes in order to enjoy successes, for one can surely program such things into one's virtual life. But since one can ensure, in virtual reality, that the challenges will never become overwhelming, and that the successes will always outnumber the frustrations, wouldn't that be a better life on all counts?

Once the virtual experience has begun, one wouldn't have any way of knowing that the experiences were only virtual, since they are (by hypothesis) 100 percent convincing. My experience of posing this question to students has been that, with only the rarest exceptions (and these are almost always due to a misunderstanding of some of the provisions of the situation), people reject the option out of hand. Such a virtual reality machine would be terrific fun for Friday and Saturday nights, students largely agree, but the idea of choosing virtual reality as a substitute for "real life" is simply out of the question.

Why might this be? The students say that it's because virtual reality is not real, but that plainly doesn't help at all. Perhaps their judgments involve a conception of a person that resembles the one sketched a minute ago: persons are not to be understood as mere passive recipients of experiences but, rather, as actors. It is not the *experience* of acting that matters, it is the fact of acting. The postulated virtual world is deeply lonely in its characterization, as well. The suggestion I'm offering here is that people do not understand themselves primarily as passive receivers of experiences of the world but as active participants in a world shared with other actors like them.[22]

This is certainly Nozick's view. Not only do we want to *do* certain things, rather than just have the experience of doing them, we want also to *be* a certain way. As he puts it, "There is no answer to the question of what a person is like who has long been in the tank. Is he courageous, kind, intelligent, witty, loving? It's not merely that it's difficult to tell; there's no way he is."[23]

I'm not sure that this helps to resolve many "big questions" about the good life, but it may go a long way toward unpacking the reaction of those who reject a life of virtual experience, however perfect, in favor of real life.

And such a conception of worthwhile human life certainly underlies my present contention that to care about a person, to respect a person, is to care about and respect at least the bare fact that she has goals, ambitions, and projects. Respecting people means respecting them as agents, as co-inhabitants of a shared world, not just as objects with properties or neural tissue with afferent nerves.

It is not necessary to applaud or otherwise appreciate the particular details of any person's projects. A society of actors, pursuing a wide array of individual and cooperative projects, will need to place limits on acceptable activity, if only to fulfill the general principle that liberty to pursue projects is to be maximally supported. But to facilitate – even barely to allow – human life, one must address the human need to act in behalf of goals that are personally motivating. To care about others only in regard to their capacity to contribute to society in general – which should be read, in all honesty, as a capacity to contribute to us and *our* projects – is to betray a deep contempt for them as persons, as well as a self-centeredness that thoroughly trashes all pretense of humanity.

Perhaps it is true that people have debts to society. Perhaps, indeed, these debts may be fairly extensive. Without some end, though, to the debt that individuals may be held to have to society, one wonders not only what room is left for respect for persons but also what value society could possibly have in the lives of persons. One also wonders what conception of society is at work in such a view. An illuminating way of understanding rights highlights the way they express the limits of the social debt borne by individuals, although this is clearly but one side of the issue.

There are important precedents for the suggestion that personal projects play a vital role in delineating human rights. Something like it may be found, in a notoriously thin form, in John Rawls's *Theory of Justice*,[24] although it is seriously undermined by the Rawlsian contention that not only unowned resources but even the talents of persons should be regarded as community property. Bernard Williams developed the "projects" theme further through the 1970s,[25] and the issues that I want to focus on have been provocatively addressed by Loren Lomasky.[26]

Without going into great detail, I wish to offer hearty endorsement to the general approach taken by Lomasky, while calling attention to certain features of his argument that appear to me either to be damaging distractions to the key idea or, in some cases, plain mistakes. For one thing, Lomasky offers a technical definition of the term "project" that is more restrictive than is necessary in his attempt to provide a grounding for rights. "Projects," in his book, are not just any old undertakings that would be covered by that term in ordinary English:

Some ends are not once-and-for-all acknowledged and then realized through the successful completion of one particular action. Rather, they persist throughout large stretches of an individual's life and continue to elicit actions that establish a pattern coherent in virtue of the ends subserved. Those which reach indefinitely into the future, play a central role within the on-going endeavors of the individual, and provide a significant degree of structural stability to an individual's life I call *projects*.[27]

Suffice it to say here that, in my view, projects need not be as grand as this in order to justify rights in general, or property rights in particular. That some such projects as these play important roles in normal human lives is undoubtedly true, and this is certainly an important consideration in what Lomasky calls "philosophical anthropology." But I do not believe this fact to be as essential to rights theory as Lomasky indicates.

Beyond this unnecessarily technical definition of "projects," it must be remarked that Lomasky argues – mistakenly, in my view – that an appreciation of the importance of personal projects in human lives leads to a renunciation of several related traditional philosophical doctrines: (1) the doctrine of the impartiality of the moral point of view; (2) the doctrine of the interchangeability of persons within utilitarianism; (3) the utilitarian doctrine that the goal of moral reflection is the maximization of general happiness; and (4) the Rawlsian doctrine that questions of justice should be settled behind an appropriately situated veil of ignorance. Any or all of these doctrines may be false, but Lomasky is mistaken, I think, in holding that their falsity follows from a full appreciation of the importance of projects – even the very grand projects that he intends – in human life. If Lomasky is right about the importance of projects, each of the doctrines listed above has well-known theoretical facility to acknowledge and incorporate this philosophically anthropological fact.

Having briefly indicated where I part company from Lomasky, I must reemphasize the importance of his effort to secure for projects their fundamental place in the justification of rights, and especially of property rights.

4. RIGHTS OF NONINTERFERENCE

I thus come to the second key principle involved in my projects-based argument for private property rights:

NONINTERFERENCE PRINCIPLE: Claims against external interference should be generally respected out of a concern that people ought not to be interfered with in projects they undertake, so long as these projects do not themselves interfere with the just projects of others.

The notion of property (and of rights in general), and the rules that adhere to property (and rights), are best understood in terms of an attempt to capture and explicate the above principle of justice. This is at least consistent with the "expressivism" of Nozick's EL: " ... Our concern for individual autonomy and liberty ... is itself in part an expressive concern. We believe these valuable not simply because of the particular actions they enable someone to choose to perform, or the goods they enable him to acquire, but because of the ways they enable him to engage in pointed and elaborate self-expressive and self-symbolizing activity that further elaborate and develop the person."[28]

What is required is a means of carving out, for each person, a realm in which activity is just and proper, a realm in which noninterference may reasonably be expected, or even demanded. Such assurance also must give some specification to the limits of the realm thus defined. With specific reference to property rights, Charles Reich has put the point well: "Property performs the function of maintaining independence, dignity and pluralism in society by creating zones within which the majority has to yield to the owner."[29]

Some rights may be held to be innate (the right to life?). Some other rights may be held to be maturational – they apply upon reaching some appropriate developmental stage (the right to full liberty?). Finally, some rights may be held to be acquired, perhaps on the basis of earlier rights (the right to some particular thing?). All of these "rights," though, are derivative from considerations of justice. It is unjust to interfere with others in projects that interfere with none of our just projects. What we are trying to do, in building up a taxonomy of rights, is to give system to this general principle of justice.

Those who argue that rights restrict freedom are certainly correct. Indeed, this is the entire point of rights: to enunciate restrictions on the "freedom" of others to interfere with morally privileged activity, whether individual or collective. The question about rights then becomes a question about how freedom ought to be restricted, and on the basis of what considerations.

So: Are there any rights that we may have that are additional to our right to life (as explicated briefly above)? I shall argue in behalf of a right that I claim is a direct descendent of the Noninterference Principle.

If there were a range of activities that could not possibly interfere with the activities of others, because no activity in that range affects others in ways that violate previously established just claims of theirs, then there would be possible, should someone undertake an activity in this new range, a direct application of the Noninterference Principle.[30] Since new activity in this area impinges nowhere on activity over which others can make just claims, activity in this area could not interfere with anyone's just claims.

I take it that it is something like this character that many people like about John Locke's rule for just acquisition of previously unowned resources. I have argued, though, that Locke's argument fails in most respects. It fails, to summarize those earlier arguments, because (1) it rests on "labor-mixing," and the labor-mixing argument is suspicious; (2) it includes a proviso or qualification that appears to be at least conceptually problematic and at worst self-defeating; and (3) it is couched in theological terms that are dubious (although these may be purged with no substantial loss of strength to the argument).[31]

But are there any untapped realms of activity? Surely there are indefinitely many, in fact. That this may seem surprising is due, I think, to a well-entrenched tendency to assume that all possible activity that does not yet have rights attached to it is somehow rightfully within the scope of community or state decision. The assumption, when stripped of obfuscation, is that whatever activity does not yet have rights assigned in and around it may rightfully *get* rights assigned by state or community apportionment. In the case of things that might be thought of as property, this comes to the peculiar (but widely accepted) assumption that whatever is not yet owned by anyone is at least quasi-owned by the state or community, since state or community is deemed to have the right to determine its disposition. But this assumption begs the question at issue, since it assumes a prior solution to the problem of property, which just *is* the problem of how things may rightly be disposed of. Unfortunately, this kind of question begging is not uncommon in the history of discourse about property rights.

5. A GENERAL RIGHT TO PRIVATE PROPERTY?

A particularly subtle version of the presumption in question (the presumption, that is, that whatever is not yet owned by anyone is quasi-owned by the state or community) is to be found in the contention that, if property rights are so important to people, then society should ensure that everyone gets some property. Jeremy Waldron entertains this possibility with considerable sympathy in his influential 1988 book, *The Right to Private Property*,[32] after arguing that the prospects for justifying private property as what he calls a "special right," in the way that both Locke and Nozick attempt to do, are bleak.[33]

Waldron's discussion depends on two distinctions among types of possible rights, one of which derives from the work of H. L. A. Hart and the other of which is Waldron's own. Hart distinguished between "special rights," which arise out of some special event or relationship, and "general rights," which don't.[34] A clear example of a special right would be one that is created by a promise. Common examples of putative general rights would be rights to life, liberty, and the pursuit of happiness.

When Hart first suggested distinguishing among rights in this way, he indicated no distinction between special rights that bind only those who were involved in the special transaction that gave rise to them, on the one hand, and special rights that don't, on the other. Waldron argues that, especially in considering property rights, this is an important distinction to make. He suggests, further, that the question of how rights arise ought to be kept conceptually clear of the question of who is bound by the rights.

Thus, for Waldron, the distinction between special and general rights focuses only on the question of origin. A second distinction, between rights *in personam*, which bind only those who are involved in the special transaction that creates the rights, and rights *in rem*, which are not so limited, is proposed. Waldron then examines the several possible combinations of these categories as represented in the following diagram:

	in personam	*in rem*
Special	I	II
General	III	IV

Two of these four categories are clearly instantiated in the moral world, Waldron argues, while two are problematic. Category I is the class of special rights *in personam*, an example of which is the standard promise. Category IV, the class of general rights *in rem*, collects things like the standard rights to life, liberty, and the pursuit of happiness.

Category III, though – the class of general rights *in personam* – which Waldron seems to think might have some instances in the moral world – looks pretty incoherent. He suggests that items in this category would have to be "limited in an *in personam* kind of way," but given his definition of "rights *in personam*," it would have to be limited, in particular, by a transaction that, by hypothesis (in the case of general rights), hasn't taken place. In any case, I will follow Waldron in ignoring Category III.

The interesting category for present purposes is Category II: the class of special rights *in rem*, since this is where Waldron takes on an entire class of property theories that includes both Locke's and Nozick's:

> On the view usually associated with John Locke and Robert Nozick, the right of an appropriator is a special right *in rem*, that is, a special right against the world. Consider the right of a Lockean farmer to the field he has enclosed and cultivated. That right (to exclude others from the field, to control it for his own benefit, etc.) is a special right inasmuch as it is not a right he is supposed to have *ab initio* or as a matter of course: it arises out of a particular contingent event in which he was involved – namely, the event of his labouring on the field. Not everyone gets around to labouring on a field, and certainly only one person can be the *first* to labour on any particular field; so the right in question is, in Hart's terms, peculiar to him who has it. But the right so acquired is nevertheless a right against all the world, and thus a right *in rem*, because, on Locke's account, once the field has been laboured on, *anyone* who interferes with it without the labourer's consent will be in violation of his duty. Similarly, on Locke's account and particularly on Nozick's, rights arising out of the sale and purchase of fields and other appropriated resources are special rights *in rem*.[35]

Waldron argues, in the end, not only that Locke's and Nozick's particular defenses of property rights as special rights *in rem* fail, but that it is simply implausible that there is anything anyone could do with as yet unowned resources that could bind the world in the way that private property rights are supposed to do. Thus, any effort to replace Locke's labor-mixing argument with some other relevantly similar argument is doomed.

Waldron is not necessarily an opponent of private property rights, however, since he thinks many of the traditional arguments in behalf of private property are rather persuasive. These persuasive arguments, though, all have a tendency to place private property rights in Category IV: They are binding on the world, all right, but no special event or relationship creates them. Like the rights to life, liberty, and the pursuit of happiness, general rights to private property *in rem* belong to everyone. We have them from

birth. And like those other more familiar general rights *in rem*, they should
be protected by a just society.

In short, Waldron finds it at least plausible that society is obliged to
see to it that everyone gets the benefits of owning private property. What
are those benefits? Waldron discusses several possibilities, among which
are (1) the possibility that owning property of one's own is valuable or
necessary for autonomy, with autonomy acknowledged as a vital human
value; (2) the possibility that owning property is valuable or necessary for
ensuring one's security; (3) the possibility that owning property is good for
building character; and so forth. It is reasonable to presume that Waldron
would place the argument offered in this essay, to the effect that private
property will find its justification in connection with its importance in the
pursuit of personal projects, on this list. If projects are so important to
people, and if private property is vital to the pursuit of projects, then we
ought to see to it that everybody gets some.

Now, there is no doubt in my mind that it would be a good thing if
everyone had the benefits of private property that could be deployed in
the pursuit of projects of theirs that didn't interfere with the just projects
of others. This is an admirable goal, and it is hard to argue with the idea
that institutions that effectively accomplish this goal would be good ones.
The story isn't all one-sided; I would have to agree with the critics of
private property that there are lots of bad things that can come from it.
Nevertheless, on balance, institutions that promote ownership of private
property are, in my view, good institutions. The difficulties arise in design-
ing institutions that can do this effectively, and those problems are largely
empirical.

It might be, for example, that an arrangement like the one proposed
by Locke, where private property rights in previously unowned resources
can be acquired by first-comers through some special act like labor-mixing,
in fact makes it more likely that third parties will be able to acquire property rights over things they value than does any other halfway manageable
scheme. The domain of things propertized is thus expanded, after all, and
the resources that now may be purchased or acquired through exchange by
people who for whatever reason weren't out there rooting among the previously unowned stuff should make more property, and perhaps improved
property, available to everyone.[36] As Nozick points out, arguments like
these need not simply be part of a utilitarian justification of property – they
might instead be deployed only to support the claim that appropriation
of private property satisfies the intent of some version of the Lockean
proviso – but they *might* be.[37]

It would be a mistake to confuse rules like labor-mixing, which are intended as rules for bringing unowned resources into the general scheme of private ownership, for rules of ownership *simpliciter*. It's not hard to imagine someone reading Locke or Nozick and thinking that, once the race for first acquisition of a finite supply of previously unowned resources is over, then anyone who didn't manage to acquire property in that race is out of luck. But that's by now a well-known mistake. Most of those resources are now *more* readily available to others, since people don't now have to follow the rules for *first* acquisition to acquire them. They can buy or trade for the resources, for example.

But still: it must be admitted that lots of very different schemes of propertization might accomplish this same end without exactly mirroring full-blown private property schemes. If our objective is to ensure that everyone has private property, there would appear to be leeway for different institutional arrangements that would maximize the opportunities for personal projects (say) through the control of resources.

There is much less than meets the eye, however, in the idea that people may have a general right to private property. Unless the idea of a "general right to private property" presumes some prior holding of property on the part of those who are to fulfill or enforce this right, the right is empty. On the presumption that it is society in general that is to enforce this right, then unless society is in control of those resources that are to be bestowed on newborns (perhaps to be held in trust until maturity) in fulfillment of their general right to own private property, the right in question is no more than deceptive rhetoric.

Now, societies can and do control resources. But the question that was addressed by Locke and Nozick had to do with how property claims arise in the first place. What is it that justifies property claims? Especially when considering which claims may justly be made over activities and resources that have hitherto been beyond the bounds of all rights claims: What justifies making the *first* such claim?

Proponents of the general rights approach too often seem to be presupposing that the very toughest justificatory questions to be found in property theory have been resolved already. They presume to know that control of the resources they plan to deploy already justly rests in some hands or other – usually in the hands of the state. But that presumption comes down to a presumption that questions of ownership have already been settled.

It may well be that state control (i.e., ownership) of all previously unowned resources is precisely what is just. But that's just the kind of claim that is supposed to be established by a thoughtfully worked out property theory, and it's the kind of issue addressed directly by attempts, like Locke's or Nozick's, at establishing what it is that must happen in order to generate rights – that is, at specifying what generates special rights. The justifiable property rights might be private, and they might not be. It won't do at all, though, to presume the solution as the basis of the analysis.

Saying that there is a general right to private property hangs on to its moral content even if it is bereft of material substance. As justified by the kinds of arguments offered by Waldron, it would still provide support to the idea that we should arrange institutions in such a way that, other things being equal, opportunities for acquiring private property are maximized. But unless there is some argument – whether this same "general rights" argument or another – supporting the contention that society itself has a right to claim as property resources that have never yet been held by anyone, then the "general rights" argument must stop there: It must stop at the point where it recommends institutional arrangements that maximize people's ability to acquire private property.[38] Since both Locke's and Nozick's work can easily be seen as attempting to outline such arrangements, they don't run afoul of legitimate "general rights" concerns.

6. PROJECTS AND APPROPRIATION

In general, then, a coherent solution to our effort to build a system of rights must not assume some prior solution. In particular, it must not assume rights on the part of the state, or on the part of the community as a whole, or on the part of any majority or minority or individual. If such groups or persons are to be acknowledged as holding rights, then this acknowledgment must emerge from the analysis. It must not be presupposed.

Carefully avoiding the assumption that the community or state has rights over all activity in advance, then, are there any realms of activity that could not possibly interfere with the just activities of others? That will be a matter of considerable controversy. How about ranges of activity that *could* in principle interfere with the just activities of others, but certainly won't as a matter of fact? Or probably won't? How should the criterion for invoking the Noninterference Principle be worded?

I doubt whether there is one answer that will suffice in considering all proposed activities. A great deal will plainly depend on the degree of risk and on the seriousness of possible rights violations. The fine print of the rules regarding activity in new areas will, in many cases, have to depend upon standard consequentialist lines of reasoning. What these lines of argument will be refining, though, is something like the idea of a basic right to noninterference, and whether the aptness of acknowledging such right need itself be a function of bringing about consequences of one kind or another is not clear. All the traditional arguments among deontologists and consequentialists about the ultimate foundation of this basic right can clearly be reconstructed in these new terms. What I hope to establish in the present discussion is simply that something like it ought to be understood as a basic right.

How does the Noninterference Principle yield property rights, in particular? It yields them via the standard observation that activity characteristically requires objects, tools, and stability of expectation in regard to their use. I have nothing new to add here. The standard, though, for deciding which objects and which tools one comes to have property rights over, and what the extent of these property rights may be, ought itself to involve the Noninterference Principle.

To take the standard Lockean situation as an example: Previously unappropriated resources may justly be appropriated for use, by individuals and (perhaps) by groups or communities, provided only that such appropriation not interfere with the justly undertaken projects of others (delineated by rights, in most cases), and that any other rules that apply to such just appropriation be followed. It is important to reemphasize that the entire set of appropriation rules will be designed to maximize scope for projects in an effective way.

Let me hasten to add that (1) this does not give any specification as to what must be done in the way of appropriating; mixing labor seems at the same time too strong a requirement (because surely the projects of native hunters and gatherers should be respected) and too weak (because indiscriminate despoliation of the land may count as labor-mixing).[39] What we want is a principle that considers these problems;[40] (2) this account does not give any answer to the question of which "bundles" of rights get assigned to the appropriator. Thus, many of the questions that have animated critics of property rights, from Proudhon to G. A. Cohen, are not yet resolved by this account. But it must be insisted that decisions about what exactly one gets when one acquires property rights are matters of justice, and not simply matters of convenience to the state, to the majority, or to anyone else; (3) the extent of just appropriation is also undetermined by this account. Interestingly, though, the projects approach may, given its characteristic logic, offer some clues about how to resolve this last problem.

Among the things contributed to the discussion of property rights by the projects approach is the emphasis on mutual respect, on the obligations placed on me by the projects of others, as opposed to apparently selfish claims of my own against the world. It is not that traditional justifications of private property rights could not take this same perspective, it is rather a question of what is emphasized.

A remaining problem for the projects approach, as it is for other approaches, is this: Given any principle of just acquisition of previously unowned resources (suitably defined to include such spooky issues as acquisition of rights over "intellectual property" and the like), what exactly is it that one gains right over? The classical problem for property theory is clearly exemplified in arguments, such as Proudhon's, that concluded that while a farmer who plants and tends a crop is surely entitled to the produce, and even to the use of the land as long as the farmer continues to work it, nothing like ownership in perpetuity comes to be deserved.

The "projects" approach offered here suggests that what gets owned is a function of the definition of the project that is alleged to justify any given acquisition claim. Which project claims are justified, in turn, will be in large part a function of potential conflict – or, more precisely, the lack of conflict – with previously justified property claims, themselves defined and characterized in terms of projects.

The approach offered here thus suggests not so much a wholesale resolution of particular property claims but a language and method to be used in the consideration of such claims. This language and method is in no way morally neutral, depending as it does at least on the two principles that I have set out and discussed here. But my hope is that many apparent critiques of private property can actually be accommodated within property theory by choosing this language and this method.

For all this qualification, however, I think we do have, in this approach, the basis for a general right to act (a right, at least, to noninterference) in all areas that have been as yet untouched, in which no rights have been, as yet, established. Where the security of the project makes it wise, appropriation proper of previously unowned resources may well be justified.

Perhaps it is simplest to describe the matter in this way: Systems of rights aim at coordinating the just claims of members of some community, broadly understood. The content of such claims depends, in part, on the possibility of this kind of coordination. But if someone wishes to take his business outside the existing community of rights and rights-holders – or outside all communities, where no coordination problem as yet, by hypothesis, exists – he must, in justice, be allowed to do this without interference. Such extensions of the moral realm into as yet external domains are themselves formative of the new moral terrain.

7. CONCLUSION

In commenting on an earlier version of this essay, G. A. Cohen took issue with what he perceived as a too-easy slide from the right to noninterference to the right to appropriate. He is right in thinking that the inference is not immediate. In support of his complaint, Cohen quoted Judith Jarvis Thomson, as follows:

> . . . it is not at all plausible to think that if something is unowned, then each of us has claims against others to noninterference with our uses of it. Having a claim to noninterference is very different from having a privilege; and it is not at all clear what I could do to an unowned thing that would generate in me a claim to noninterference with my uses of it.
>
> Ownership includes not merely privileges, not merely claims, but powers as well, such as the power to make other people have powers. What could I do to an unowned thing that would generate in me the power to make other people have powers in respect of it?[41]

Cohen might as well have quoted any one of an entire tradition of thinkers, from at least Proudhon to Waldron.

What I have tried to show here, however, is precisely how to argue for the move from noninterference to appropriation. Your right to my noninterference is to be based on an understanding of the importance of projects to persons. What I am to refrain from interfering with – that is, what you acquire a right to when you acquire a right to my noninterference – will be defined in terms of the requirements of your project, on the one hand, and the previously established rights of others, on the other.

The Noninterference Principle yields also a right of transfer of alienable rights, among them rights to transfer property. Wherever people severally agree to exchange or otherwise transfer rights that they have, and wherever such exchange or transfer violates no previously established rights or just claims of others, then the principle demands that this cooperative activity be free of interference from others.

Finally: Many who have written about property rights[42] have argued that acquisitions and transfers, where they improve the positions of the people who engage in them, may frequently violate the principle of Noninterference mentioned earlier in this essay. They are alleged by some authors to do this in all "competitive" situations, since they leave others at a competitive disadvantage. They also may "deprive others of opportunity."[43]

This criticism is hard to fathom for two reasons that I shall simply mention, rather than discuss. First, the rights of first acquisition and transfer discussed here derive directly from the Noninterference Principle, quite independent of any reference to competition. Perhaps, if "competitive situations" are special, consideration of their special character will lead to special rules of application in those situations. I have no intuitions whatsoever about how one might propose to do this, short of simply abolishing all competition. Indeed, it is not even clear to me that capitalism, which some of those who offer this critique seem to think of as a near paradigm of this kind of situation, is really "competitive" at all in the required sense. Much depends, I think, on how one understands the term "capitalism."[44]

Second, it is hard to understand why it would be unfair or unjust, given that one is in a competitive situation, to gain advantages over others as part of the competition. Imagine a chess game, in which both parties have been playing by the rules, and in which one party objected that the seizure of his queen was "unfair." What could be meant by that in such a situation, beyond a mere expression of frustration (or, perhaps, a joke)? Again, the argument seems to amount to a claim against competition as such, if it has any force at all. Yet no argument against competition, in general, is characteristically offered by those who take this approach. Perhaps it is a supposed necessary character of competing in capitalist economies that makes the situation different from chess, and which allows entry for accusations of unfairness. But, again: No defense of the alleged necessity of the relevant kind of competition under capitalist regimes is typically offered, anyway, against the claim that people are perfectly free to cooperate with one another, and no defense is offered for the claim that there is any unfairness involved at all.

Let me summarize, in any case, the small progress that I hope to have made in this essay. We have not yet arrived at a full-fledged substitute for the labor-mixing principle, but I have suggested that consideration of the role of personal projects in human life (a role emphasized in all of Robert Nozick's work) will play a central justificatory role in establishing whatever principle of first acquisition emerges. Focusing on the importance of projects to human life and to human personality will preserve much of the intent of Locke's labor-mixing principle, while giving full consideration as well to the projects of nonlabor-mixers, both historical and current. The insistence on alteration of things is eliminated altogether.

I have not provided a foolproof criterion of acquisition, transfer, or anything else, any more than Nozick has so far been able to do. I am convinced, in fact, that any rule is bound to have loopholes.[45] But the approach to property taken here avoids, I think, some of the more glaring problems of earlier approaches.

Notes

[1] Various versions of this essay were read and discussed at West Virginia University, Bowling Green State University, SUNY at Buffalo, and the University of Waterloo. Earlier versions were delivered at the meetings of the Ockham Society, Oxford University, the International Society for Value Inquiry in Moscow, the Tenth International Social Philosophy Conference in Helsinki, and at a meeting of the Rochester Area Political Thought Forum, University of Rochester. While I am grateful to all of the participants in these various sessions for their comments and criticisms, I owe special debts to G. A. Cohen, who was my commenter at Oxford, and to Roger Crisp, Jan Narveson, Sharon Ryan, David Schmidtz, Danny Shapiro, David Suits, and Naomi Zack.

[2] Robert Nozick, *Anarchy, State, and Utopia* (New York: Basic Books, 1974), p. ix.

[3] Ibid.

[4] ASU, especially pp. 167–82 and 268–71.

[5] This is the strategy adopted in John T. Sanders, "Justice and the Initial Acquisition of Property," *Harvard Journal of Law and Public Policy*, 10 (1987). See especially pp. 367–68, where this issue is discussed, and footnote 2 at the bottom of p. 368.

[6] Sharon Ryan's comments on an earlier version of this essay were instrumental in helping me sort out a plain inconsistency in my thinking. I confess, though, that I'm still not sure whether or not it's best to extend rights jargon to other animal species.

[7] ASU, p. 39.

[8] I am opposing here a line of thought that has been worked out by Jan Narveson, among others. See especially Narveson, "Animal Rights Revisited," in H. Miller and W. Williams (eds.), *Ethics and Animals* (Humana Press, 1983), pp. 45–60; Narveson, "A Case Against Animal Rights," *Advances in Animal Welfare Science* (The Humane Society of the United States, 1986); and Jan Narveson, "Morals and Animals," *Moral Matters* (2nd edition), pp. 133–42 (Peterborough, Ont.: Broadview Press, 1999).

[9] Such an approach would seem to settle the question of whether nonhuman animals can have rights for Hobbesians. They don't, unless some sense can be made of hypothetical agreements between humans and members of other species.

[10] *The Examined Life: Philosophical Meditations* (New York: Simon and Schuster, 1989), pp. 286–87.

[11] EL, p. 287.

[12] See also John T. Sanders, "The State of Statelessness," in John T. Sanders and Jan Narveson (eds.), *For and Against the State: New Philosophical Readings*

(Lanham, Md.: Rowman and Littlefield, 1996), pp. 255–88, and Gerald F. Gauss, "Goals, Symbols, Principles: Nozick on Practical Rationality," this volume.

[13] "Justice and the Initial Acquisition of Property," op. cit.

[14] The arguments in question are to be found not only in Locke's *Second Treatise* but also in the *First Treatise*. See Peter Laslett (ed.), *Locke's Two Treatises of Government* (Cambridge: Cambridge University Press, 1960).

[15] See Schmidtz, "When Is Original Appropriation *Required* ?," *The Monist* (October 1990): 504–18, and Schmidtz, *The Limits of Government: An Essay on the Public Goods Argument* (Boulder, Col.: Westview Press, 1991), pp. 15–32.

[16] See Charles Darwin's introduction to Ernst Krause, *Erasmus Darwin* (London: J. Murray, 1879), p. 45.

[17] In "The Institution of Property" (*Social Philosophy and Policy*, 1994), Schmidtz elaborates his discussion of these matters considerably, suggesting (roughly) that the proviso *allows* appropriation when demand does not exceed the carrying capacity of the commons, then *requires* appropriation when demand exceeds carrying capacity. The "proviso" is plainly not functioning as a proviso if (as seems plausible) it works like that.

[18] ASU, pp. 178–9.

[19] ASU, pp. 174–5.

[20] "The Nature and Value of Rights," *Journal of Value Inquiry*, 4 (1970), p. 252.

[21] ASU, pp. 42–5. See also David Schmidtz, "The Meanings of Life," this volume.

[22] Roger Crisp has suggested in personal correspondence that, since one can imagine an experience machine on which one could still make autonomous choices, the case made in the text might be stronger if one imagined that a chip – one that makes all your decisions for you in such a way as to maximize pleasure, success, or whatever – is implanted in your head.

[23] ASU, p. 43.

[24] Rawls, *A Theory of Justice* (Cambridge, Mass.: Harvard University Press, 1971).

[25] See especially "Persons, Character and Morality," in Williams, *Moral Luck* (London: Cambridge University Press, 1981). See also "A Critique of Utilitarianism," in J. J. C. Smart and Bernard Williams (eds.), *Utilitarianism: For and Against* (London: Cambridge University Press, 1973).

[26] Especially *Persons, Rights, and the Moral Community* (New York: Oxford University Press, 1987).

[27] Lomasky, op. cit., p. 26.

[28] EL, p. 287.

[29] See Reich, "The New Property," *The Yale Law Journal*, 73 (1964). As Gerald Gaus and Loren Lomasky observe, this in no way distinguishes property rights from any others. See Gaus and Lomasky, "Are Property Rights Problematic?," *The Monist*, 73 (1990), pp. 492–3.

[30] This formulation is an idealization. Application in the real world will have to interpret it in light of claims made about interference. I shall address some such claims, briefly, in Section 6.

[31] See Sanders, "Justice and the Initial Acquisition of Property."

[32] Jeremy Waldron, *The Right to Private Property* (Oxford: Clarendon Press, 1988), pp. 106ff.

[33] Waldron's argument against the possibility of "special rights" justifications of private property is ably countered, I think, by A. John Simmons, "Original Acquisition Justifications of Private Property," in Ellen Frankel Paul et al. (eds.), *Property Rights* (Cambridge: Cambridge University Press, 1994), pp. 63–84. As Simmons argues, what Waldron calls "special rights *in rem*" (and what will be referred to below as "Category II rights") are in general far more familiar and considerably less repugnant than Waldron suggests. The conventional way in which pick-up softball games acquire playing space is an excellent example (Simmons, p. 83). In what follows, my own aim is to address the positive reasons advanced by Waldron for thinking that there might be a general right to property.

[34] H. L. A. Hart, "Are There Any Natural Rights," in Jeremy Waldron (ed.), *Theories of Rights* (Oxford: Oxford University Press, 1984).

[35] Waldron, The Right to Private Property, pp. 108–09.

[36] Schmidtz's arguments in "The Institution of Property" are especially useful here.

[37] ASU, p. 177.

[38] I am indebted to Danny Shapiro for an annoyingly reasonable argument that helped me see that my earlier line of thought on this point was incomplete.

[39] See "Justice and the Initial Acquisition of Property," pp. 388–9.

[40] And others – such as the fact that labor-mixing is just incoherent as a means of acquiring some of the rights that are now regarded as property rights.

[41] Judith Jarvis Thomson, *The Realm of Rights* (Cambridge, Mass.: Harvard University Press, 1990), p. 325.

[42] See, for example, Lawrence C. Becker, *Property Rights: Philosophic Foundations* (Boston: Routledge and Kegan Paul, 1977), p. 43.

[43] Becker, op. cit., p. 43.

[44] For more on this, see John T. Sanders, "The State of Statelessness," pp. 276–8.

[45] For further discussion of such problems, see Sanders, "Justice and the Initial Acquisition of Property," pp. 397–8.

4 | Nozick's Libertarian Utopia

LOREN E. LOMASKY

I. INTRODUCTION

Whatever the attractions elsewhere of utopia-spinning, it may seem decidedly out of place within libertarian theorizing. No privileged good incumbent on individuals or societies is acknowledged by libertarianism. Rather, it is the theory quintessentially committed to leaving people alone to direct their lives as they themselves see fit, not as some edifying copy-book might dictate to them. Philosophers and assorted gazers on stars may harbor pet prescriptions and ingenious nostrums for how life might be better – even *best* – lived. Fair enough; they are at liberty to try in the marketplace of ideas to peddle their wares to willing consumers. But even should one such conception of the good attract overwhelming attention and support, its authority extends only to those who voluntarily subscribe to its dictates. Anyone is free to embrace whatever mode of life appeals, provided only that it does not incorporate rights-violating activity. The result is that within a libertarian framework there can be no preferred conception that merits the honorific, *utopia*.

Alternatively, we might say that libertarian utopia is not some one privi-leged pattern of social relations but, rather, any order incorporating full re-spect and regard for the rights of individuals. Understood in that way, utopia is not some one especially felicitous arrangement but rather a full instantia-tion of the principles governing the processes through which arrangements of any sort might emerge. It is, in a word, libertarianism well-practiced. But while this interpretation of *libertarian utopia* may be consistent enough with libertarianism, the utopian element seems to have dropped out. To enjoy a libertarian utopia is simply to be possessed of libertarianism. By similar accounting, a Hobbesian utopia is a regime in which sovereignty is unlimited and absolute, a Rawlsian utopia one in which the two principles of justice have been given effect. Willy-nilly, all theories of politics have been rendered utopian. A potentially informative designation has thereby been emptied of content, and significant structural differences among

59

competing brands of political theories have been elided. Indeed, the so-called libertarian utopia appears to be more scandalous than the others. For example, Rawls declares "In justice as fairness men agree to share one another's fate ... to avail themselves of the accidents of nature and social circumstance only when doing so is for the common benefit."[1] That lends some plausibility to reading *A Theory of Justice* as utopian, for to take as morally primary an overarching fate that unites all agents and that constitutes in some measure for them a joint success or failure is to announce a view that bears at least a family resemblance to other utopian exercises that would meld the many into a harmonious, admirable one. By way of contrast, libertarian transactors bear their own several, undistributed fates, and one point – arguably the central point – of the libertarian structure is that persons' implication in the success or failure of others, absent specific ties of contract or affection, is minimized. In this sense, we might think, no species of politics is less utopian than libertarianism.

Is it settled, then, that Robert Nozick should have titled his libertarian manifesto *Anarchy and State*? Not necessarily. For several reasons, the actual title might, after all, be the better one. First, it is more mellifluous. Second, and more substantively, it has the virtue of assertively presenting a libertarianism with a human face. "One *must not* violate the rights of others!" Thus, a social order in which each is free from interference is mandatory. Well, yes, but for all that the imperative conveys, this might be the political equivalent of cod liver oil. No doubt respect for rights fends off the worst that human beings can and do visit on each other – Hobbes's state of nature, the Gulag – but it doesn't in any obvious way hold forth the promise of anything very lovely. People who scrupulously refrain from violating others' rights may nonetheless be glum, unfriendly, flinty, humorless. Like the stereotypical Prussian officer, they may be disposed to follow the orders that justice passes along but not to flavor them with any discernable measure of warmth or compassion. This sort of reflection prompts indictments from both the left and right by critics of liberalism who find it wanting as a creed that can inspire and uplift human beings. Contemporary communitarians, for example, claim that liberal rights to self-determination are a thin gruel that fails to provide the spiritual sustenance and sense of a meaning to one's life that are afforded by communal ideals and commitments. Humming the same tune but with slightly different rhythms are exponents of manifest national destiny or divinely dictated imperatives. Liberals can and must resist these sorts of blandishments, but as a matter of salesmanship, if nothing else, it will be helpful if they can supplement the dour directives of a deontology that speaks mainly in an idiom of "Thou shalt not"s with depictions of goods that attract and enliven. A libertarianism that weaves into its garment of side constraints some utopian threads may thereby be better fortified to deflect illiberal broadsides.

A third reason to believe that utopian considerations are not alien to libertarianism, especially the libertarianism of Nozick, is that when eventually he comes to disown the theory of *Anarchy, State, and Utopia*, the grounds he advances can plausibly be read as invoking utopian considerations:

> The libertarian position I once propounded now seems to me seriously inadequate, in part because it did not knit the humane considerations and joint cooperative activities it left room for more closely into its fabric. It neglected the symbolic importance of an official political concern with issues or problems, as a way of marking their importance or urgency, and hence of expressing, intensifying, channeling, encouraging, and validating our private actions and concerns toward them. . . . There are some things we choose to do together through government in solemn marking of our human solidarity, served by the fact that we do them together in this official fashion.[2]

The critique is not transparent, but it seems to be an indictment of libertarianism not on grounds of any particular injustice done to specifiable citizens but rather because of some unity deficit afflicting laissez-faire arrangements. That is, even if individuals are doing tolerably well severally, they underachieve with regard to what they (don't) do jointly. Although utopia has not yet been formally characterized in these pages, Nozick's attention to what is done together rather than what is enjoyed separately puts his concerns at least in the immediate neighborhood.

For these reasons, if the libertarianism of ASU merits being taken seriously, then so, too, does its utopian coda. Accordingly, Section II stipulates an understanding of what it is for a political order to be both libertarian and utopian. Section III is the heart of the essay. It begins by reviewing the antithesis of libertarian society developed in ASU's penultimate chapter, "Demoktesis," and then shows how such extreme collectivism is inverted to generate the concluding "A Framework for Utopia." I argue that the strategy for realizing utopia can usefully be understood as an extension and strengthening of familiar forms of liberal toleration. Section IV suggests that Nozick can be seen as developing ideas foreshadowed by an earlier libertarian utopianism, that of J. S. Mill. Section V argues that a line often taken up by critics of liberalism is even less forceful than usual when the target is a Mill-Nozick libertarian utopianism. The essay concludes with a brief examination in Section VI of the later Nozick's utopian counterlibertarianism.

II. CONSTRUING UTOPIA

I assume for the sake of this exposition that "utopia" is not simply an honorific to be accorded to a social order in virtue of its being skillfully designed
and regulated. That is not primarily because of any ordinary language strictures about proper deployment of the term, but because so doing would
render utopian reflection epiphenomenal, nothing above and beyond ordinary theory construction. Accordingly, I stipulate the following four conditions as necessary for a political order to be in the running as a libertarian
utopia.

1. Utopia is *synergistic*. The success measure of the society as a whole is not
    merely the additive sum of the success measures of the individuals who
    make it up. Rather, their various efforts constitute a whole the value of
    which is greater than that of its parts. This can be understood in either
    of two ways. In the first, the society as a whole is deemed to be an entity
    that possesses ends, projects, and volitions, thereby having a good of its
    own that takes precedence over that of the individuals who comprise
    it. This sort of organicist conception is inadmissible in a liberalism
    that takes individual men and women to be the bearers of moral sta-
    tus. The second understanding sees individuals in society as benefitting
    from spillover effects due to their standing in the relationship of *fellow
    citizen* to those among whom they live. On this conception, social rela-
    tions matter not because they constitute some putative organic whole
    but because they confer on individuals dividends above and beyond
    opportunities to transact in furtherance of personal projects. If these
    dividends are not merely occasional and incidental but systemic and
    substantial, they underpin a liberalism that can also be utopian.

2. The framework of the political order is a *local maximum*. That is, if it
    were altered along any dimension things would be made worse. The
    point of this condition is to capture the idea of utopia as superlative, as
    surpassing feasible alternatives. A stronger condition still would be to
    insist that the framework be a *global* maximum, the best of all possible
    forms of social life. I believe this to be too strong because it rules out the
    existence of several radically different social forms, each of which is a
    remarkably successful instantiation of its kind but which are responsive
    to such different goods that they are not meaningfully comparable. So,
    for example, it may be useful to appraise the libertarian minimal state
    against the more-than-minimal state of democratic redistributivism but
    not against a monastic community organized around a common faith.

3. Utopia is in *equilibrium*. That is, it possesses homeostatic defenses against crashing and burning when subjected to pressures from within or without. Political orders, for better or for worse, don't endure forever, but they are structures within which people can reasonably expect to live out complete lives, They are less like roman candles than steady, luminous beacons. Being inherently self-sustaining counts in favor of a regime's utopian standing; carrying the seeds of its own destruction counts against. We appraise a social order not as a time-slice, or even as a series of time-slices, but as a temporally continuous entity constituted by its history and prospects.[3]

4. The ends to which people swear allegiance and the roles and relationships they take on will mostly be a matter of their own uncoerced choices. I say "mostly" because the opportunities open to individuals and how they respond to these opportunities are also a function of the natural endowments they possess, their early acculturation, vagaries of circumstances encountered and, most important, their dependence on the assent of equally self-determining others. The weight to be assigned to these factors and the implications that follow are extensively debated in the literature. Those issues cannot be taken up here, but it is stipulated that the shape taken by a society be that which emerges from the multitude of uncoordinated choices taken by the individuals that make it up, not vice versa. This is the stipulation that accounts for the putative utopia's character as libertarian.

I turn next to how these stipulations are to be realized.

III. CONSTRUCTING UTOPIA

By the time we arrive at the third triad element of ASU, it may seem that all the essential work of developing a full libertarian theory has been completed (or, if it has not been, then the preceding arguments stand in need of patching rather than supplementation by a new philosophical initiative). In the first part of the book, Nozick demonstrates to his satisfaction that the minimal state can emerge from the anarchic background of the state of nature without violating fundamental moral strictures and, moreover, that the result thereby achieved constitutes an improvement from the perspective of securing individuals' rights. In the second part, he argues against Rawls, Marxists, and assorted proponents of an extensive redistributive apparatus that political structures more capacious than the minimal state do incorporate impermissible encroachments on rights, and are, therefore, illegitimate. Many readers who grant the cogency of those two argumentative strategies will take the moral credentials of libertarianism to have been validated. Nozick, however, sees an escape hatch that needs to be closed. Even if all extant more-than-minimal states come into being and maintain themselves via massive trains of rights violations, this does not constitute a demonstration that they must do so. Might there be a rights-preserving avenue via which the minimal state could be transformed into a more-than-minimal state, specifically into the redistributive democratic state? Pursuit of that question is the burden of the remarkable ninth chapter, "Demoktesis."

Candidates and Elections

Recall that the derivation of the minimal state is hypothetical, an account of processes by which its institutions *could have* emerged. It is not presented as a historical model of the evolution of any actual minimal state, of which there are none, nor is it in any obvious way a blueprint for how we might move from current insufficiently just arrangements to those that do better by way of attending to the rights of individuals. If Nozick's analyses are correct, then there are possible worlds in which rights-preserving transformations yield as their equilibrium outcome the minimal state. But what is the upshot for *this* possible world, one with a decidedly nonideal history? It is not altogether clear what Nozick takes the answer to be. But perhaps he intends something like this: If a social order is such that it could emerge only as a consequence of violating peoples' rights, then it is rejected on grounds of its injustice.[4] If a social order could emerge without violating people's rights, then it is a *candidate* for acceptability. If there exists only one candidate, then it is chosen forthwith. But if two or more candidates emerge, then some mechanism is required to choose among them. Let us call this mechanism an *election*. Because all eligible candidates have satisfied the deontological criterion of not necessarily incorporating rights violations, the election will be decided by appealing to some other standard. Let us call the process of appealing to proffered standards the *campaign*.

The function of hypothetical histories is, in the first instance, to determine which are the eligible candidates. But when invoked as elements of a campaign, they also can help swing an election. Suppose that in one hypothetical history people wax in knowledge, fellow-feeling, and aesthetic appreciation, while in another they stagnate. It is plausible, all else being equal, to call for the election of the more dynamic society. Of course, all else may not be equal; the histories may have alternative versions in which they run different courses, and there may be yet undiscovered narratives featuring heretofore unpublicized favorite sons to nominate as candidates. Therefore, we should be careful not to put more weight on hypothetical histories than they can bear; nothing close to an algorithm for choice among regime-types is on offer. It is, though, important to observe that they can serve not only as (in)justice detectors but also as indicators of overall attractiveness.[5]

The minimal state is the sole candidate throughout the first eight chapters of ASU, but the story told in "Demoktesis" probes eligibility possibilities for democratic redistributive regimes. As Nozick tells it, progression away from the minimal state comes about because people wish to achieve heightened efficiency in capitalizing on positive externalities potentially forthcoming from others' choices. By giving away or trading rights to various kinds of activities that one might perform (the color of paint selected for the exterior of one's house, the quantity of one's whisky consumption, etc.), individuals surrender and gain stakes in each other that take the form of full or partial entitlements to determine how they behave. Concerns to lessen transaction costs leads to increasing standardization of holdings until everyone has precisely one share in everyone, including in oneself. These partial ownership rights are exercised via elected representatives whose powers may be unlimited or may be bounded by checks that preserve for individuals some of the moral space within which they had formerly exercised sovereign self-direction. Voilà! – the (much) more-than-minimal state has been realized through justice-preserving transactions.

Is the outcome plausible? In one sense it certainly is: The institutions of the regime so generated bear considerably greater resemblance to the political furniture of actual societies than does the minimal state. In another sense, it is wildly implausible; the transformative steps are highly artificial when compared with those that had yielded the minimal state. That latter implausibility may not matter, though, if the point is simply to demonstrate the *possibility* of a morally licit path for the emergence of a democratic redistributive state. There must, then, be an election. My suggestion is that Nozick's "Utopia" section is best understood as the campaign for the minimal state.

The Platform of Libertarian Utopia

Turning now to the major themes of that campaign, we observe two central features that render Nozick's libertarian utopia both libertarian and utopian.

First, it is libertarian in that the various ideals of the good represented therein are voluntarily subscribed to by individuals acting in consort with willing others. No one is enlisted by an exercise of force majeure into communities directed toward ends for which she holds no regard. Rather, she is at liberty to attempt to collaborate with those who will have her as a partner in their designs and they are at liberty to try to secure her consent. Community membership, then, is analogous to market transactions insofar as they are constituted by unanimous agreement.[6]

Second, it is utopian insofar as persons are recipients of more than that for which they bargain. This point is more implicit than explicitly argued in Nozick's treatment, but it is what lends to the libertarian utopia whatever charm it possesses beyond the familiar "markets work" refrain. Development of this thought will not be straightforward, but its starting point is familiar from every first year microeconomics text. People are not interchangeable; they differ in their talents, circumstances, opinions, and preferences. The constituents of a satisfactory life for one individual will not be identical to those for all others, perhaps not for any others. This platitudinous observation underscores the desirability of the division of labor in economic markets. More significant in the present context, it supports the desirability of affording individuals a wide liberty to act on behalf of those ends to which they themselves subscribe rather than ends which are validated by some standard external to their own valuations. When you and I go out to eat at a restaurant, we are each likely to dine better if you order the particular dishes that you crave and I the dishes that I want rather than my ordering for you and you for me. (This is not to deny, of course, that we may be able to increase our consumer surpluses yet further by agreeing to share a bottle of wine or by offering each other tastes of our different delectables.) In the typical case each person knows better than does anyone else her likes and dislikes, has a better idea of her own optimal tradeoffs (calories for succulence, portion size for dollars), greater zeal for advancing the ends that are her own rather than those of another, more attentiveness to costs that she herself will bear than those that will be borne by others, and so on.

The upshot in the realm of economic theory is private property and enforceable contracts. In liberal political philosophy it is possession by all competent agents of zones of limited sovereignty within which they are self-determining and immune from coercion. The perimeter of that zone is established by the rights people possess. On some accounts these rights are entirely negative, rights to noninterference; on other accounts they also incorporate certain claims to positive provision. The details aside, a theory will not qualify as liberal unless it affords primary recognition to the exercise of individual discretion.[7] Actors are understood to be motivated by their own conceptions of the good, and they are restrained by principles of justice in their dealings with others because the mutual recognition of such restraints allows each to do better according to his own conception of the good than would be the case if they were unrestrained. No ties of affection or fellow-feeling are assumed. So, for example, Rawls models the contractors in his original position as mutually disinterested rational maximizers.[8] Similarly, Gauthier describes them as *nontuistic*,[9] meaning thereby that their utilities are independent. And Nozick's own rights-bearers edging their way from the state of nature to dominant protective agencies to the minimal state are presented throughout the transition as avid custodians of their own ends.

Critics of liberalism frequently indict this model as *atomistic*. That charge is not typically rendered very precise, nor are the communitarian and/or collectivist alternatives offered in its stead. (Further specification and discussion is offered in Section V.) Liberals frequently respond that rights-bearing individuals are, of course, free to establish one with another relations for mutual benefit, and that for all but a handful of anchorites or misanthropes the creation of rich webs of sociality is an important characteristic of human lives. That response is certainly correct, but it may be deemed not to go far enough. For on this picture all benefit-conferring associations are both external and instrumental; the value of the attachments is derivative from the service provided to one's own preferred conception of the good. If a better offer, a more efficient route to the advancement of one's own utility function becomes available, then one is morally at liberty, indeed rationally obliged, to accept. The system of transaction for the sake of benefits that are, even if mutual, individually realized may strike an observer as crabbed, parched, insufficiently social. If others are valued only insofar as they are potential contractual partners, then has not one violated the Kantian injunction to treat humanity in their person as well as one's own not merely as means but as ends in themselves?

Three sorts of responses suggest themselves. First, one may opt for some sort of collectivism, recognizing a trans-individual entity the good of which trumps or entirely subsumes individual goods. Second, one may bite the bullet and embrace a liberalism that is not only individualistic but ruggedly so. Third, one may advance a liberal individualism that is integrative, in which the whole adds up to more than the sum of its parts. This third strategy can properly be characterized as liberal utopianism because it exhibits a society as attractive not merely because its various constituent members are doing well according to their own particular standards of right functioning, but in virtue of their hanging together in the way that they do.

Plato's Republic is not libertarian, but it is utopian if any political order is. It displays an (alleged) overall social good that is not identical to but instead supervenes on the proper functioning of each of its several parts. Plato, of course, can avail himself of various moves that are closed off to liberals. He recognizes supra-individual wholes and an impersonal, author-itative Form of the Good that is the one-size-fits-all universal standard of value. Liberal theorists demur on both counts. The puzzle for them is, then, securing the utopianism without sacrificing the primacy of individuals' preferences and projects.

As attentiveness to positive externalities generates a route to the more-than-minimal state, so too does it offer entry to libertarian utopia. Being able to direct one's life according to one's own conception of the good is, liberals are wont to say, necessary for living well. But a conception of *which* good? Only fanatics recognize just one way of life as being valuable, and it is very nearly as single-minded to acknowledge just one as holding out prospects of value-for-oneself. Without presuming overly much in disputed realms of value inquiry, it can be maintained that an indefinitely wide array of goods is potentially directive of human activity. That one is motivated in one's choices only by a very limited set of these should not be allowed to obscure the existence and attractiveness of the others. It is an instance of self-inflicted epistemic blindness to suppose that the only goods that exist are those that enter into one's own projects.

Some philosophers maintain the existence of *moral dilemmas*, situations in which one's available options are such that whatever one chooses one does wrong. These are sometimes called "tragic choices." Whether or not dilemmas of that sort genuinely obtain, we can recognize the existence of a different sort of dilemma, one in which whatever one does he forfeits an opportunity to advance some enormously attractive alternative good. That will be the case when X is valuable and Y is valuable, but X and Y are not compossible. It may be maintained that this is not a genuine dilemma be-cause choice among goods is merely to select among permissibles. Perhaps, but that should not disguise the fact that the opportunity cost of X is Y forgone, and that if Y is truly of great value, then giving it up is valuation-ally expensive. To be sure, the pain of sacrificing Y will be assuaged by the recognition that acquiring X constitutes full or more than full compensa-tion. Indeed, if X is more valuable than Y, then it seems out of place to speak of sacrifice at all. To "sacrifice" two $20 bills to receive a $50 note is the sort of sweet service that the dutiful man of prudence will cheerfully endure. But if X and Y are radically distinct in kind such that nothing like the sort of enhancement that Y offers to a life is provided by X, then to select X is genuinely to forgo some good for which X is not a satisfactory substitute (although it may be adequate *compensation*).

If there exist *incommensurable values*, then the dilemma is further sharpened. To say that X is incommensurable with Y is to maintain that it is neither the case that X is better than Y, that Y is better than X, nor that X and Y are equally valuable. There is no deeper good to which they can be reduced, no numeraire through which to provide a meaningful comparative measure.[10] Incommensurability of value often takes center stage in discussions of tragic choices, such as the one faced by Antigone, when she must decide whether to respond to the urgings of kinship by giving her fallen brother a proper burial or instead to express political allegiance by observing the king's command to do no such thing. Such tragic choices are instances of the first sort of moral dilemmas mentioned above. But incommensurability can equally evidence itself in *joyful choices*, decisions concerning which of two luminous goods to pursue. Someone may have a nose for philosophical argument but also a nose for fine clarets. To pursue the practice of philosophy will close off opportunities to develop a rich and fulfilling career as a professional wine taster, and vice versa. Wholehearted devotion to either way of life is possible, but not to both. In this case, the tradeoff is significant but not total; someone who philosophizes may develop cellar skills in his spare time. But other species of incommensurability more radically exclude partaking in the other value. There is goodness in the life of quiet, intense contemplation, and there is also value inherent in an adventurer's derring-do, but the one excludes the other. Similarly, a calling to humble service is incompatible with entrepreneurial cut-and-thrust. Even if time and energy, resources and talent were unlimited, one could not have everything that is worth having.

Four Stages of Liberal Toleration

One way to respond appropriately to what is recognized to be of positive value it to work to achieve it in one's own activities. But as noted above, if an understanding of the range of value as broad, diverse, and largely uncombinable within the range of one life is accurate, then this strategy is feasible only for a minority of genuine values. Another mode of fitting response is to endorse pursuit of these goods by others. Perhaps *I* won't save the rain forest, study Sumerian script, or break the record for most consecutive baseball games played, but I acknowledge the worthiness of these activities insofar as I endorse their performance by others. Within the theory of liberalism the paradigmatic expression of endorsement is *toleration*.

It is important to distinguish among weaker and stronger types of endorsement. At its weakest, endorsement is the pledging of restraint consequent on receiving restraint from others. It is something of a stretch to call this endorsement, because it may indicate only that one's degree of loathing and disdain for the other person's projects is not so great as to move one to abrogate the articles of peace that protect both her and you. I call this *tolerance as restraint*; it is the intolerant person's toleration.

Toleration is more positive if it represents an acknowledgment that, although the other person's ends and affections as such mean nothing to oneself, because they are genuinely and authentically subscribed to by that individual it is appropriate that she act on them. On this version, the tolerant person is not someone who succeeds in overcoming temptation to interfere but rather one who supports people's devotion to their personal projects as such, not predicating that support on shared affection for the ends in question. In contrast to tolerance as restraint, we may call this *tolerance as respect for autonomy*.

Respecting autonomy constitutes moderate endorsement. A stronger form is suggested by the human bestiary assembled for examination on p. 310 of ASU:

> Wittgenstein, Elizabeth Taylor, Bertrand Russell, Thomas Merton, Yogi Berra, Allen Ginsburg, Harry Wolfson, Thoreau, Casey Stengel, The Lubavitcher Rebbe, Picasso, Moses, Einstein, Hugh Hefner, Socrates, Henry Ford, Lenny Bruce, Baba Ram Das, Gandhi, Sir Edmund Hillary, Raymond Lubitz, Buddha, Frank Sinatra, Columbus, Freud . . . Bobby Fischer, Emma Goldman, Peter Kropotkin, you, and your parents. Is there really *one* kind of life which is best for each of these people?

The question is rhetorical, and the reader quickly assents to Nozick's suggestion that there can be no one society that is best for each of these individuals. If we don't wish to see them bumping into each other too often and too violently, we do well to allow each ample scope for unimpeded action. This is a reflection prompted by the ethics of tolerance as restraint. We may also observe that because each has very distinctive ideas about what is worth doing and the style in which it ought to be done,[11] they must be afforded adequate scope to work out these conceptions in order to be able to live lives that they will view from the inside as satisfactory. This is a reflection prompted by the ethics of tolerance as respect for autonomy. Additionally, though, we can observe that this is not the sort of group that might be assembled by Gallup to provide representative opinions for some forgettable poll. Rather, it is an assemblage of *powerhouses*, of dazzling characters who manifest glamour, rebelliousness, wisdom, wit, piety, passion, compassion, conviction, creativity, irony, involvement, detachment, competitiveness, charity, grace. The one thing they are not is average. They are utterly different one from another, yet they are alike in manifesting human aspirations and characters that can be seen to be valuable even by those whose own lives are directed by different conceptions of a good. Even those we might take to be more trouble to humankind than they were worth *almost* make up for their great failings with their great virtues.

I believe that the star quality of the assemblage is integral to Nozick's utopian aims, for it suggests a third species of toleration, what I shall call *tolerance as regard*. It exemplifies not only respect for the autonomy exhibited in the other's projects such that achievement of her end is judged to be good for her but also that the contents of a life lived in that way are objectively valuable. A libertarian framework that encourages and protects the flourishing of diverse strains of valuable activity is better with respect to its product, all else equal, than one that allows scope only for a smaller range of types. One has reason to prize being part of such a society not only because the freedom it affords is good for oneself but because it is good, period. Its overall goodness is a function of supporting a diversity of particular goods that are incommensurable and that cannot coherently be objects of pursuit within one life but that can coexist in a regime of ordered liberty. Note that it is not diversity as such that is being welcomed (as is so much the fashion within contemporary public moralisms of a mostly mindless cast) but, rather, a diversity of modes of activity that are intrinsically valuable. Of course, reasonable people can differ concerning questions of value, and if you were populating the bestiary of laudable human types you might well choose to omit some of the ones Nozick includes and to insert some others strikingly different from any of the individuals represented there. But toleration as regard will have some sort of grip on anyone who believes that representation of more rather than fewer species of goods is itself to be welcomed as a good even if it is not specifically a good for oneself.

There is one further rung to be climbed, for these ruminations on impersonal value can swing around again to the observer, yielding a fourth and strongest version of toleration. If people around you are leading diverse lives, many of which are responsive to genuine goods – albeit not the ones that provide a major thrust to the activities in your own life – then the society you share with them is better for their presence. But for that same reason, *you* are better for their presence. You gain *epistemically* by being made more sharply aware of the variousness of the springs of worthwhile human action. Almost certainly, there will be some lessons for oneself to be taken away from the successes and failures of their projects. There also are *affective* gains to be had insofar as one is inspired, uplifted, or merely entertained by episodes from others' biographies. And despite some risk of giving an appearance of wishing to appropriate unearned profundities, we might say that there are *spiritual* gains to be had by voluntarily identifying with others whose projects differ substantially from one's own. By freely taking on a valuational stake in their lives, one achieves indirect association with goods to which one has no direct practical connection, goods from which one would otherwise be altogether exiled. Free-riding on the commitments and concerns of others widens and deepens one's links to that which is worthwhile. To endorse the existence of diverse forms of good lives within one's society because they indirectly contribute to the value of one's own life can be called *toleration as vicarious achievement*. It is stronger than the tolerance of regard, because it adds to the judgment that these other modes of life are indeed valuable the further thought that the value they hold out is, crucially, also value to oneself.[12]

A libertarian society, then, will not automatically qualify as utopian no matter how sedulous its respect for rights. If individuals left to their own devices form societies that are stolid, stultifying, and insipid, then they may exhibit perfect justice one with another but are deficient with regard to other important human virtues. That seems clear. A less clear-cut case will be if within the libertarian framework many diverse individuals and subcommunities of individuals are nurtured, but they carry on with as much independence as circumstances will allow. Each respects the autonomy of others and thereby acknowledges that it is fitting that they pursue the ends that are distinctively their own, but those foreign ends elicit no regard or resonance in one's own valuations. In such a case, I would be inclined to say that this is a successful libertarian society, but that it is not *maximally successful*; it is not a libertarian utopia. That is because the good of the society is merely the sum of the good of the parts. What is missing is synergy. For each agent, the existence of the divergent others is dispensable without loss. Unlike social relationships that exhibit toleration as regard and, especially, toleration as vicarious achievement, there are no positive externalities to be had.

This reflection finally brings us back to the derivation of the more-than-minimal state in "Demoktesis." There, too, the motivating concern was a wish to capture positive externalities, and so this becomes the major issue on which the election campaign will be waged. Is it the minimal or the more-than-minimal state that holds out the better prospects for how human beings might do well with regard to managing external benefits (and costs) of sociality? The answer surely depends in large measure on what degree of liberal toleration is to be had. If not even tolerance as restraint is reliably forthcoming from the parties, then a much-more-than-minimal state may be necessary to secure even rudiments of civility. This proposition is well understood by Hobbes and by contemporary inhabitants of the Balkans. If, however, stronger degrees of toleration are on offer, then the libertarian version surely wins the beauty pageant. Basic respect for autonomy enables pursuit of individual projects within a liberal order, but autonomy in any recognizable guise is the first casualty of a social arrangement in which everyone effectively owns a piece of everyone. Recall, though, that toleration as respect for autonomy still leaves us on the far side of libertarian utopia. When accompanied by tolerance as regard and as vicarious achievement, a liberal order shines with a further luster. It affords positive externalities that are ubiquitous and reciprocally enjoyed but which are available only within a regime hospitable to self-direction and voluntary association. Against this, the utopian credentials of communitarian conformism seem thin indeed.

IV. MILL AS UTOPIAN PREDECESSOR

One possible line of criticism of Nozick's libertarian utopia is that it is unrealistic, insufficiently grounded in human nature, too distant a long shot to merit a wager. This chapter refrains from taking up and directly responding to that sort of criticism. Another possible line of criticism is that, in attempting to mate liberalism with utopianism, Nozick breeds a monster, a creature heretofore unknown. Whatever the merits of liberalism, historically it has always presented its case by way of improving on the state of nature, not by serving copious portions of pie in the sky. Indeed, one of the chief merits of liberalism, some will say, is its sober avoidance of utopian temptations.

This is to overlook important strands of liberal theorizing. It fails, for example, to take account of the utopian liberalism of Rousseau, for whom the polity acting in consort is more than the sum of its constituent particular agents. But because, as noted in the preceding section, it as at just this juncture that Rousseau's utopianism tends to drown out his liberalism, the omission is pardonable, perhaps praiseworthy. Less dispensable, however, is the liberal strand most notably represented by J. S. Mill's *On Liberty*.[13]

It finds the primary justification of a liberal order in the flourishing of the characters of free men and women rather than the society's fidelity to deontological strictures of rights and duties.

Mill announces an explicitly utilitarian standard of appraisal, but its application is notoriously evasive, for the standard to which ultimate appeal is made invokes "utility in the largest sense, grounded on the permanent interests of man as a progressive being."[14] This seems to incorporate essentialism and a non-hedonistic component of utility, both at odds with Mill's official program as announced in *Utilitarianism*. But rather than belabor notorious difficulties in Mill interpretation, I shall simply assume for present purposes that there is some sort of serious attempt being made here to justify a libertarian order in terms of its product. What I wish to point out here is how similar in spirit to the utopian themes of ASU are Mill's deployment of the notions *experiment in living* and *person of genius*.

The term "experiments in (or "of") living" is misleading. Almost never are we to conceive of these as deliberately designed tests of some hypothesis; they do not attempt to hold all but the crucial variable constant; to the extent there is a control group it is the entire experience of the remainder of human civilization; the experimenters are themselves the experimented on. Moreover, it does not seem to be the case that these "experiments" are capable of decisively validating or invalidating a way of life for anyone other than the individuals who experience it.[15] Rather, what they do is graphically inform (or remind) the observer what it is like to pursue that sort of good in that sort of way. The more numerous and diverse these experimental practices, the greater is the service they provide in shielding us against the oppressive weight of servitude to custom. Experiments in living are of much service to the boldly adventurous but are of yet far more importance to the cautiously conventional person. By attending to the example of the iconoclast or innovator one learns (or learns more firmly) that the conventional is not a dictum of necessity but one choice among innumerable other possible choices. One whose cognizance extends even minimally beyond the ambit of one's own self and circle confronts the implicit question, "Why am I doing *this* rather than *that*?" To the extent that the query elicits an active response, the individual is elevated beyond the level of mechanistic conformism. The value of experiments in living is, then, predominantly a function of the vividness of the impression they make on observers and only secondarily, if at all, in terms of comparative judgments of value that might be derivable therefrom.[16]

As with Nozick's libertarian utopia, here, too, the existence of a multiplicity of parties pursuing diverse ends serves the common good. People whose ways differ from one's own are not to be tolerated only because that is the price exacted for one's own freedom but because insofar as they enjoy untrammeled liberty (subject, of course, to the condition that they not harm others), they generate substantial positive externalities. As with Nozick's libertarian utopia, the merits of the Millian free society are built on toleration as regard and toleration as vicarious achievement. If anything, Mill is even more insistent than Nozick on the magnitude of the moral stakes. Against a vibrantly plural liberal society, he juxtaposes the rigor mortis of Asiatic stagnation, most especially that of China. Although the Orient is by no means inferior to the West in the quality of its sages and philosophers, and although early on it came into possession of institutions and habits at least as functional as those enjoyed anywhere else in the world, the petrification of these practices has shackled the peoples who live under them and utterly sapped their vitality. It is to our nonconformists that we owe the comparatively greater vigor of our own culture. If anything, they are to be subsidized rather than restrained.[17]

Most of all is this true of *persons of genius*. These are those rare individuals (rarer in his own time, Mill thought, than in preceding epochs) who do not simply pick and choose among previously explored avenues for living but who pioneer radically new theories and practices that can then profitably be taken up by less inventive others. Their contribution can hardly be overestimated: "[T]hese few are the salt of the earth; without them, human life would become a stagnant pool. Not only is it they who introduce good things which did not before exist; it is they who keep the life in those which already exist."[18] Interpretations of Mill that take him to be offering a fundamentally perfectionist argument here are, I believe, mistaken. Free institutions are not being endorsed as the cost that must be borne in order to produce rare instances of transcendent human greatness. Rather, those great individuals are to be valued in themselves but even more so as a propellant or catalyst for those many others who lack a capacity for radical inventiveness but who can be stimulated by those who do in ways that bring to fruition their more modest potentials. Mill's account may be élitist, but it is not upwardly redistributionist: Transactions under conditions of freedom between the most gifted and their lesser brethren are positive-sum but disproportionally beneficial to the latter. Without wishing to strain parallels between eminent libertarians a century apart, Mill's persons of genius are reminiscent of Nozick's listing of strikingly individual personalities. Neither group does well for itself in a one-size-fits-all cookie cutter society and, more important still, under conformist-collectivist conditions, they will be prevented from conferring the cornucopia of positive externalities that they dispense in a regime of liberty.

But if this is so, one wonders, why will the nongeniuses, the vast majority in all social classes that constitute civil society, act to constrict and stifle a source of so much potential profit to themselves? How can sentiments so sharply at odds with rational self-interest prevail? Although Mill does not offer a direct response, several passages from the "On Individuality" discussion are suggestive, perhaps most of all where he complains:

> [S]ociety has now fairly got the better of individuality; and the danger which threatens human nature is not the excess, but the deficiency, of personal impulses and preferences. . . . In our times, from the highest class of society down to the lowest, everyone lives as under the eye of a hostile and dreaded censorship. Not only in what concerns others, but in what concerns only themselves, the individual or the family do not ask themselves, what do I prefer? Or, what would suit my character and disposition? Or, what would allow the best and highest in me to have fair play and enable it to grow and thrive? They ask themselves, what is suitable to my position?[19]

That is, instead of acting as self-owners, they behave as if everyone has a share in them. This is Demoktesis not as a fancifully ingenious "how it could happen" story but as sober-minded social commentary on the poisonous fruits of collectivist conformism. We thus observe a further parallel between Mill and Nozick: For each, the libertarian utopia is an unbegrudging reciprocal showering of positive externalities, and for each the counterutopia is a crabbed and cautious claiming and being claimed by others.

V. UTOPIAN DEFENSES AGAINST CRITIQUES OF LIBERALISM

It is not possible within the compass of this essay to take up the multitude of charges that have been levied against liberal society. Many critics decry liberalism because it does not pay obeisance to the one dominant good that they themselves have espied and are eager to bestow on benighted humanity with or without its assent. Various theocracies and totalitarian enthusiasms fit this description, and the reasons why liberals resist their manifestos are too palpable to need presentation here. A more interesting type of critique claims to take up liberalism on its own terms and find it hollow at the core. What is wrong with liberal society is that it is overwhelmingly more liberal than it is a society. Liberalism, we are told, is built on an "atomistic"[20] edifice of "possessive individualism."[21] It is populated by *luftmenschen* who lack moral gravity because they are "unencumbered selves"[22] undefined by ties to anything external to their own egos.

It is clear that atomism, lack of encumbrance, and so on are taken by the critics to be pathological conditions, less clear why that is so. It may simply reflect a temperamental conservatism that is uncomfortable with the ceaseless churning and unpredictability of a society based on contractual association rather than status. As such it is a nostalgia for the fixity of premodern communities possessed of a monolithic view of the good life mandatory for all.[23] As a statement of the critics' own tastes this may be unassailable, but it has no implications for those more at home with modernity.

A potentially more fruitful way to interpret the criticism is that it opposes against liberalism's allegedly straitened conception of what it is to live well a more capacious alternative. Taking a cue from the poet/preacher John Donne's declaration that "No man is an island," the critic maintains that the individualism central to liberalism leaves each capable of achieving only that degree of success that can be enjoyed by someone who manufactures out of whole cloth ends for himself (it doesn't matter if we change the metaphor to ends selected off the rack featuring this season's ready-made fashions) and then pursued by himself and for himself. This is a model not only asocial but one that verges on solipsism insofar as it pictures the individual as lord of his own valuational universe. What it hubristically abandons is precisely that which for most people is fundamental to their capacity to lead meaningful lives: acknowledged membership in a wider community whose triumphs and tragedies are by extension one's own.

In other contexts, I have attempted to respond to this sort of communitarian challenge by pointing out that there is nothing that prevents liberal individuals from framing their projects around cherished and enduring relationships with others and, indeed, that for most people these sorts of ties are central to their conceptions of what it is to live well.[24] Liberal individuals can avail themselves of the goods of communal association while remaining free to abrogate such ties should they find it necessary to do so. That remains a satisfactory counter, but I have now come to believe that it can be buttressed by attention to utopian considerations. The critic views liberal society on the model of market arrangements in which there are no externalities. But a liberalism in which toleration is not confined to respect for autonomy but extends to regard and vicarious achievement will be one in which some men are isolated islands but many are not; they have access to moral bridges that connect them not to some specious mainland (whose territory would that be?) but, rather, to the innumerable other island outposts of value that the wit and will of free persons can scout out and settle. These bridges go, of course, in both directions. Not everyone will achieve an abundance of social linkages, and some people may not admit them at all, but that, too, is the sort of choice that within a free society is open to individual discretion. To characterize such an order as "atomistic" is, at best, highly misleading.

The critic is certainly correct in maintaining that people who are radically dissociated from each other will fail to secure crucial benefits of social relationship. One way of addressing this problem is the "Demoktesis" strategy of each owning shares in everyone else. Insofar as it takes collective judgments of value as primary, it bears affinity to communitarian programs. Another way is to gamble that people associating consensually with each other will more often than not generate externalities that are positive. That is the wager taken up by libertarian utopianism.

VI. NOZICK'S COUNTERLIBERTARIAN UTOPIANISM

So why, if the prospectus for libertarian utopia are so attractive, does its formulator disown it? I am unable to say. But a quick look at the author's own remarks on the matter reveal that neither is he. In Section I, I cited Nozick's original "recantation" of libertarianism ostensibly grounded on utopian considerations. That this is not a passing fancy is indicated by his offering an essentially identical critique some four years later:

> The political philosophy presented in *Anarchy, State, and Utopia* ignored the importance to us of joint and official serious symbolic statement and expression of our social ties and concern and hence (I have written) is inadequate [here citing the aforementioned passage from *The Examined Life*].[25]

The idea appears to be something like this: In a libertarian polity people acting on an individual basis may offer symbolic expression of their deepest values (through liturgical performances, remembrance in memoriam, acts of stylized recrimination, etc.), but they do not do so jointly and together. The closest approximation would be if they were unanimously to agree to come together in performance of such a rite, but the existence of high transaction costs and, of course, the fact that we almost never achieve such unanimity in valuation means that for practical purposes Nozick is correct in saying that "joint and official serious symbolic statement" is absent in a libertarian polity. Whether he is correct, though, in maintaining that the absence is important to us is another question. One wishes first to ask: Who is the "us"? Presumably it excludes those who lack an appetite for the symbolic. But it also excludes those for whom joint symbolic activity is indeed important but for whom that function is best fulfilled within units smaller than the society as a whole: in families, synagogues, colleges, fraternal societies, and so on. With the partial exception of the first of these,[26] such associations are voluntary and typically on a small enough scale so that benefits of intimate association not present in vast, impersonal associations are forthcoming. One need not deny all value to the existence of official national days of celebration such as an annual Thanksgiving Day – or even National Pickle Week – to observe that we have been given no reason whatsoever to suppose that joint expressive activity will not proceed tolerably well within libertarian society.

That is not to deny that some people will find their own symbolic expressions diminished by the opting out of other citizens. Were the abstainers to be enrolled by some means or other (evangelizing; conversion at the point of a sword; conversion at the point of a ballot box) in the joint performance so as to swell the numbers involved, that would provide such people with positive externalities. Thus they will regard a liberal order as less than optimal, as a way-station to a fuller enjoyment of the benefits of sociality. They will, if they are terribly clever, reflect that if, for example, everyone were to own equal shares in everyone else.... It does seem that the later Nozick may have had second thoughts not only about the satisfactoriness of libertarianism but also about (what nearly every reader of ASU will have taken to be) the palpable unattractiveness of Demoktesis. Could his thought have taken so drastic a turn in the interim? I confess that although the evidence points in that direction, I cannot bring myself to believe that Nozick has embarked on so ill-starred a journey.

Besides, the Demoktesis route to joint performance is fanciful. There is no realistic prospect of universal enrollment via a sequence of voluntary agreement. In the actual world, such joint undertakings are the product of democratic voting in which majorities secure outcomes that are binding on all. Thus, weighing against the putative positive externalities to be achieved through universal enrollment are the negative externalities showered on unwilling others. The entire history of liberal thought and practice teaches us that these are apt to be substantial and divisive. For that reason, any satisfactory system of collective decision making through democratic practices will have to be constrained by constitutional provisions that check the capacity of majorities to impose their wills on reluctant minorities.[27] Indeed, attentiveness to the magnitude of specifically expressive factors within the operation of democratic institutions in large-number electorates such as those of all modern nation-states and most of their subsidiary political units suggest further reasons for limiting rather than expanding the scope of collective decision making.[28] To put the matter as noncommitally as possible, it is by no means obvious that attentiveness to the importance of symbolic expressive activity counts against rather than in favor of libertarian structures.

Perhaps when all is said and done we might conclude what will have seemed apparent to many at the beginning of this discussion: Utopia is in the eye of the utopian beholder. This observation was developed with brilliance and panache by the earlier Nozick in his ASU construction of utopia as a framework for utopias. For all that he subsequently has had to say, I believe that the result still stands.[29]

Notes

[1] John Rawls, *A Theory of Justice* (Cambridge, Mass.: Harvard University Press, 1971), p. 102.

[2] *The Examined Life* (New York: Simon and Schuster, 1989), pp. 286–7.

[3] Aristotle proposes similar strictures with regard to estimating the flourishing of an individual human life. See *Nicomachean Ethics*, Bk. I.

[4] This is probably too simple. Suppose that regime-type A can emerge only via rights violations, but the same is true for types B, C, D . . . and that these are the only regime-types that can feasibly be instantiated (i.e., all the better possible forms are predictably unattainable or unmaintainable). Then we may be obliged to endorse a social order that necessarily incorporates injustices.

[5] See ASU, pp. 293–4.

[6] "Analogous" rather than "equivalent to," because most communities also will have some members who enter through birth rather than consent. On any liberal account, utopian or otherwise, children raise special theoretical difficulties. Locke wrestles with these in his *Two Treatises on Government*; many other influential liberal tracts simply ignore the problematic status of children. Because the issue is endemic to all liberal theorizing and, I believe, to most of liberalism's competitors, this essay follows the ignorers' strategy. But see Loren Lomasky, *Persons, Rights, and the Moral Community* (New York: Oxford University Press, 1987), pp. 152–87, for suggestions concerning how libertarianism in a somewhat utopian mode can accommodate children.

[7] Rousseau may be judged to be an exception insofar as he takes the central function of political structures to be the eliciting of a *general will* rather than as serving as an arena for the interplay of particular wills. Better, I think, is to withhold from Rousseau designation as a liberal theorist, at least with regard to this aspect of his account.

[8] *A Theory of Justice*, p. 144.

[9] David Gauthier, *Morals by Agreement* (Oxford: Clarendon Press, 1986).

[10] The literature on value incommensurability is substantial. A major progenitor is Isaiah Berlin's classic essay "Two Concepts of Liberty," in *Four Essays on Liberty*

(London: Oxford University Press, 1969). A take on the significance of incommensurability for liberalism at variance from the one presented in this essay is developed by Joseph Raz, *The Morality of Freedom* (Oxford: The Clarendon Press, 1986).

[11] Although to the best of my knowledge only one on Nozick's list epitomized a career by singing "I did it my way," virtually all of the others are entitled to join in the chorus.

[12] This is to stretch the concept of tolerance to the breaking point – or beyond it. To acknowledge the well-directedness of the commitments of others, to identify with their achievements and thereby indirectly to win their goods as goods for oneself is, it can be argued, better understood as a practice of celebration rather than toleration. I take the point but retain the somewhat misleading terminology, because it emphasizes the continuity of the four stages. If the last of these is not, strictly speaking, toleration, then it is a transcendence of toleration by a liberal virtue yet more excellent.

[13] As Mill himself indicates with the epigram that leads off *On Liberty*, another important representative of this strand is Wilhelm von Humboldt's *The Limits of State Action*.

[14] *On Liberty*, ed. Gertrude Himmelfarb (Harmondsworth: Penguin Books, 1974), "Introductory," p. 70.

[15] See, Mill's discussion of the epistemic status of other people's experience in the chapter "Of Individuality," p. 122. Mill does, however, show some sympathy for the claim that there is no call to countenance experiments in lives of drunkenness and licentiousness because the crushing weight of past experience has refuted the hypothesis beyond need for continued testing. See Chapter IV, "The Authority of Society and the Individual," pp. 147–8.

[16] Mill seems to be taking a rather different stand in *Utilitarianism*, in which he attributes to the reports of "men of experience" a credible empirical basis for comparing various pleasures as to their higher and lower quality. Whether the two books can be rendered consistent on this matter is a question to take up on some other occasion.

[17] In the *Apology*, Socrates claims that the proper "punishment" for his nonconformist deeds is a lifetime public subvention at a place of honor. To enroll him on this basis as yet another libertarian utopian would, perhaps, be to gild the lily.

[18] "Of Individuality," p. 129.

[19] "Of Individuality," p. 125.

[20] See Charles Taylor, "Atomism" in Shlomo Avineri and Avner de-Shilit (eds.), *Communitarianism and Individualism* (New York: Oxford University Press, 1992), pp. 29–50.

[21] C. B. McPherson, *The Political Theory of Possessive Individualism* (Oxford: Clarendon Press, 1962).

[22] Michael Sandel, *Liberalism and the Limits of Justice* (Cambridge: Cambridge University Press, 1982).

[23] See, for example, Alasdair MacIntyre, *After Virtue* (Notre Dame, Ind.: University of Notre Dame Press, 1981).

[24] See Loren Lomasky, "Civil Enough: Toward a Liberal Theory of Vice (and Virtue)," in Robert Fullinwider (ed), *Civil Society, Democracy, and Civic Renewal* (Lanham, Mass.: Rowman and Littlefield, 1999), pp. 273–94.

[25] Robert Nozick, *The Nature of Rationality* (Princeton, N.J.: Princeton University Press, 1993), p. 32.

[26] Although entering families through birth is not voluntary, subsequent determinations to uphold the significance of kinship ties is a matter for ongoing assent.

[27] The *Federalist Papers* are a classical statement of this concern. A contemporary classic offering the same moral is James Buchanan and Gordon Tullock, *The Calculus of Consent* (Ann Arbor: University of Michigan Press, 1962).

[28] The argument for this conclusion is developed at length in Geoffrey Brennan and Loren Lomasky, *Democracy and Decision: The Pure Theory of Electoral Preference* (New York: Cambridge University Press, 1993).

[29] I am grateful to Michael Ridge and David Schmidtz for thoughtful comments on a previous draft. The original stimulus for this essay was a twenty-fifth anniversary conference on *Anarchy, State, and Utopia*, sponsored by Liberty Fund of Indianapolis, Indiana, and held in Cambridge, Massachusetts, during December 1999. Its vigorous yet collegial discussions not only analyzed the idea of libertarian utopia but, in large measure, manifested it.

5 | Non-Consequentialism and Political Philosophy

PHILIP PETTIT

Robert Nozick[1] did political theory a great service when he showed how a theory of natural rights, such as John Locke[2] endorsed, could be invoked in defense of a libertarian theory of the state; in particular, could be invoked in defense of such a theory without defeating itself in the exercise by giving even greater support to anarchism. The result is that his book now stands unchallenged as the most coherent statement available of the case for a rights-based defense of the minimal, libertarian state.[3]

But there are two challenges that the invocation of natural rights in defense of the state must face, not just one. Those who invoke natural rights certainly have to show that their approach does not slide into a rights-based defense of a sort of anarchy, and I am happy to concede that Nozick establishes something close to this result. But they also have to show that the approach does not slide into a defense of the state that is ultimately based, not on a non-consequentialist theory of rights – and not, more generally, on a non-consequentialist theory of any kind – but, rather, on a consequentialist theory of goals that the state ought to try to promote.

My contention in this chapter is that Nozick does not establish that his invocation of natural rights is proof against this consequentialist challenge and, more generally, that it is difficult to see how any non-consequentialist political philosophy could be proof against it. Political philosophy is that branch of ethics or moral philosophy that tells us what the state should be and should do, assuming that the state is to be given a legitimate monopoly of force in a society.[4] The problem of developing a non-consequentialist political philosophy that does not ultimately devolve into a consequentialist theory is analogous to a problem that arises in ethics more generally but the political problem, as we shall see, is a particularly pressing one. The fact that it does not figure much in the debates between consequentialists and their opponents is a surprising lacuna in the literature.

The paper is in three sections. In the first, I offer an account of non-consequentialism in political theory, showing why the rights-based approach adopted by Nozick is non-consequentialist in character. And then, in the following two sections, I look respectively at two variants on the con-sequentialist challenge. The first is the familiar question as to why the state should have to treat certain principles as constraints, not as goals. I call this the treatment problem, since it asks why the state should treat principles in a certain way: viz., as constraints rather than as goals. The second is the less frequently posed question as to why the state should have to treat these principles in particular, and not some other set, as constraints. I call this the selection problem, since it focuses on why we should select one set of principles rather than any other as the principles that ought to constrain the state.

1. PRINCIPLES, CONSTRAINTS, AND RIGHTS

Non-Consequentialism and Consequentialism

As a theory of personal morality, non-consequentialism comes in many forms. Deontologists hold that agents ought to discharge certain duties: they ought to tell the truth, keep their promises, be non-violent, and so on. Kantians say that agents ought to act on the categorical imperative – act only on a maxim that they could accept as a general law of behavior – or ought to treat other people always as ends, never merely as means. Virtue ethicists say that they ought to manifest certain virtues in their behavior. Contractualists assert that they ought to conform to principles that no one could reasonably object to as the bases of social life. Theorists of special obligation say that they ought to deal in a certain way with those who are bound to them, such as their children, spouses, and friends. Rights theorists maintain that they ought to respect certain rights that others have against them. Egoists say that they ought to try and advance their own welfare. And so on.

What is the common thread in these positions? All non-consequent-ialists speak, at whatever level of abstraction, about what any or every agent ought to do or be; in that sense they are universalists. All non-consequentialists prescribe neutral principles of behavior or psychology or relationships for such agents: that they act on the categorical impera-tive, manifest certain virtues, nurture their friendships, respect the rights of those they deal with, advance their egoistic ends, and so on; the prin-ciples are neutral in the sense that they can be understood in the same way by everyone. And all non-consequentialists say that the right thing for an agent to do is to instantiate the prescribed principles – so far as they are co-instantiable – in their own behavior or relationships or psychology. In particular, they say that that is the thing to do even if instantiating a principle in their own life means, because of the perversity of the agent's circumstances, that the principle will be less fully realized than otherwise in the world as a whole.

Non-consequentialism extends naturally from personal to political morality: from the theory of what private agents – personal or associational – ought to do and be to the theory of what the state ought to do and be. It holds, in every form, that there are universal principles that any state ought to instantiate in its own behavior or relationships or, if this is thought relevant, psychology. And it insists that the state ought to instantiate such a principle even if doing so means, because of the perversity of circumstances, that the principle will be less satisfied in the world as a whole: say, less satisfied among its own citizens.

Consequentialism takes two steps away from this position in ethics and politics.[5,6] The first step is to assert that there are certain potentially shared values by means of which possible states of affairs can be ranked, though perhaps not completely. These may be the neutral principles in behavior or relationships or psychology that the non-consequentialist favors; states of affairs may be ranked as valuable, in other words, so far as they involve everyone's acting on the categorical imperative, everyone's manifesting certain virtues, everyone's nurturing his or her friendships, and so on. Or the values for ranking states of affairs may be neutral outcome-principles that are more detached from how people behave: principles to the effect that happiness should be maximized, for example, or uninhabited wilderness preserved.

The second consequentialist step is to say that the right choice for an agent to take in any decision is one of those choices, assuming there is at least one – assuming incomplete ranking is not a problem – that promote the overall realization of such values or principles. Promoting overall realization may mean acting in a way that actually leads to the highest level of realization or acting in a way that maximizes the expected level of realization; I sidestep this source of ambiguity here. I also abstract from the question of whether consequentialism should be extended beyond the realm of action and choice to the domains of motives, rules, decision-procedures and so on.[7]

The basic difference between consequentialists and their opponents, under this account, is that while each side privileges certain general principles – treats them as values, as it is natural to say – they differ on what this privileging involves. The consequentialist side says that the important thing for any agent – for people or associations or states – is to promote the realization of those principles in the world at large, while the opposing side says that the important thing is rather for those agents to instantiate the relevant principles in their behavior or relationships or psychology. Consequentialists say that privileged principles should be treated as consequences or goals to be promoted, non-consequentialists that they should be treated as constraints to be instantiated or respected.

Nozick's Application of the Distinction to Rights Theory

This account of the divide between consequentialism and non-consequentialism derives, in its essentials, from points made by Robert Nozick in Chapter 3 of ASU. The core idea appears in his contrast between goal-centered and constraint-centered theories. The goal-centered or consequentialist theory holds up various patterns that ought to be advanced by agents. The constraint-centered view holds up various principles that ought to be respected by them, even if respecting the principles means that they are less well respected overall.

In his book, Nozick puts the account to use in describing what is involved in believing, as a non-consequentialist, that the state is bound by certain rights, and in defending that belief. The rights by which he thinks that the state is bound are the rights associated with Locke's state of nature; in their core, rights not to suffer harm to one's life, health, liberty, or possessions (ASU, 10). He argues that to be a rights theorist in the Lockean tradition is to hold that the principles associated with respecting relevant rights are constraints on the state. They are principles such that the state ought to instantiate them in its behavior toward other agents, in particular toward its own members. And they are principles such that the state cannot justifiably fail to instantiate a given principle simply because an opportunistic breach promises to promote the overall realization of that principle better than conformity would do. "The side-constraint view forbids you to violate these moral constraints," he says; and it forbids this, even if a violation would "lessen their total violation in the society" (ASU, 29).

This account makes two features of rights more perspicuous than they were before the appearance of Nozick's book. First, the insistence that rights are constraints, not goals, explains the sense in which a right counts as a trump, in Ronald Dworkin's phrase.[8] A right may not be a trump in the extreme sense that nothing ever justifies a breach of the right; few rights will have the infinite weight required for being a trump in that sense. But every right, by the suggested account, will be a trump in at least this sense: that the overall promotion of respect for the right will never justify a breach of the right. Every right will be an asset held by people such that they can invoke it to protect themselves against those who would trample on them in the name of maximizing the very principle associated with respecting the right. Consider the right to freedom of speech, for example. This right, qua right, can be invoked against a state that would silence a fascist group, even when the group, if allowed freedom of speech, is likely to stir up populist passions and drastically reduce freedom of speech among minorities.

The other feature of rights that becomes particularly clear, under this account, is that endorsing a theory of rights in the proper, traditional sense is to be distinguished from being a consequentialist about rights. One would be a consequentialist about certain rights if one thought that the state – or any other agent – should promote the principles associated with respecting those rights, even if that meant that it does not instantiate respect for the rights in its own behavior or relationships or psychology. This is "something like a utilitarianism about rights," Nozick (ASU, 28) argues; "violations of rights (to be minimized) would replace the total happiness as the relevant end state in the utilitarian structure." Thus, a state that is prepared to silence a political group in order to promote freedom of speech – say, in order to stop the group popularizing racist attitudes – does not endorse the right of freedom of speech as a constraint on its own activity; it merely treats such freedom – the enjoyment of the right – as a goal that should be promoted.

Not only does Nozick give a perspicuous characterization of non-consequentialism and use this to make clear what is involved in holding the state to Lockean rights. He also raises in the sharpest possible way the problem that any such rights theory must face: that of showing that whereas Lockean rights argue for the minimal as against the non-minimal state, they do not argue for anarchy as against a state of any kind. "The fundamental question of political philosophy, one that precedes questions about how the state should be organized, is whether there should be any state at all" (ASU, 4). His deservedly celebrated answer to that question is that if we imagine a Lockean state of nature in which people respect one another's rights and suppose that those people are rational, then we will be able to see that without ever having to breach such rights those people would be rationally led to establish something close to the minimal state. I have discussed this argument elsewhere and won't address it further here.[9]

2. THE TREATMENT QUESTION: WHY TREAT THESE PRINCIPLES
AS CONSTRAINTS?

The Issue

How will consequentialists react to non-consequentialism in political theory? Specifically, how will they react to the claim that certain principles – say, the principles associated with respecting Lockean rights – have to be instantiated, at whatever promotional cost, by the state? They will inevitably ask, "Why treat these principles as constraints?" That question, as we shall see, has two readings, each associated with a distinct challenge. In this section we take it as a question as to why non-consequentialists should think that the principles they privilege should be treated as constraints to be instantiated rather than as goals to be promoted. Hence, the italics in the title question.

The question for Nozick, then, is why the Lockean rights that he prizes should be taken as pointers to principles that the state should instantiate, rather than as pointers to principles that the state should do its very best to promote. This question is more telling in political theory than in ethics generally, as the state may often be in a position where, in principle, it can best promote the enjoyment of Lockean rights – or any principles that are plausibly hailed as constraints – by itself offending against some of those rights. It may be objected that the state cannot ever be safely entrusted with such a promotional task but I put aside that objection for the moment.

We naturally describe situations in which an individual can best promote a certain principle by breaching it in his or her own behavior or relationships or psychology as perverse. The situations that come to mind are those where an individual can scandalize others by breaching the principle and can thereby induce them not to follow suit; and those where, for equally unlikely reasons, the individual can reduce the opportunity for others to follow suit by breaching the principle in his or her own case. But situations where the state can best promote a principle, in particular a principle of the sort associated with Lockean rights, by itself breaching the principle are much easier to imagine.

Consider the principle associated with freedom of speech or freedom of association or anything of the kind. Or consider the principles linked with other broadly Lockean rights such as the right not to be arbitrarily harmed or deprived of one's possessions or held in detention. We already saw that the state may be in a position where, faced with an increasingly influential fascist group, it is clear that freedom of speech will be better served overall in the society if it now deprives this group of freedom of speech. And a similar point will hold in regard to the other rights. There are many possible cases where a preemptive, rights-breaching strike by the state – be this an exercise of violence or coercion or intimidation or incarceration – will promise to reduce the incidence of such breaches generally. If the state punctiliously instantiates the relevant principle in its own behavior – respects the right – it will often have to face the prospect of seeing that right much more grievously breached on the part of others than it would be if it itself were less punctilious. Montesquieu surely had this sort of situation in mind when he wrote: "The usage of the freest peoples that ever lived on earth makes me believe that there are cases where a veil has to be drawn, for a moment, over liberty, as one hides the statues of gods."[10]

In response to this possibility, then, consequentialists will insist on the question of why, to take Nozick's own view, the state should have to treat Lockean rights as constraints rather than as goals. Non-consequentialists may avoid having to make a response by arguing that they are only interested in ideal theory: that is, in the theory of how the state should be and behave, assuming that those who live under it will fully comply with its laws; assuming, in particular, that the state will not have to consider breaching the privileged principles in order to mitigate the effect of breaches by others.[11] But while it may be perfectly proper for non-consequentialist theorists to restrict their attention for certain purposes to ideal theory, they cannot postpone forever the issue that we have raised. So how then are they likely to respond?

Two Responses That Collapse into Consequentialism

There are three responses I can envisage non-consequentialists making. One will be to object that the state cannot be entrusted with promotional tasks of the kind in view here; this is the objection that I put aside above. The idea is that the power that state officials would be given by entrusting them with the preemptive, opportunistic discretion envisaged would be so great as to corrupt the most virtuous individuals and that it would lead overall to a worse result than that associated with a severely constrained state. It would lead in the end to more violation of the rights in question, not less.

The second response that non-consequentialists may make is closely related to this first line and may be considered in tandem with it. The response I have in mind says, if the state instantiates rights-related principles, even at a promotional cost to the overall satisfaction of those principles, it will thereby promote a further more important goal better than it would have done by being given a power of breaching the principles opportunistically. Non-consequentialists might argue, for example, that by being punctilious in its treatment even of the fascist group we imagined, the state can thereby induce a confidence among its citizenry that they do not live at the mercy of the state they have created: that it is not a Leviathan in their midst but an inherently respectful and constrained agency.

The problem with both of these responses is that they play into the hands of consequentialists. They each argue that the reason it is good that the state should be bound to instantiating or respecting certain rights-related principles is, in the end, a consequentialist consideration. The consideration in the first case is that binding the state to suitable rights-related principle will actually reduce the overall level of rights-violation, since an unbound state is likely to run amok. And the consideration in the second is that binding the state to such rights-related principles is required for the cause, not of reducing overall rights-violation, but of promoting some further more important goal.

Under either response to the challenge raised, non-consequentialists represent the constraints to which they would bind the state as conditional constraints of a kind that consequentialists will be happy to acknowledge. They are constraints that the state must honor so far and only so far as that is taken to be the best way of advancing the ultimate goal by which things are assessed, whether that goal be the non-violation of the rights in question or the promotion of some further good. The constraints no longer represent the categorical imperatives imagined by non-consequentialists but get turned into hypothetical imperatives of the kind that consequentialists or teleologists routinely support. Nozick is prepared to tolerate a certain conditionality in Lockean constraints, suggesting that 'they may be violated in order to avoid catastrophic moral horror' (ASU, 30). But – defensibly or not – he thinks that such suspendability under catastrophe is to be distinguished from the smooth dependence that would come with a consequentialist perspective (PE, 495).

As a consequentialist, I have no difficulty in thinking that it may be best, from the point of view of the overall good by which the performance of a state is to be judged, to bind the officials of the state to certain constraints. I have argued elsewhere that the goal of promoting freedom as non-domination – freedom in the sense in which it requires not being under the power of another, even the power of a benign other – requires that officials of the state be constrained in such a manner.[12] It requires that officials not be allowed, on the basis of their own calculations as to what will best promote freedom as non-domination, to breach the constraints that are laid on their behavior in the name of precisely that goal. If non-consequentialists take any such line then they give up on their distinctive commitment. They require officials of the state to be bound by certain constraints, but only on the understanding that imposing this requirement best serves their ultimate, consequentialist goal.

So much for the first two responses that I said non-consequentialists may make to the challenge raised in this section. Before turning to consideration of the third, I should add that just as they cannot invoke any other goal or telos in support of the constraints they would impose on the state, so non-consequentialists cannot invoke Robert Nozick's own notion of symbolic utility or value as something by reference to which they might hope to justify imposing constraints.[13] We can imagine someone's arguing that by recognizing Lockean rights as constraints on its behavior, the state can symbolize the importance of people's enjoying a certain immunity in relation to the state. Maybe so. But those who use this argument remain steadfastly within a consequentialist frame of thinking. There may be actuarial difficulties about how consequentialists are to count symbolic consequences in their calculations, because these consequences are sensitive to the very reasons for which actions are taken (NR, 55–6). But the argument that the state should recognize certain constraints for the sake of the symbolic value of doing so remains a characteristically consequentialist argument, not one that can be happily endorsed by any adherents of Lockean rights.

A Third Response, and Its Problems

So what is the third response that non-consequentialists may make to the question as to why the principles they prize should be treated by the state as constraints, not as goals? The line I have in mind argues that there is something about acting on persons – specifically, perhaps, about the state's acting on persons – that requires a commitment to treating relevant principles as constraints. This is the line that Nozick actually takes when he himself addresses the question in *Anarchy, State, and Utopia* as to why the state should treat Lockean principles as constraints. Where the state treats those principles as constraints, it denies itself the possibility of ever violating an individual's right to X for the sake of maximizing satisfaction of that right overall; where it treats them as goals, it retains the discretion to make such opportunistic violations. But, Nozick (ASU, 30–33) argues, the state is required to respect each individual as a separate person – to treat them as an end, not merely as a means to achieving any distinct goal – and this requirement would be breached if the state retained the discretion to violate a given individual's right to something, merely because that was the best path to minimizing violation of that right overall. Thus, the state that aims to treat people always as ends – in a word, to respect people – must treat the Lockean principles as constraints on its behavior, not just as regulative goals. "Side constraints express the inviolability of others, in the ways they specify. These modes of inviolability are expressed by the following injunction: 'Don't use people in specified ways'" (ASU, 32).

Nozick has much of interest to say on the question of why it is important that people enjoy the sort of inviolability that they would have under a regime where everyone satisfies Lockean constraints. The line along which he is led is one that receives further development in other works (PE, Ch. 6). "I conjecture that the answer is connected with that elusive and difficult notion: the meaning of life. A person's shaping of his life in accordance with some overall plan is his way of giving meaning to his life; only a being with the capacity to so shape his life can have or strive for meaningful life" (ASU, 50).

But to my consequentialist eye, this line of argument misses an obvious objection. I am happy to grant that the enjoyment of Lockean inviolability is of the greatest importance to human beings, being connected with the possibility of having a meaningful life. But that in itself does not show that the state ought to honor Lockean constraints in cases where breaching them would be the best way of minimizing violations of the constraints overall. It does not show that the state should treat the principles involved as constraints rather than as goals.

If people's enjoying non-violation of their rights is important, then it is important that they enjoy non-violation of those rights at anyone's hands, not just at the hands of the state. But why, then, shouldn't the desirability of such non-violation not allow the state to violate the rights of some people, if it can thereby increase the amount of non-violation that is enjoyed by people overall? It may compromise the possibility of those it affects having a meaningful life, but it will presumably facilitate the enjoyment of a meaningful life on the part of an even greater number of others.

Nozick and non-consequentialists generally need to do more than show that there is reason why the state should respect people as separate individuals, and not sacrifice them for the benefit of others. Consequentialists like me certainly will agree with that. They need to show, more specifically, that there is reason why the state should respect people as separate individuals, and not sacrifice them for the benefit of others, even when a certain form of sacrifice it might impose on some would be a way of blocking the imposition by third parties of an even greater level of sacrifice on others.

I hasten to add that I do not favor a policy under which the state might routinely impose harm on some in order to avoid others suffering an even greater harm – or a greater number of others suffering the same harm – at the hands of third parties. But my own reason for taking this view is not that constraints against harm have a sacred status as constraints, only that they have to be satisfied by any state that is likely to be able to promote certain palpable goods: say, the good of enjoying freedom as non-domination. My own reason, in short, is consequentialist in character.

I think that it is going to be very difficult for non-consequentialists, however, to hold the line against the challenge under discussion. They will have to produce a non-consequentialist argument for why the state should be bound to certain constraints, even when the principles enforced by the constraints can be more fully promoted by an opportunistic breach. And apart from rehearsing favored mantras to the effect that two wrongs do not make a right, it is hard to see what they can effectively do. The problems that arise for Nozick's argument will threaten any attempt on the same lines.

Non-consequentialists may appeal to intuition, of course, and argue that it is a datum of moral sense that it is just wrong for the state, or any agent, to resort to opportunistic breaches of whatever constraints are prescribed for the state. Nozick of *Anarchy, State, and Utopia* sometimes seems to take this line, as in the opening sentence of the book. "Individuals have rights, and there are things no person or group may do to them (without violating their rights)" (ASU, ix). But appealing to intuition at this fundamental level is not going to make an impact on opponents and amounts to little more than a refusal to join debate.

3. THE SELECTION QUESTION: WHY TREAT *THESE PRINCIPLES* AS CONSTRAINTS?

The Issue in General

The problem to be raised in this section is formulated in the same question that we addressed in the last section but with a different principle of emphasis. The question is no longer, why should the state treat relevant principles – say, those associated with Lockean rights – as constraints rather than as goals. Granted that some principles are to be treated as constraints, the question rather is, why should the state treat these principles in particular – these principles and not others – as constraints. Where the earlier issue is a question of why to treat the principles as constraints, here the question is how to select those principles that are to be given that sort of treatment.

The Issue with Property-Rights in Particular

The selection question is particularly pointed with the Lockean principles that Nozick discusses in *Anarchy, State, and Utopia*. He sets out the principles he has in mind in this passage, discussing Locke's *Two Treatises of Government*.

> Individuals in Locke's state of nature are in "a state of perfect freedom to order their actions and dispose of their possessions and persons as they think fit, within the bounds of the law of nature, without asking leave or dependency upon the will of any other man" (§.4). The bounds of the law of nature require that "no one ought to harm another in his life, health, liberty, or possessions" (§.6). Some persons transgress these bounds, "invading others' rights and . . . doing hurt to one another," and in response people may defend themselves or others against such invaders of rights (Ch. 3). The injured party and his agents may recover from the offender "so much as may make satisfaction for the harm he has suffered" (§.10); "everyone has a right to punish the transgressors of that law to such a degree as may hinder its violation" (§.7); each person may, and may only "retribute to [a criminal] so far as calm reason and conscience dictate, what is proportionate to his transgression, which is so much as may serve for reparation and restraint. (ASU, 10)

The Lockean state of nature, Nozick suggests, is "a nonstate situation in which people generally satisfy moral constraints and generally act as they ought" (ASU, 5). And so the state will be justified, he tells us, to the extent that it would have arisen by a process involving no morally impermissible steps from that situation. The idea is that if we think that the Lockean principles – the principles displayed in Locke's state of nature – are morally compelling, then we will find the state that would emerge under Nozick's derivation as morally compelling, and certainly as morally permissible.

But what if we do not think that the Lockean principles are uniquely compelling? What if we are open to the possibility that certain other principles are morally superior? In that case, Nozick's derivation will do nothing to persuade us that the state ought to treat the Lockean principles, as distinct from our preferred principles, as constraints – or indeed as goals. Even if we grant that some principles should be treated by the state as constraints, we will ask "why treat *these principles* as constraints?"

The Lockean principles allow of a variety of different interpretations – they constitute a family of different principles, not a single set – and in any case they are not the only principles that we might imagine people satisfying in a relatively peaceful, well-organized state of nature. The point is particularly obvious with the principles whereby people are said not to harm one another in their possessions. For it is notorious that the rights of property to which Locke directs us are not specified in unambiguous detail and are not the only rights of property to which we might consider holding a state.[14,15]

Nozick himself, with characteristic candor, draws attention to the indeterminacies in Locke's formulation of property rights and to the alternative sets of rights that we might imagine. A system of property rights will determine the different titles to ownership and the discretion available to owners as to how the things they own may be used. Nozick makes clear that Locke is not unambiguous on either matter, as appears for example in the fact that the famous proviso on ownership – that there should be "enough and as good left in common for others" (ASU, 178–82) – can be interpreted in a number of different ways.

More important, however, Nozick also makes clear that there are many different possible systems of property rights possible, ranging from private systems of the kind illustrated by Locke to systems of collective property where "a group of persons living in an area jointly own the territory, or its mineral resources" (ASU, 178). He spells out some of the variations possible in the following passage.

> The central core of the notion of a property right in X, relative to which other parts of the notion are to be explained, is the right to determine what shall be done with X; the right to choose which of the constrained set of options concerning X shall be realized or attempted. The constraints are set by other principles or laws operating in the society; in our theory, by the Lockean rights people possess (under the minimal state).... This right of selecting the alternative to be realized from the constrained set of alternatives may be held by an *individual* or by a *group* with some procedure for reaching a joint decision; or the right may be passed back and forth, so that one year I decide what's to become of X, and the next year you do (with the alternative of destruction, perhaps, being excluded). Or, during the same time period, some types of decisions about X may be made by me, others by you. And so on. (ASU, 171)

Given that many systems of property rights are possible, it is obvious that Nozick must face the question raised in this section as well as that which was raised in the last. Not only will he have to explain why the Lockean principles are to be treated by the state as constraints, and not as goals. He also will have to explain why it is the Lockean principles – in particular, the Lockean principles in property holding – that are selected for such treatment, and not some others.

The Plausibility of a Consequentialist Answer

I suggested with the treatment question that the most plausible answer available will take us back to a consequentialist perspective. The best way of explaining why certain principles should be treated by the state as constraints is to show that only by doing this will the state be able to promote some important value or goal. I make a similar suggestion with the selection question. The best way of explaining why it is the Lockean principles in property that a state should treat as constraints, for example, will be by showing that if the state privileges the Lockean principles in that way it will do better in securing and advancing certain palpably desirable consequences than it would do by privileging any rival set.

Nozick himself draws attention at a number of points to how natural it is to think in consequentialist terms as we consider the question, crucial to political theory, as to which system of property rights should be put in place in a society. Thus, he seems to tell us that what we need for assessing different systems is precisely the sort of theory that would give us information about the consequences each would have. Having said that a property right gives us a constrained set of uses an owner may make of something and an account of the exclusionary and shared ways in which ownership may be enjoyed, he goes on to add

> We lack an adequate, fruitful, analytical apparatus for classifying the types of constraints on the set of options among which choices are to be made, and the types of ways decision powers can be held, divided, and amalgamated. A theory of property would, among other things, contain such a classification of constraints and decision modes, and from a small number of principles would follow a host of interesting statements about the consequences and effects of certain combinations of constraints and modes of decision. (ASU, 171)

A little later he even rehearses the consequential considerations by reference to which he thinks that a private as distinct from a collective system of ownership is to be justified:

> It increases the social product by putting means of production in the hands of those who can use them most efficiently (profitably); experimentation is encouraged, because with separate persons controlling resources, there is no one person or small group whom someone with a new idea must convince to try it out; private property enables people to decide on the principle and types of risks they wish to bear, leading to specialized types of risk-bearing; private property protects future persons by leading some to hold back resources from current consumption for future markets; it provides alternate sources of employment for unpopular persons who don't have to convince any one person or small group to hire them, and so on. (ASU, 177)

Nozick maintains that within a Lockean theory these considerations serve to determine how we should understand the proviso that there should be "enough and as good left in common for others." Within the theory, then, they are not designed to offer "a utilitarian justification of property." But this comment says nothing to argue against the plausible idea that it is considerations of this kind that show why we should want the state to privilege Lockean principles in the first place, rather than principles of any other kind.

Nozick's line of thought about property indicates why it is natural to try to resolve the question under discussion – the question of why the state should privilege these principles rather than those – on a consequentialist basis. The non-consequentialist commitment to having the state treat certain principles as constraints leaves the question as to why the theory should select the set of principles it actually selects from among the alternative sets possible. And a natural way to answer that question would be to say that at this level the theory goes consequentialist. While it maintains that the state should treat the principles as constraints, and not as goals – and is in this respect non-consequentialist – it selects the principles that it holds up as constraints on the grounds that the state's treating them as constraints will do better in consequentialist terms than its treating any alternative principles as constraints.

Not only is a consequentialist answer to the selection question plausible, as it is plausible with the treatment question. One and the same consequentialist view can provide an answer at once to the two questions. Thus, we may think that the goal of promoting something like freedom as non-domination justifies the state in selecting certain principles as those it ought to implement and that it requires the state to implement them in the fashion of constraints: any attempt to treat them as goals is likely to be counterproductive.

The problem that we have been discussing in connection with property-rights arises also in regard to other rights that non-consequentialists will want to have the state respect. As there are many different systems of property rights, so there are many different systems of rights related to liberty and even life. The literature on the different interpretations of liberty and on the different ways of understanding rights to life shows that, as there is no easy response to the selection problem in the case of property, so there is going to be no easy response to it in these areas either. And what is true of life, liberty, and property is going to be true in even greater measure for those principles related to reducing and rectifying offences against life, liberty, and property. In every case, there are going to be many possible sets of principles available for the state to treat as constraints – or as goals – and in each case, then, there will be a substantial question as to which set should be preferred.

Contractualism Does not Offer a Sustainable Alternative

We might well leave the discussion at this point, but opponents will argue that I should look beyond Nozick's work for other ways in which the selection question might be treated by non-consequentialists. Is there any distinctively non-consequentialist way, then, in which political philosophy might hope to argue that certain principles, and not others, should be selected for being made into constraints on the state?

One familiar line will be that if the state – or the people or the society or the tradition or whatever – has bound itself in an historical contract to honoring certain constraints, then that will provide a non-consequentialist basis of selection. I am happy enough to concede the point, at least for present purposes. The concession is not going to provide any consolation for non-consequentialists, for no people in history is on record as having made the sort of contract that would be required.

This observation leads, however, to the obvious question. Might hypothetical contracts serve to justify the selection of certain principles in a non-consequentialist way? John Rawls argues in *A Theory of Justice* that the state should be constrained by certain principles of justice, because these are principles we would each have chosen to constrain it by, in the so-called original position: in the position where we choose social arrangements under a veil of ignorance as to our chances of doing well or badly under the arrangement chosen. And in a related manner Tim Scanlon[16] suggests that the right principles by which to constrain the state are, roughly, those to which no one could raise an intuitively reasonable objection within an enterprise of mutual cooperation. Might such approaches give non-consequentialists a way of dealing with the selection issue?

I think not. The first thing to observe is that any such approach will inevitably identify a general feature that some principles have and others lack, and will recommend the principles that have it over those that don't. In Rawls's case, the feature by which his principles of justice are singled out as principles the state should treat as constraints is that they are fair: in particular, fair in the sense in which the fact that they would be chosen under a veil of ignorance testifies to their fairness. In Scanlon's case, the feature by which any proposed principles would be singled out is the fact that they are mutually justifiable in a distinctive way: no one could reasonably object to them as a basis of cooperation. (There is a question in interpreting Scanlon as to whether the justifiability of principles in this sense is the property of being substantially such that no one could reasonably object to them as a basis of cooperation or the purely subjunctive property of being such that, without any substantive base explaining the fact, no one could reasonably object.[17] But that difference in possible construal is not relevant for present purposes.)

Given that any hypothetical contractual procedure will select and recommend certain principles on the grounds that they possess a general property of some sort, we can state the problem with arguing that hypothetical contracts can provide a non-consequentialist answer to the selection question. The property envisaged – say, fairness or mutual justifiability – is presumably one that the principles selected are held to realize in a manner that makes them preferable to alternatives. Organize the state and the society around this set of principles, so the idea must be, and there will be more fairness or mutual justifiability than would obtain under any of the alternatives. But the rationale for selecting the principles, stated in this way, is clearly consequentialist. The hypothetical contract favored articulates what is thought to be the crucial property to look for in relevant principles – Rawls's contract articulates one property, Scanlon's another – and the principles actually recommended are selected on the grounds of promising to promote that property best.

In identifying the principles that will serve fairness or mutual justifiability best, there is a tendency to do ideal theory: to identify the principles that would serve best under conditions of universal acceptance and compliance. But this does not take away from the point I am making. Rawls's contractors ask in the original position after which principles they would rationally prefer to have operate in an ideal society and he argues that they would prefer the two principles of justice; they would require officials of the state, and ordinary citizens, to treat those principles as constraints. But the contractors might well give a different answer to the question as to which principles they would rationally prefer to have operate in a society that is said to incorporate such and such shortfalls from ideal acceptance and compliance. Contractualists in the spirit of Rawls should presumably hope that they would opt for the principles that would do best by fairness in that particular world.

Rawls will argue of course – and Scanlon may argue in an analogous way – that the principles that ought to be treated as constraints in the actual, imperfect world are those that would maximize fairness in an ideal society, even though when they do not maximize fairness in the actual one. But what argument is available in support of this line? If what matters is fairness or mutual justifiability, and if there is more of it to be had in the actual world by imposing one set of principles rather any other, then why not go for that better-performing set of principles? Why not do so, even if another set would have done better in the non-actual world envisaged in ideal theory? All of the arguments rehearsed in discussing the treatment question are available at this point to deny hypothetical contractarians the possibility of arguing that they have a sustainable, non-consequentialist basis for dealing with the selection issue.

Another Perspective on this Critique of Contractualism

For those who are not persuaded of these remarks on contractualism, I add a further, deeper-running line of criticism. This is not essential to my purposes but it may help to persuade some skeptical readers that the position I am taking has a good deal to be said for it.

In my earlier characterization of non-consequentialism and consequentialism I argued that while each approach embraces general principles – neither privileges any person or place or other entity by name – the first argues that agents ought to instantiate such principles, treating them as constraints, the second that it ought to promote them in the manner of goals. This means that from the point of view of the agent who conforms to a non-consequentialist theory, whether a certain scenario is to be preferred to another – whether it is better in moral terms from his or her point of view – will depend on how that agent behaves in that scenario: on what principles they instantiate in their behavior. Looking at two abstractly described scenarios, then, this agent will not be able to form a moral preference as to which should be brought about before learning who he or she is in those scenarios: before turning the abstract scenarios into centered scenarios where the person is identified as this or that agent. By contrast, of course, the agent who conforms to consequentialist theory will be able to rank abstract scenarios without reference to who he or she is; the morally preferable scenario will be that in which the preferred principles are maximally realized, even if in that scenario they are the agent who does least well by those principles.

Let us agree, then, that non-consequentialism cannot rank abstract scenarios, only centered ones. It cannot rank possible ways things might be except from the point of view of an agent whose identity and role in each of the different situations under assessment is fixed and manifest. The lesson gives us another, useful perspective on the question of whether contractualist approaches to the selection question are genuinely non-consequentialist.

I argue that they are not, on the grounds that those approaches are all meant to provide us with the ability to rank abstract scenarios. We are invited to endorse a contractually articulated ideal like fairness or mutual justifiability and to rank the abstract scenarios associated with different sets of principles in terms of the ideal. But this exercise is exactly the sort of assessment that non-consequentialists, with their emphasis on how a designated agent does by way of instantiating a certain ideal, cannot endorse. It belongs firmly in the camp of consequentialist approaches.

Notice, by contrast, that historical contractualism would provide a non-consequentialist line on the selection question by the criterion I am introducing; the problem here is that there are no historical contracts available for non-consequentialists to invoke. Were we to identify ourselves as a people or society or state – as a collective agent of an intertemporally stable variety – and were we to have made an historical contract of some kind in the past, then we could argue that from our point of view the centered scenario in which we remain faithful to that contract – impose principles of the kind supported by the contract – is to be preferred to all others. In arguing this, we would be thinking in a distinctively non-consequentialist way, abjuring any ability to assess abstract scenarios and any interest in pursuing assessment of that sort. We would be operating on a non-consequentialist basis in dealing with the question as to which principles ought to be selected as the principles that officials of the state, and ordinary citizens, ought to treat as constraints.

Hypothetical contractarians cannot help themselves to any argument of this kind. They might claim to focus on the state or the people as a collective agent and to ask in a non-consequentialist way as to why that agent should select certain principles to impose on itself as constraints. But if it can argue for the selection of one set of principles over others only on the grounds that those principles would have been chosen in a certain counterfactual situation, even chosen by that very state or people, then that is not going to provide a basis of obligation akin to the obligation imposed, intuitively, by an historical contract. Why should any agent think itself constrained in a non-consequentialist way by a contract it would have made in certain circumstances, as distinct from a contract that it made in the course of its actual history?

The Issue in Ethics Generally

I have been arguing that whereas there is a natural, consequentialist answer available for the selection question, as there is an answer of this kind available for the treatment issue, there is no reply available that looks to be at once plausible and non-consequentialist. The difficulty, I want to stress, is not just a technical one. It stems from a very deep feature of non-consequentialism and in order to emphasize that claim I end by considering a way in which it surfaces for non-consequentialism in ethics generally, not just in political philosophy.

Every non-consequentialist position takes a given set of principles as established or authoritative and argues that those principles ought to be treated as constraints, not as goals. The principles in question may be principles whereby parents pay special attention to their children, friends care for one another in a distinctive way, those who make promises give privileged consideration to the promisees, people who are engaged directly with others acknowledge the claims of those others in a way that privileges them over third parties, and so on. There is a clear issue as to whether such principles should be treated as constraints on the parties immersed in the relevant practices, or whether they should be treated as goals. This is an issue that arises within the practices in question, be they practices of parenting, friendship, promise-keeping or face-to-face civility. But that internal issue is paralleled by an external question to do with whether the principles and practices in question should indeed be taken as given principles, already established or authoritative. This is the selection question as distinct from the treatment question.

Should we have an insulated family sphere or expose that sphere in greater measure to initiatives within civil society? Should we institute or sustain principles of friendship that allow friends to make claims on one another that are detrimental in various ways to the interests of third parties?

Should we make promise-keeping sacred to the point that people may be forced to keep even promises or contracts that beggar them? These are all instances of the selection question, though they are raised now in a context that is not distinctively political. The questions are serious and can hardly be ignored by any one who claims to be committed to the moral enterprise.

Yet those questions, so it appears to me, do not allow of resolution along non-consequentialist lines. For what distinguishes non-consequentialism is the insistence on the fact that it is morally right to instantiate certain principles rather than to promote them; or, more generally, an insistence that the moral point of view allows the assessment of centered but not of abstract scenarios. And non-consequentialism in that sense has to give way to consequentialism when it comes to the question of which principles should be selected as fit to be treated as constraints, whether in this area or in that. As the selection problem confounds non-consequentialism in political philosophy, then, so it confounds non-consequentialism more generally. Non-consequentialists may keep putting off recourse to consequentialist considerations. But if they are serious about pursuing questions of justification to the limit, they cannot put it off forever.

Notes

[1] R. Nozick, *Anarchy, State, and Utopia* (Oxford: Blackwell, 1974).

[2] J. Locke, *Two Treatises of Government*, ed. P. Laslett (New York: Mentor, 1965).

[3] For his own later criticisms, see R. Nozick, *The Examined Life* (New York: Simon and Schuster, 1989), pp. 286–92.

[4] R. Nozick, *Philosophical Explanations* (Oxford: Oxford University Press, 1981), p. 503.

[5] P. Pettit, "A Consequentialist Perspective on Ethics," in *Three Methods of Ethics: A Debate*, M. Baron, M. Slote, and P. Pettit (eds.) (Blackwell: Oxford, 1997).

[6] P. Pettit, "Non-consequentialism and Universalisability." *Philosophical Quarterly*, 2000, 50: pp. 175–90.

[7] P. Pettit and M. Smith, "Global Consequentialism," in *Morality, Rules, and Consequences: A Critical Reader*, Brad Hooker, E. Mason, and D. E. Miller (eds.) (Edinburgh: Edinburgh University Press, 2001), pp. 121–33.

[8] R. Dworkin, *Taking Rights Seriously* (London: Duckworth, 1978).

[9] P. Pettit, *Judging Justice* (London: Routledge, 1980).

[10] C. d. S. Montesquieu, *The Spirit of the Laws*, A. M. Cohler, B. C. Miller, and H. S. Stone (eds.) (Cambridge: Cambridge University Press, 1989), p. 204.

[11] J. Rawls, *A Theory of Justice* (Oxford: Oxford University Press, 1971).

[12] P. Pettit, *Republicanism: A Theory of Freedom and Government* (Oxford: Oxford University Press, 1997).

[13] R. Nozick, *The Nature of Rationality* (Princeton, N.J.: Princeton University Press, 1993).

[14] B. Williams, "The Minimal State," in *Reading Nozick: Essays on Anarchy, State, and Utopia*, J. Paul (ed.) (Totowa, N.J.: Rowman and Littlefield), p. 32.

[15] T. M. Scanlon, "Nozick on Rights, Liberty, and Property," in *Reading Nozick: Essays on Anarchy, State, and Utopia*, J. Paul (ed.) (Totowa, N.J.: Rowman and Littlefield), pp. 124–6.

[16] T. M. Scanlon, *What We Owe to Each Other* (Cambridge, Mass: Harvard University Press, 1998).

[17] P. Pettit, "Two Construals of Scanlon's Contractualism," *Journal of Philosophy*, 2000, 97: pp. 148–64.

6 | Goals, Symbols, Principles: Nozick on Practical Rationality*

GERALD F. GAUS

1. A PUZZLE: THE RELATION BETWEEN NOZICK'S THEORY OF PRACTICAL REASON AND HIS LIBERTARIANISM

Although Robert Nozick has made seminal contributions to many areas of philosophy – value theory, ethics, the philosophy of science, epistemology, and metaphysics, to name just a few – the libertarian political philosophy articulated in *Anarchy, State, and Utopia* remains the most famous.[1] It is not clear precisely what is his current evaluation of that libertarian philosophy, but in two important passages in the late 1980s and early 1990s, he partially disavowed it. In *The Examined Life*, he wrote:

> Within the operation of democratic institutions . . . we want expressions of the values that concern us and bind us together. The libertarian position I once propounded now seems to me seriously inadequate, in part because it did not fully knit the humane considerations and joint cooperative activities it left room for more closely into the social fabric. . . . There are some things we choose to do together through government in solemn marking of our human solidarity. . . .[2]

In *The Nature of Rationality*, he makes a similar observation:

> Symbolic meaning . . . is a component of particular ethical decisions. . . . It has been argued that the symbolic meaning of feeding someone, giving sustenance, enters into the discussion of the ways in which the lives of direly ill people permissibly may be terminated – turning off their artificial respirator

* Versions of this chapter were presented to the International Society for Utilitarian Studies, The International Economics and Philosophy Society, The American Political Science Association, and to the Law Faculty at Universidad Torcuato Di Tella. I would like to thank Scott Arnold, Joshua Cohen, Ben Eggleston, Jonathan D. Halvorson, Benjamin Gregg, Eric Mack, Douglas MacLean, Guido Pincione, Geoff Sayre-McCord, David Schmidtz, Horacio Spector, and Fernando Tesón for their comments and suggestions.

but not halting their food and starving them to death. The political philosophy presented in *Anarchy, State, and Utopia* ignored the importance to us of joint and official serious symbolic statement and expression of our social ties and concern and hence . . . is inadequate.[3]

In both passages, Nozick's repudiation of libertarianism is based on the importance of *expressing commitments* and *symbolic meanings*. Apparently, one function of public policy is to officially express our joint commitments or symbolize our concern for each other. Nozick thus tells us that minimum wage laws might be understood as symbolizing our concern for the poor (NR, 27).

In *Anarchy, State, and Utopia*, symbolic rationality does not appear. That argument is focused on the contrast between reasons derived from goals and those derived from rights (or, more broadly) principles. Famously, Nozick insisted that rights cannot be reduced to goals. He took as unproblematic that we can have a reason to advance a goal. His question in *Anarchy, State, and Utopia* is whether we can have a reason to perform act *A* when *A*-ing does not advance any goal. Can it be rational to respect rights when they are what he calls "side constraints" on the pursuit of our goals (ASU, 28)? Nozick explicitly worried that this is irrational, "Isn't it *irrational* to accept a side constraint *C*, rather than a view that directs minimizing the violations of *C*?" (ASU, 30). In defending the rationality of acting on rights as side constraints, he appealed to the notion of action on principle: "Side-constraints upon action reflect the underlying Kantian principle that individuals are ends and not merely means . . . " (ASU, 31).

The libertarian theory of *Anarchy, State, and Utopia* thus presupposed a defense of principled rational action that, apparently, cannot be reduced to goal-directed action. Nozick's later repudiations of his libertarianism, sketchy as they are, clearly focused on the incompleteness of that theory of practical reason, stressing the need to incorporate symbolic and expressive rationality. At least in Nozick's eyes, adopting a wider view of practical reason was critical in abandoning his libertarianism. In *The Nature of Rationality*, Nozick presents a systematic account of this wider conception of rationality, including accounts of goal pursuit, symbolic expression, and principled action. This chapter explores that wider view of rationality.

Section 2 considers Nozick's account of goal-directed rationality, Section 3 examines his innovative discussion of symbolic rationality, while Section 4 analyzes the role of principles in rational action. Having critically examined the relation between these three core elements of practical rationality, I will briefly return in Section 5 to the relation between the theory of practical reason and Nozick's political philosophy.

2. GOAL-DIRECTED RATIONALITY

2.1. A Tiny Step for Humeans?

Although *Anarchy, State, and Utopia* stressed the possibility of principled rationality, and *The Nature of Rationality* makes much of symbolic rationality, it needs to be emphasized that for Nozick, as for most contemporary philosophers, instrumental rationality lies at the heart of practical reason. "Instrumental rationality is within the intersection of all theories of rationality (and perhaps nothing else is). In this sense it is the default theory, the theory that all can take for granted, whatever else they think. . . . The question is whether it is the *whole* of rationality" (NR, 133). Indeed, Nozick thinks, "it is natural to think of rationality as a goal-directed process. (This applies to both rationality of action and rationality of belief)" (NR, 64). So, according to the basic "instrumental conception, rationality consists in the effective and efficient achievement of goals, ends, and desires. About the goals themselves, an instrumental conception has little to say" (NR, 64). "At present, we have no adequate theory of the substantive rationality of goals and desires, to put to rest Hume's statement, 'It is not contrary to reason to prefer the destruction of the whole world to the scratching of my finger'" (NR, 140).

On this last issue, Nozick presents his account as mildly revisionist. He takes "a tiny step beyond Hume," arguing that the constraints "on how preferences hang together that are formulated in the standard Von Neuman-Morgenstern conditions or their variants that decision theory presents" – such as transitivity – constitute criteria of rational preferences. Nozick's strategy is to advocate a set of coherence requirements for rational preference structures. He then adds a more adventurous claim: a "preference or desire is rational only if (it is rationally coherent and) it is arrived at *by a process* that yields rationally coherent preferences and desires" (NR, 148). This is part of Nozick's overall strategy of combining internalist and reliablist justifications: the rationality of a belief/desire is a function of both (1) its relation to the other elements of the system of beliefs/desires (internalism) and (2) the reliability of the process by which it was formed (reliablism).

Without taking issue with reliablism in general,[4] it is especially puzzling as a theory of rational preference. To better see its problems, consider Nozick's claim that

> A person lacks rational integration when he prefers some alternative x to another alternative y, yet prefers that he did not have this preference, that is, when he also prefers not preferring x to y. When such a second-order preference conflicts with a first-order one, it is an open question which of these preferences should be changed. What is clear is that they do not hang together well, and a rational person would prefer that this not (continue) be the case. (NR, 141)

We loosely use the terms "preference" and "desire" as synonyms; in many places Nozick uses them interchangeably.[5] Let us, then, take a standard case where this story appears to make sense: a desire to get drunk. We can imagine a person with a desire to get drunk, and also with a desire to get rid of his desire to get drunk. There appears to be a conflict of desires – an irrational inconsistency. Suppose we also know that the desire to get drunk is one that leads to many such inconsistencies in the person's system of desires and that this desire is produced by a desire-forming process *IH* (impulsive hedonism) that typically produces these sorts of troublesome desires. Nozick's reliablist condition would seem to indicate that desires formed by *IH* are not rational.

Although we often talk about ordering desires, or ordering preferences over things ("I prefer beer to wine"), strictly speaking such conflicting desires or preferences for things are not irrationally inconsistent. No irrationality is manifested by desiring both to get drunk and to stay sober. We cannot always do both, but that is the case with many of our desires. Nor is there anything irrationally inconsistent about sometimes preferring beer to wine, and sometimes preferring wine to beer. It is perfectly rational to prefer wine to beer if I am confronted with bad beer and great wine; and even a wine connoisseur might select a cheap-beer-plus-a-ten-thousand-dollar side payment to a fine wine. Our desires or preferences for objects or experiences are constantly conflicting; we cannot say that a process that produces such conflicting desires is in any way irrational. This includes a clash between first- and second-order desires. There is nothing irrational about liking beer and desiring that I didn't like beer, but instead cultivate a taste for wine, which would impress my highbrow friends. I cannot simultaneously satisfy both, but neither can I satisfy both my preferences to go out tonight and to refrain from going out so that I can write. I am *ambivalent* about going out tonight: I want to satisfy that preference, but I also wish I didn't have it so that I would stay home and write. It is irrational knowingly to entertain inconsistent beliefs, but it is neither unusual nor irrational to be ambivalent about values or desires.[6]

Certainly no consistency requirement such as Nozick mentions in the above quotation can be inferred from abstract decision theory, if we understand preferences to range over goods, goals, actions, experiences, and so on. What *are* strictly subject to rational consistency constraints on a decision theoretic view are preferences over states of the world, or total outcomes of one's choices. It does indeed violate standard conditions of rational choice to (1) prefer the world where I drink good wine and forgo the bad beer at three o'clock today and (2) prefer the world where I drink the bad beer and forgo the good wine at three o'clock today. If these are complete descriptions of my options, and are the ways I rank the outcomes, then I cannot say what best maximizes the satisfaction of my preferences. Note, though, that the inconsistency does not arise from any inconsistency among elements of my set of desires, understood as the things that I like, the goals that I seek, or actions I desire to perform. The rational inconsistency results simply from the way that I rank combinations of these satisfactions in terms of possible states of the world.

This being so, the *process* that produces either a rationally consistent or inconsistent preference ordering is *not* the process that allows desires, likings, or goals *into one's set* of things that are liked, or goals that are sought. Desire and preference formation, then, are fundamentally disanalogous to belief formation; a reliablist theory of belief is explicitly concerned with the process by which a belief enters one's system of beliefs. *Any* desire for *x* or preference for *x* over goods, goals, actions, or experiences can enter into one's value system without any rationality-impugning inconsistency whatsoever. The *process* that produces rationally consistent preferences is that capacity by which individuals rank outcomes that combine different mixes of preference satisfaction, which crucially involves the way in which they trade off the satisfaction of some preferences for others depending on the opportunity costs of satisfying them. But this process just *is* practical rationality: taking conditions such as consistency, transitivity, and so on as reasons to order preferences over total outcomes.

Even if we reject the claim that a preference for an object, experience, action, goal, and so on can be judged rational or irrational in virtue of the process by which it enters into our system, this analysis still has gone quite a ways beyond Hume.[7] Reason is far more than a slave of the passions. Rationality requires agents to rank, in accordance with consistency, transitivity, completeness, and so on, states of affairs with different mixes of satisfactions of desires. This in turn requires building a tradeoff rate or utility function that manifests an agent's consistent rankings of bundles of preference satisfaction.[8] Reason's role of producing coherent choices out of a mass of conflicting desires is thus constructive and regulative. The conclusion remains important: Even instrumental reason presupposes a conception of reasoning that is not about how we are best to achieve our desires, but how we are to sort them out so as to make consistent, effective, choice possible.

2.2. Causal and Evidential Reasoning

Nozick is well known for his analysis of the Newcomb problem.[9] In this familiar problem, an agent confronts a situation with two boxes. The first box is clear, and so the agent can see it contains $1,000; the second is opaque. The agent can choose to take the contents of one box or both. So far it is an easy choice – take both boxes, so assuring oneself of at least a thousand dollars, plus whatever is in the opaque box. The agent also knows, however, that an extremely reliable predictor has put the money in the boxes. She has put a million dollars into the opaque box if and only if she predicts you will choose it alone; if she predicts that you will choose both, she has left the opaque box empty.

According to Nozick, if one employs a simple principle of expected utility the agent will simply calculate the utility of each option's possible outcomes, weighted by their likelihood, and then add these up. Since, however, the outcomes are not necessarily probabilistically independent of the action the agent performs, a more adequate evidentially expected utility principle (*EEU*) calculates the expected utility of actions by taking account of the conditional probabilities of the outcomes, given that the agent performs that action (NR, 43). Now, Nozick has famously argued, an agent employing *EEU* will reason that given the information about the predictor, the probability of getting a million dollars conditional on choosing both boxes is extremely low, whereas the evidential expected utility of taking only the opaque one box is high, so *EEU* recommends choosing only the opaque box. This seems counterintuitive to many: after all, at the time of choice, the million dollars is either in the opaque box or not, and so the agent's decision to take one or two boxes at that time cannot affect what is in them. So why not still take both?

Some advocates of expected utility theory have argued that an adequate understanding of it gives the "right" answer – that the agent should take both boxes.[10] But insofar as act *A* being a *cause* of an outcome is distinct from A being a *sign* of an outcome,[11] there is case for distinguishing two conceptions of goal-directed rationality. Whereas evidential expected utility focuses on the signs that an action maximizes the achievement of one's goals, causal expected utility (CEU) focuses on probability that one's action will have a causal role in achieving one's goals. Thus, Nozick has argued that EEU instructs the agent to take only the opaque box, whereas CEU directs the agent to select both, since an inspection of the causal chains connecting the agent's choices to outcomes indicate that the action with the highest expected causal utility is to choose both boxes.

The extensive literature on this issue has generated a variety of cases for and against EEU and CEU. Exemplifying the tendency to combine divergent views that we witnessed in his attempt to combine reliablist and internalist conceptions of rational preference (§2.1), Nozick seeks to accommodate both. "I suggest that we ... say not merely that we are uncertain about which *one* of these two principles, CEU and EEU, is (all by itself) correct, but that both of these principles are legitimate and must be given its respective due" (NR, 45). For Nozick, an indication that both principles have some pull on us is the way in which our intuitions respond to changes in the values in the Newcomb problem. If the amount in the clear box is $1, he maintains, even "two boxers" sympathetic to CEU see the virtues of EEU, whereas if we raise the amount in the clear box to $900,000, even those inclined to EEU are apt to take both boxes. Although some commentators have doubted the existence of a general tendency to switch principles depending on the values, empirical evidence indicates that choices in Newcomb problems are indeed dependent on both the reliability of the predictor and the magnitude of the values at stake.[12] In any event, Nozick's solution is to endorse a meta-decision theory that encompasses both CEU and EEU. What Nozick calls the "decision value" (DV) of act A is the "weighted value of its causally expected utility and its evidentially expected utility, as weighted by that person's confidence in being guided by each of these two kinds of expected utility" (NR, 45). Hence, provisionally, we can say, $DV(A) = Wc \times CEU(A) + We \times EEU(A)$.

2.3. The Connection and Flow Metaphors

Both EEU and CEU are goal-directed theories of practical rationality: Both understand rational action as directed toward the satisfaction of goals or desires. EEU sees a rational action as one that, given the relevant signs, is *indicated* to be the best option given one's goals, while CEU identifies rational action as a type of action that *causes* the state of affairs in which one's goals are best achieved. Whereas *EEU* is goal-directed but not instrumental (it tells us what to choose given our ends, but does not claim that the best action is an instrument to achieving our ends), *CEU* is both (NR, 137). I shall not comment here on Nozick's combination of causal and evidential decision theory insofar as it is intended as a solution to the Newcomb problem or a meta-decision theory; some of its difficulties have been discussed by others,[13] and the literature on the general problem is vast. So far as I know, what has gone largely unnoticed is *the way* in which Nozick explicates the difference between causal and evidential reasons. According to Nozick, reasons are "connections" between outcomes and goals (or desires) (NR, 49). As he puts it, utility "flows" along reasons. What distinguishes, then, evidential from causal reasons is the nature of the connections; in one case utility flows along causal connections (NR, 27), in the other it flows along evidential routes.

This conception of reasons recurs throughout *The Nature of Rationality* but is never really explicated; like so much of what Nozick says, it remains suggestive, indeed, metaphorical.[14] Nevertheless, metaphorical as the idea is, it is at the heart of his goal-directed theory of practical reason. And if we take the trouble to explicate it, we will uncover the paradoxical nature of Nozick's goal-directed theory of reason.

2.4. Goals and Utility's Backwash

How might we explain the flow metaphor? Well, given that both *EEU* and *CEU* are goal-directed accounts of practical reason, the place to begin is with the sought-after end, the goal (or value) of action. The goal or value, V, then, has utility – let us say, more generally, that it is valenced: It is normatively charged. Let us signify this by $V+$. Now, the question is how do we link up that goal with reasons for action? Hobbes – a proto-causal theorist – points the way: We engage in a "train of regulated thoughts," reasoning back from a desired effect to the "means that produce it."[15] Suppose, then, that we reason in this way, and conclude that act A causes $V+$, or $A \rightarrow V+$. But note that at this point it is simply a discovery of reason that the desired effect can be accomplished by performing A; $A \rightarrow V+$ is a fact about the world. Act A thus far has no utility or valence itself; reason has simply connected it with a valenced goal. At this point Nozick postulates what we might call a utility backwash: "utility can flow back, be imputed back, . . . along causal connections" (NR, 27). So the fact that $A \rightarrow V+$ produces a flow-back of valence: normative charge travels back along the causal link, producing a charged act A – call it $A+$. The utility backwash, then, shows why A

matters, how it gets valenced or infused with utility. It now seems clear why we have not simply a reason to *believe* that $A \rightarrow V+$, but a reason to *A*. *Mutatis mutandis*, the same applies to evidential connections. We should note that on Nozick's account, the type of valence or utility that infuses the act depends on the channel along which the utility has flowed back; if the utility flows back along evidential routes it produces one type of utility (i.e., evidential utility), whereas if it flows back along causal paths it produces a different type of utility. So in the process of washing back toward the act, the nature of the utility changes.

When acting instrumentally, then, the agent's action *manifests a present value*. Because *A* has been charged by the utility backwash, when the agent performs the instrumentally rational act $A+$, her action is not simply for the sake of a goal – a future value – but is informed by value *now*. But to do $A+$ because $A+$ is valenced is in an interesting way non-consequential in character, one's $A+$-ing itself is valuable. All instrumental acts thus presuppose acting for present value. This important point is easily misunderstood. We must distinguish:

> *Cognitive instrumentalism*: If (i) Alf has goal $V+$, and (ii) Alf has well-grounded belief that $A \rightarrow V+$, then (iii) the belief that $A \rightarrow V+$ itself gives Alf a reason to *A*.
>
> *Backwash instrumentalism*: If (i) Alf has goal $V+$, and (ii) Alf has a well-grounded belief that $A \rightarrow V+$, then (iii) the value (utility) of $V+$ backwashes to *A*, producing $A+$, hence (iv) $A+$-ing is valued and thus (v) Alf has a reason to $A+$.

Backwash instrumentalism presupposes that instrumental action always itself embodies value. According to backwash instrumentalism, a reason for action always involves *acting on a present value*, not simply acting for the sake of a future value. The causal beliefs infuse *A* with value, and so allow one to act on the value, but in themselves the causal beliefs do not provide reasons for action. Paradoxically, then, instrumentally rational action is always action performed for a present value.

It might be thought that my analysis takes the flow metaphor too seriously (although, we shall see, it forms a theme of *The Nature of Rationality*). Why not simply opt for cognitive instrumentalism? Note that cognitive instrumentalism requires that a belief that $A \rightarrow V+$ itself provides an agent with a reason to act. But the claim that beliefs themselves provide reasons for action appears anti-Humean.[16] It seems, then, that the Humean account of instrumental rationality is faced with a dilemma. By contrast, it can insist that beliefs alone cannot provide motivating reasons to act.

This, though, leads to backwash instrumentalism, and the paradoxical claim that rational action is never really simply for the sake of its consequences. In order to show that action can be purely instrumental, a Humean might adopt cognitive instrumentalism, that is, that a person acts simply for the reason that his action achieves a goal. But if so, then beliefs do, after all, provide *reasons that move to action*, and the Humean account converges with a more Kantian-inspired theory. Thus, despite all its problems, something like the flow-back theory is necessary for a resolutely Humean theory according to which beliefs themselves never provide reasons that move to action.

3. SYMBOLIC REASONS

3.1. Symbolic Flow-Back

We have seen that on Nozick's account of goal-directed reasons, utility can flow back along evidential and causal paths. He also insists that it can flow back along *symbolic* channels. In general, Nozick believes that A symbolizes X if A *stands for* X. Appealing once again to the flow-back theory, Nozick argues that if X is valued, then the value flows back through the symbolizing relation to A, giving "symbolic utility" (SU) to A (NR, 26–7). Thus, an evaluation of the rationality of an act must not only consider the causal and evidential utilities at stake, but the symbolic, too. We arrive, then, at Nozick's final formula for the overall decision value of an act: $DV(A) = Wc \times CEU(A) + We \times EEU(A) + Ws \times SU(A)$. The overall decision value with respect to A is the weighted value of A's causally expected utility, plus the weighted value of its evidentially expected utility, plus the weighted value of its symbolic utility.

The "standing for" relation is the crux of symbolic rationality. In order to grasp symbolic rationality, we need to get clear about the ways in which one thing can stand for another. Following Charles Peirce's theory of signs, James H. Fetzer distinguishes three ways in which A might stand for X.[17] (1) A might stand for X in the sense that it resembles X; call this the iconic relation. As Fetzer points out, "Statues, portraits, and photographs are icons in this sense...." (2) "Any things that stand for that which they stand for by virtue of being either causes or effects of that which they stand for are known as indices." Thus "Dark clouds that suggest rain, red spots that indicate measles... are typical indices in this sense." Note here that if A causes X, or is evidence of X, then A is a sign of – it stands for – X on Peirce's theory as an indicator of it. This would seem to make the "standing for" relation the most general; both varieties of goal-directed reasons – causal and evidential – are instances of the standing-for-qua-indicator relation. (3) Last, "Those signs that stand for that which they stand for either by virtue of conventional agreements or by virtue of habitual associations between those signs and that for which they stand are known as 'symbols.'" Note that on Peirce's view symbolizing is simply one type of "standing for" relation.

3.2.   Freudian Symbolism: Making Sense in a Crazy Sort of Way

Nozick's conception of symbolic rationality focuses on the third type of "standing for" (with room for the first); causal and evidential rationality are subsumed under the second. Consider the central case of the third, Peirce's notion of a symbol – in particular the case of psychological association between A-ing and a value, V. Nozick explicitly refers to the way that such symbolic rationality is part of Freudian psychology:

> Freudian theory must hold not only that actions and outcomes can symbolize still further events for a person but also that they draw upon themselves the emotional meaning (and utility values) of these other events. Having a symbolic meaning, the actions are treated as having the utility of what they symbolically mean; a neurotic symptom is adhered to with a tenacity appropriate to what it stands for. (NR, 26)

Let us, then, reflect on the nature of the Freudian project. Freud tells us that the aim is to make "sense" of symptoms.[18] Consider the case of a nineteen-year-old girl with obsessional sleep ceremonies:

> The big clock in her room was stopped, all the other clocks or watches in the room were removed, and her tiny wrist-watch was not allowed even to be inside her bedside table. Flowerpots and vases were collected on the writing table so that they might not fall over in the night, and disturb her in her sleep. . . . The pillow at the top end of the bed must not touch the wooden back of the bedstead. . . . The eiderdown . . . had to be shaken before being laid on the bed so that its bottom became very thick; afterwards, however, she never failed to even out this accumulation of feathers by pressing them apart.

At this point the behavior is simply incomprehensible. In a way that seems consistent with Nozick's symbolic utility, Freud appeals to symbolic connections to make sense of it:

> Our patient gradually came to learn that it was as symbols of female genitals that the clocks were banished from her equipment for the night. Clocks and

watches – though elsewhere we have found other symbolic interpretations for them – have arrived at a gradual genital role owing to their relation to periodic processes and equal intervals of time. . . . Flower-pots and vases, like all vessels, are also female symbols. . . .

She found out the central meaning of her ceremonial one day when she suddenly understood the meaning of the rule that the pillow must not touch the back of the bedstead. The pillow, she said, had always been a woman to her and the upright wooden back a man. Thus she wanted – by magic, we must interpolate – to keep man and woman apart – that is, to separate her parents from each other, and not allow them to have sexual intercourse. . . .

If a pillow was a woman, then the shaking of the eiderdown till all the feathers were at the bottom and caused a swelling there had a sense as well. It meant making the woman pregnant; but she never failed to smooth away the pregnancy again, for she had been for years afraid that her parents' intercourse would result in another child. . . .

Should it be the case that these are the actual symbolic connections – some iconic, some simply associational – then we have made a sort of sense of it all, in a crazy sort of way. As Freud notes, these are "wild thoughts." Admittedly, if "wooden bedstead = father," and "pillow = mother," then we can see a sort of crazy logic in keeping bedstead and pillow apart. But it hardly seems that Freud's account demonstrates that the girl has a good reason to keep the pillow and wooden bedstead from touching, or to smooth out the quilt. To be sure, it is important to her that her parents do not sleep together and have another child, but how can *that* give her reasons to make sure the pillow and bedstead do not touch and to make sure the quilt is smoothed out? As Freud suggests, false magical beliefs would actually help make sense of the whole affair, since we could then understand it as a case of (false) causal reasoning: The girl thinks keeping the pillow and bedstead apart will actually do something useful.[19]

If we put aside erroneous goal-directed reasoning, what is the nature of the link between the action (keeping the bedstead and pillow apart) and the value (that her parents do not have intercourse)? The answer seems simply that she associates them in her mind. This, though, hardly seems a *rational* connection. If any such associational link necessarily constitutes a rational (symbolic) connection, the dictum that "the laws of reason are the laws of thought"[20] becomes true in a surprising way. According to the associationist tradition in psychology – indebted to David Hartley and Hume, but going all the way back to Aristotle – consciousness can be explained in terms of laws governing the association of ideas, such as resemblance, contiguity, coexistence, succession, and so on.[21] Now if our mind forges such associational links between two elements such that we think of one standing for the other, then on Nozick's account this link is ipso facto a rational connection. Rationality reduces to psychology.

To be sure, associational symbolic links can explain *why* we develop preferences. Our obsessional girl has a preference to keep the pillow and the bedstead apart because she associated that with her desire to keep her parents apart, and so, we might say, seeing the pillow and bedstead apart "pleases her." But now we simply have a brute preference for keeping them apart, and a psychological tale as to how that preference developed. What we cannot say is that her goal of not having a competing sibling itself gives her a reason to make sure the pillow and the bedstead do not touch and to smooth out the quilt.[22] And that is why Freud believes that once a rational person sees *the sort of sense behind it all*, her obsessions will fade.[23]

3.3. Communicating and Expressing Through Symbols

Have I missed something important about symbolic expression? As Nozick points out, "A large part of the richness of our lives consists in symbolic meanings and their expression, the symbolic meanings our culture attributes to things or the ones we ourselves bestow" (NR, 30). Now, we need to distinguish symbolic *meaning* from symbolic *rationality*. It certainly is true that the richness of culture is associated with a system of meanings that allows one thing to stand for another. The question is not whether we have symbolic meanings – thought itself can be understood as a semiotic system.[24] And it is certainly true that symbols are constitutive of our goals: We could not think, and that includes conceiving of goals, without a system of symbolic meanings. Our question, however, is not whether thinking creatures must possess systems of meanings, but whether acting solely on the basis of symbolic links to our values is rational. Can symbolic *action* be rational?

Begin with a single-person case. Alf has a commitment to the poor. Let us say that in Alf's mind, caring for the poor is habitually associated with making sure his pillow never touches his bedstead. In his mind, the latter stands for the former. I have been arguing that Alf's commitment to the poor does not give him a reason to worry about the placement of his pillow. But now let us say that Alf wants to *show* that he cares about the poor. This is a different goal than helping them. If Alf has a general value of caring for the poor, one thing he may do is help them, another thing he might wish to do is communicate this value, perhaps simply to show the sort of person he is, to get the record straight about his values, or to induce others to adopt the value. The use of shared symbols is essential for this communicative act. If there is conventional rule that "*A* stands for *V*," or if there is an iconic relation such that anyone who sees *A* will see it as a stand-in for *V*, then the goal of communicating *V* will give you a reason to *A*.[25] If we employ a transmission theory, we can say that the expressive utility of communicating your commitment to *V* flows back along symbolic connections to action *A*.[26] Communicating through shared symbols is thus a type of goal-directed rational action. Shared symbols provide conventional or iconic pathways to assert or show things to others. In the cases that seem intuitively appealing – we want to symbolize our commitment to freedom, God, or human life – the symbols are ways to reveal these commitments with others. One of their functions is, thus, as a tool to achieve our communicative ends. This does not make them unimportant, but it is hard to see why "symbolic rationality" should be placed alongside goal-directed rationality as a distinct idea.[27]

Cannot a person ever practically rationally use symbols in a non-communicative way? What if a person uses symbols to express something to himself? A person who is trying to stop smoking might break a cigarette in half every morning to symbolize breaking the habit. Perhaps the person is trying to express to himself that he really wants to quit: He is trying to convince himself that he is a quitter. We already are on the margins of rationality in case like this; it hardly is a crystal-clear case of rational action. If he does not believe already that he is a quitter, how can he convince himself that he is one? If we go one step further, to a person who has no communicative intentions, even to himself, but just breaks the cigarette because in his mind it is linked to stopping smoking, then we seem to be back to the obsessional girl.

Perhaps this example is too odd. Take a much more conventional link: the symbol represented by the American flag. To many, this symbolizes freedom, a rich history, and valor in war; it thus seems to many that they have reasons to act toward the flag in ways that express respect for these values. Here we appear to have a solid example of symbolic reasons. To focus on the purely symbolic (non-communicative) feature of the flag, however, we must abstract from the flag's function as a shared symbol that allows us to communicate our commitment to these values to each other. Abstract too from what psychologists have called "functional autonomy"[28] – the way in which the flag, valued for its communicative functions, may become cherished for its own sake. What remains is pure symbolic meaning: the individual's association of the flag with these values. In the relevant case she does not seek to communicate her values to others nor does she care for the flag itself; in her mind the flag "stands for" these values. Does this in itself give her a reason, for example, to not use the flag as a rag to sop up spilled beer when she is at home alone? If so, then why shouldn't our nineteen-year-old girl make sure the bedstead doesn't touch the pillow?

Some insist that the flag case is very different from that of the pillow and bedstead. Whereas the latter is an idiosyncratic association that provides no reason to act, the former is a shared convention that does generate a reason to action. Thus, it is said that a patriot does indeed have a symbolic reason to treat the flag with reverence even when alone (and no one will know what she does), while the nineteen-year-old girl has no reason to keep the pillow and bedstead apart. Underlying this view may well be a certain theory of meaning, according to which meanings are inherently social, and so there is no such thing as a private meaning or symbol. Even if we accept the view that there is no such thing as private symbolic meaning – which on the face of it seems quite false, as Freud's account of the bedtime ritual indicates – there is still a puzzling jump from "conventionally, A means V" to a "person who values V has a reason to A in light of this symbolic connection." That is, there is still a gap between shared *meanings* and *reasons* to act. Conventionally, "D-O-G" stands for a group of canines, but even if I love dogs, the conventional meaning does not itself give me a reason to act – to utter the word "D-O-G." I use that conventional meaning to communicate (and to formulate plans and goals regarding dogs). Indeed, it is precisely the communicative nature of a system of meanings that explains the importance of shared conventions, for only shared conventions can provide the basis for communication. But if we insist that symbolic action is rational apart from communicative intentions, it is mysterious why the distinction between the conventional and the personal should bear so much weight. *Apart from the role of symbolic meanings in communication*, why should it be the case that (a) if only for me "A stands for V" I do not have a reason to A just because I value V, but if (b) in the minds of enough other people, "A stands for V" I then do have a reason to A just because I V?

4. PRINCIPLES AND REASONS

4.1. Are Principled Reasons So Different?

Principles or rules identify general classes of action and require or prohibit particular acts falling under the general descriptions.[29] Act A thus stands to principle P in something like a token-to-type relation. To A because of a P is to A because it instantiates the general principle P, that is, is an instance of it.[30] Thus, we have something like the schema:

Principle P is a reason to perform act A because A instantiates P.

It is often thought that this instantiation relation is somehow odd: How can the fact that A is an instance of P give us a reason to A? In contrast, it is commonly thought that, intuitively, it is obvious how pursuing a goal gives us a reason to act – the *promoting* relation links what matters to us with the act.

Our examination of Nozick's account of goal-directed rationality in Section 2 calls into question this way of distinguishing principled and goal-directed reasons. According to the utility flow-back account of goal-directed reasons, goal-directed action always presupposes action done on the grounds of an occurrent value. This suggests that at the foundation of all goal-directed action is a relation of the form:

Goal G is a reason to perform act A because G produces value V in A – A embodies V.

This, though, moves goal-directed rationality very close to principled or rule-directed rationality. Whatever the puzzling feature of principled action, it cannot be the instantiation relation. The relation "A instantiates P," is the same general type of relation as "A embodies V." In both cases, the action embodies a more abstract or general concern: with principles the action is a case of the principle, with goal-directed action, the action, via utility backwash, is infused with the general value attaching to the goal. At the foundation of both principled and goal-directed reasons, then, is a similar relation between the action and the feature that generates the reason to perform it: The action *embodies* the relevant reason-generating property – in one case the principle, in the other the value. If principled reasons are harder to grasp than goal-directed ones, it must be because, somehow, it is harder to see why principles should matter to people in a way that guide their actions. The issue, then, comes down to why principles matter, not the oddness of their link to actions.

4.2. The Intellectual Functions of Principles

In explaining why principles matter to us, Nozick stresses their functions. Once again he adopts a goal-directed account: Principles are important largely because they help us achieve our goals. While acknowledging that "Principles ... provide one means to control and reshape our desires," he adds that "Kant asked too much of them ... when he divorced them from their connection to desire and expected them to generate actions solely from respect for principle itself" (NR, 138). Nozick asks for less – principles perform crucial functions in helping us to advance our cognitive and practical goals.

Nozick first considers the intellectual function of principles – the benefits of organizing our systems of beliefs so that specific cases fall under general principles. Principles, he sensibly argues, test our specific judgments – if a specific judgment does not conform to an adequate general principle, our confidence in it decreases. "Failure to uncover an acceptable general principle that yields some judgment in particular may mean that there is no such acceptable principle, in which case that particular judgment is mistaken and should be abandoned" (NR, 4). Again appealing to his general transmission theory of reasons (§§2.3, 3.1), Nozick tells us that "Principles are transmission devices for *probability* or *support*, which flow from data or cases, via the principle, to judgments and predictions about new observations or cases whose status otherwise is unknown or less certain" (NR, 5). And Nozick speculates that moral principles may work in essentially the same way. "Writers on ethics frequently state that ethical principles must be formulated using general terms only.... This feature might enable a principle to license an inference to a new case, hence enable new normative judgments to be supported by previous ones" (NR, 5). There is certainly much to this, as is testified by the widespread acceptance of reflective equilibrium as a way to formulate moral principles and to evaluate individual judgments.[31]

Let us see how this works by again focusing on the transmission theory of reasons. The basic idea is that we have made individual judgments $\{j_1 \ldots j_n\}$, each of which has a level of confidence associated with it; suppose that the average level of confidence of $\{j_1 \ldots j_n\}$ is f. Principle P is a law-like statement; because $\{j_1 \ldots j_n\}$ falls under P, "probability or support ... flows from data or cases, via the principle, to judgments and predictions about new observations or cases whose status is otherwise unknown or less certain." Now it is not altogether clear whether (1) the lines of transmission are frictionless, so that we have degree of confidence f in a new judgment entailed by P, (2) whether some support is lost in the transmission, such that our level of confidence in a judgment entailed by P is less than f, or (3) whether the ability to formulate a law-like P to cover $\{j_1 \ldots j_n\}$ increases the average level of confidence, so that our confidence in a judgment entailed by P is greater than f. All three seem plausible in some cases. Many understand reflective equilibrium as conforming to (3): The systematization of our judgments under general principles *adds* to our confidence in the set. As Nozick remarks, "A theorist gains confidence in his particular judgments (or side in a controversy) when he can formulate a general principle or theory to fit it ..." (NR, 4). By contrast, suppose we possess a set of individual judgments with an average confidence level of f, and P explains (accounts for, etc.) them, but our confidence in P itself – that it is the correct systematization – is less than perfect, we are not certain of it. Since the adoption of P is an additional source of error, it would seem that a judgment entailed by P would have a confidence of less than f, since some of our confidence is lost because we are uncertain of P. If both of the preceding two relations hold, there may be countervailing effects: Some aspects of the transmission to P may increase our confidence above f while others push it under f, the final confidence being a function of these two inverse tendencies. Lastly, there may be neither amplification nor reduction of confidence, but frictionless transmission: P allows us to transfer f to a new judgment from a set of previous ones.

Whichever transmission relation or relations are endorsed, a circularity problem arises. Take the simple case of frictionless transmission. Suppose that at the first iteration $\{j_1 \ldots j_n\}$ has an average confidence level of f, which is frictionlessly transmitted, so not amplified, to P, which can now transmit f to new cases "or cases whose status otherwise is unknown *or less certain.*"[32] Suppose, then, that j_n had a confidence below the average, f. Thus, by employing P in relation to j_n, we raise our confidence in j_n to f, and that in turn raises the average confidence in $\{j_1 \ldots j_n\}$ to above f. That means the confidence level transmitted to P is now above f. Thus, P can now be reapplied to j_n, whose confidence level was exactly f, raising it to above f, which raises the confidence of judgments entailed by P even further above f, and so on.

Perhaps, though, it might be insisted that if the judgment under examination is j_n, then that judgment should not be included in the set of judgments whose support flows through P back to j_n. So now we have the set $\{j_1 \ldots j_{n-1}\}$, whose average confidence is f, and then we can raise our confidence in j_n to f by appeal to P. That will solve the circularity issue, but now note that we can vastly increase the confidence of all our judgments by starting out with a set of only those that are most certain, and then formulating a principle that transmits *that* high level of confidence to all "less certain" cases.[33]

4.3. Practical Principles: Using Symbols to Achieve Goals?

Nozick's analysis of the practical function of principles follows from this account of their intellectual function. Practical principles, he tells us, help in overcoming "temptations, hurdles, distractions, and diversions" so that we can better pursue our long-term goals and interests (NR, 14). This, of course, is a general problem in the theory of goal-directed reasoning that has attracted widespread attention.[34] As Nozick sees it, the crux of the problem is time preference (a preference for the near over far, simply because it is near) and the way it can lead us to abandon goal-pursuing plans to the long-term detriment of our goals. Suppose at time t_1, I form a plan: In order to write decent philosophy tonight, I decide that I should not drink Australian red wine with dinner, as it tends to make me think that my bad arguments are pretty convincing. If I can get to t_3, my goal will be satisfied: I will have written without being under the philosophy-impairing influence of Australian red. But at t_2, my preferences may be such that then I prefer drinking the wine to working unimpaired tonight, so that at t_2 it is rational to drink the wine. But that means I shall not work unimpaired tonight, and both t_1 and t_3 I prefer working unimpaired to drinking the wine. "Everyone sees succumbing to the smaller reward during the time interval t_2 as a problem, an irrationality, or an undesirable shortsightedness" (NR, 23).[35] Can I have a reason to ignore my t_2 preference for Australian red wine?

Nozick argues that having a principle – for example, "Do not drink wine when I want to write" – can do the trick:

> By adopting a principle, we make one action stand for many others and thereby change the utility or disutility of this particular act. This alteration of utilities is the result of exercising our power and ability to make one action stand for or symbolize others. . . . Adopting the principle forges . . . [a] connection, so that the penalty for violating the principle this time becomes the disutility of violating it always. (NR, 18–19)

Note that Nozick explains principled reasons in terms of symbolic reasons. The principle symbolically relates tonight's wine consumption to all other cases of drinking when I want to write afterwards. My drinking wine tonight "now stands for the whole class" (NR, 17). "By adopting this principle, it is as if you have made the following true: if you do this particular action in the class, you will do them all. Now the stakes are higher" (NR, 17). The idea, then, is that if I always drink wine before working, I will never write decent philosophy in the evening, and that is a cost of wine drinking that is clearly unacceptable. So it must be that my attraction to having wine at t_2 on any given night depends on my supposition that I will abstain on other nights – it is this supposition that the symbolic connection undermines. The symbolic connection forges a tie between this and other nights, the disutility of drinking on all the other occasions *flows* to this single case, thus giving me overwhelming reason not to drink tonight.

Nozick thinks this also explains the way ethical principles function in relations between people. "A principled person can be counted upon to adhere to his principles in the face of inducements or temptations to deviate" (NR, 9). Deontological principles, then, might be at least partially explained as ways to achieve smooth coordination by assuring others that one can be counted on to act in the principled way despite temptations to cheat. One might expect that Nozick would draw on this idea to show why it may be rational to cooperate in a prisoner's dilemma: If *this* act of defection stands for *all* acts of defection, and if I can see that the consequences of constant defection are terrible, then I might rationally adopt a principle that instructs me to cooperate with those who also adopt the cooperative principle. And because we are principled, we can rationally count on each other not to defect in individual cases.[36] Interestingly, however, Nozick instead appeals directly to the symbolic value of "being a cooperative person," and how acting on this symbolic reason may endorse a cooperative strategy in a prisoner's dilemma.[37] Overall, Nozick understands moral reasons as crucially, though not entirely, symbolic:

> There are a variety of things that an ethical action might symbolically mean to someone: being a rational creature that gives itself laws; being a lawmaking member a kingdom of ends; being a rational, disinterested, unselfish person; being caring; living in accordance to nature; responding to what is valuable; recognizing someone else as creature of God. The utility of these grand things, symbolically expressed *and instantiated* by the action become incorporated into that action's (symbolic) utility. Thus, these symbolic meanings become part of one's reason for acting ethically. Being ethical is among our most effective ways of symbolizing (a connection to) what we value most highly. (NR, 29–30)[38]

4.4. Principles: Instantiating or Symbolizing?

In the above passage, Nozick refers to both the symbolizing and instantiating relation between moral concerns and specific acts. These are different. If *A* instantiates *P*, it is a case of *P*. The principle identifies a general class of actions, and *A* is a member of that class. If, then, *P* is a sort of moral concern, then *A* is itself an instance of that concern. It is not simply associated with the moral concern, nor does it express the moral concern: it is a case of it. That is very different from saying that, either by conventional, habitual, or iconic links, the act is seen as a stand-in for the moral concern. Once we distinguish these, a strong case can be made (pace Nozick) for identifying the instantiation, not the symbolic, relation as fundamental to principled action.

Understanding the relation between practical principles and the acts that fall under them as basically symbolic raises puzzles. Once again the problem – this time, with symbolic reasons – stems from Nozick's transmission theory. Nozick's account of practical principles is analogous to his account of the intellectual role of principles. Just as intellectual principles transmit support or warrant from a set of judgments to an individual judgment, practical principles transmit utility from a set of acts to an individual act. The principle "Always A" symbolically transmits the combined utility of acts $A_1 \ldots A_n$ to each act in the set; each act stands for the whole set. Now it must be right that in a case of principled reasoning more is at stake than the value of this specific act; that is why a principled person will perform specific acts that themselves have little value. Nozick, then, seems entirely correct that in principled deliberation whether to X, more is at stake than the value of X. The worry is that his account puts too much at stake: *every case is at stake in each case.*

Suppose that there are two sets of actions that have the same overall non-symbolic utility: say 100. The first set is composed of three possible acts, $\{A_1, A_2, A_3\}$, each one of which contributes equally to achieving the 100 units of utility. If I perform simply A_1 I will get 33.3 units, if I perform both A_1 and A_2, I receive 66.6. The second set has one thousand acts $\{B_1 \ldots B_{1000}\}$, each one of which contributes an equal amount to the achievement of the 100 units (each contributes one-tenth of a unit). On Nozick's symbolic transmission account of the principles "Always A" and "Always B," the utility of the entire set is symbolically transmitted to each member of the set. It follows that I have equally strong principle-based reasons to perform A_2 and B_2, even though A_2 is a much more important opportunity to help achieve utility than B_2. If I adopt principles as a way to achieve my goals, and I have to choose whether to A_2 or B_2, it seems most implausible to say that my principles give me equally strong reasons to A_2 and B_2, and so I presumably should be rationally indifferent.

Note also that on Nozick's transmission theory, it would appear that the strength of one's reason to perform a specific act is dependent on one's estimate of the utility of the total set of acts. Suppose I now see A_2 not as an element of a set of three with a total utility of 100, but as an element of a set of twelve with a total utility of four hundred: My reason to conform to the principle "Always A" seems to be in some sense four times as strong – 400 units of utility are symbolically transmitted to A_2. But that means that the strength of one's reasons will typically be dependent on one's estimate of the size of the set of possible acts symbolically related. Principles do not seem to operate in this way.

Explaining principled action in terms of symbolic reasons seems mistaken on five grounds. (1) We have seen (§3) that symbolic reasons are problematic indeed; they are most sensible when connected with communicative intentions, but then they seem to be a species of goal-directed reasons. Action based solely on symbolic connections seems irrational. (2) Just because the most sensible case of a symbolic reason concerns the communication of one's values, and because communication often, perhaps typically, relies on shared rules that constitute the meanings of communicative acts, symbolic actions typically presuppose rules and principles rather than vice versa. Shared symbolic connections are rule governed: symbols presuppose rules. (3) I have argued (§4.1) that the instantiation relation, which seems the correct model of the relation between a principle and an action that it calls for (and which is noted by Nozick in the quotation at the end of §4.3), is not an especially odd one, which somehow needs to be explicated in terms of more familiar ideas. As I argued, the basic relation between action and concern presupposed by instantiation is very close to Nozick's own account of goal-directed reasons.

(4) As Nozick himself suggests, symbolic reasons themselves often presuppose the instantiation relation. "Sometimes an action may symbolically mean something by being our best instantiated realization of that thing, the best we can do" (NR, 33). More generally, Paul Moser has suggested that in Nozick's theory of reason, the key to understanding how one thing can symbolize another may be the idea of classifying actions together as of the same type (NR, 17).[39] Nozick indicates that action A_1 stands for all others in the set $\{A_1, A_2, A_3\}$ because it is the same type of action. If so, however, the token-to-type relation is presupposed by symbolic reasons. Rather than principled reasoning being derived from the symbolic, the opposite seems nearer the mark. (5) Finally, recall that Nozick's examination of goal-based rationality (§2.1) revealed that even it presupposes certain principles, such as transitivity, consistency, and so on. If so, in an important sense, all rationality presupposes principled rationality. In sum, rather than seeing principled reasons as somehow derived from goal-based and symbolic reasons, there seems a much stronger case within Nozick's own general theory of rationality for seeing principled reasons as basic, goal-based reasoning as presupposing principled reasons, and symbolic reasoning as being derivative of goals and principles.

5. PRACTICAL RATIONALITY AND POLITICAL PHILOSOPHY

This chapter opened with Nozick's two repudiations of *Anarchy, State, and Utopia*'s libertarian doctrine, both of which stressed the importance of symbolic and expressive reasons in politics. Someone seeking to bring Nozick back into the libertarian camp may be tempted to respond to these repudiations by pointing out that simply acknowledging the importance of symbolic reasons by no means entails that politics is the proper sphere for acting on them. That symbolism is important to us does not mean that it is a politically appropriate activity. Perhaps actions based on symbolic reasons are only at home in the voluntary "utopian" associations that Nozick made room for in Part Three of *Anarchy, State, and Utopia*. I think this tempting libertarian response underestimates the importance of symbolic reasons in Nozick's later writings. We have seen that Nozick closely links the ethical to the symbolic: symbolic expressions are not simply part of what gives life meaning, they are fundamental to rational ethical action. Indeed, we have seen that principles are explicated in terms of symbolic reasons. This suggests that the principled side-constraints that Nozick appealed to as the basis of his libertarianism in *Anarchy, State, and Utopia* are themselves based on symbolic reasons; there is no getting away from appeal to the symbolic in the moral realm. The symbolic cannot be exiled to utopias. To be sure, saying that the principled morality of *Anarchy, State, and Utopia* is based on symbolic rationality does not in itself imply the justification of the other sorts of political symbolic reasons that Nozick seeks to admit in *The Examined Life* and *The Nature of Rationality*. There certainly can be an argument for allowing Lockean symbolic reasons but not, say, symbolic reasons based on concern for others. But Nozick's theory of rationality posits no basic theoretical divide between the principle of respecting persons and symbolic caring. It is plausible indeed to suspect that, once the symbolic basis of so much of the moral is appreciated, political theory may be forced to admit symbolic "expressions of the values that concern us and bind us together." In many ways, that is what rational ethical action is all about.

Throughout this chapter, I have been skeptical of according to symbolic rationality this foundational role. It seems far more problematic than either goal-based or principled reasoning. Indeed, as I have indicated, it seems reasonable to understand symbolic reasons as derived from communicative goals, rules regulating the public meaning of symbols, and the instantiation relation whereby one thing stands for others of the same type. Consider, then, this alternative theory of practical reason and its relation to the libertarianism of *Anarchy, State, and Utopia*. On this alternative account, the fundamental divide in the theory of rational action – as it was in *Anarchy, State, and Utopia* – is between goal-based and principled reasons for actions. Moreover, we have seen that principled reasons are not especially odd creatures; if we accept Nozick's flow-back view of goal-based reasons (§2.3), both principled and goal-based reasons presuppose an embodying relation between what matters and the act (§4.1). Furthermore, insofar as goal-based reasoning itself presupposes principles of consistency (§2.1), goal-based reasoning presupposes principled reasoning. And since this view – in contrast to Nozick's later theory – does not render principles derivative of goals and symbols, it makes sense of justifying political principles in a society that does not share common goals. All this indicates that the view of rights as side constraints defended in *Anarchy, State, and Utopia* is not rationally suspect. To be sure, this theory of practical rationality in no way implies the Lockean principles defended in *Anarchy, State, and Utopia*, but it provides the rational foundations for it. Insofar as symbolic reasons enter into this account, they are derivative: They are ways for us to communicate our diverse goals to each other, and thus seem entirely at home in personal voluntary action and in the utopias Nozick explores in Part Three of *Anarchy, State, and Utopia*.

The libertarianism of *Anarchy, State, and Utopia* has a number of problems. Ironically, however, Nozick seems to reject it because of one of its strengths: its underlying theory of practical rationality.

Notes

[1] Robert Nozick, *Anarchy, State, and Utopia* (New York: Basic Books, 1974).

[2] Robert Nozick, *The Examined Life* (New York: Simon and Schuster, 1989), pp. 286–7.

[3] Robert Nozick, *The Nature of Rationality* (Princeton, N.J.: Princeton University Press, 1993), p. 32.

[4] I consider the problems of reliablism in *Justificatory Liberalism: An Essay on Epistemology and Political Theory* (New York: Oxford University Press, 1996), pp. 26ff.

[5] He distinguishes them on NR, p. 144, but that does not affect the point here.

[6] I consider in more depth the nature of ambivalence and conflict among values, and what sorts of consistency conditions can be imposed on values, in my *Value and Justification* (Cambridge: Cambridge University Press, 1990), pp. 219ff.

[7] For a detailed discussion of Von Neuman and Morgenstern's axioms, and their relation to instrumental rationality, see Jean Hampton, *The Authority of Reason* (Cambridge: Cambridge University Press, 1998), Chs. 7 and 8.

[8] For a fuller treatment of goal ranking, see my "Why All Welfare States (Including Laissez-Faire Ones) Are Unreasonable," *Social Philosophy & Policy*, vol. 15 (Summer 1998), 1–33.

[9] Robert Nozick, "Newcomb's Problem and Two Principles of Choice," in *Rationality in Action*, Paul K. Moser (ed.) (Cambridge: Cambridge University Press, 1990), pp. 207–34.

[10] See, for example, Ellery Eells, *Rational Decision and Causality* (Cambridge: Cambridge University Press, 1982).

[11] See Jordan Howard Sobel, *Taking Chances: Essays on Rational Choice* (Cambridge: Cambridge University Press, 1994), p. 152.

[12] See Paul Anand, *Foundations of Rational Choice Under Risk* (Oxford: Clarendon Press, 1993), p. 41. For a doubter, see David Christensen, Review Essay of "Robert Nozick, *The Nature of Rationality*," *Noûs*, vol. 29 (1995), pp. 259–74.

[13] See, for example, Christensen, "Nozick, *The Nature of Rationality*," pp. 260–63.

[14] There are obvious comparisons here with his ideas of ethical "push" and "pull." See Robert Nozick, *Philosophical Explanations* (Oxford: Clarendon Press, 1981), Ch. 5.

[15] Thomas Hobbes, *Leviathan*, ed. Michael Oakeshott (Oxford: Blackwell, 1948), p. 15 (Ch. 3).

[16] As Stanley Benn and I have argued. See S. I. Benn and G. F. Gaus, "Practical Rationality and Commitment," *American Philosophical Quarterly*, vol. 23 (July 1986), pp. 255–66.

[17] James H. Fetzer, "Signs and Minds, An Introduction to the Theory of Semiotic Systems," in *Aspects of Artificial Intelligence* (Boston: Kluwer Academic Publishers, 1988), pp. 133–61. All quotations from Fetzer in my text are from p. 135.

[18] Sigmund Freud, *Introductory Lectures on Psychoanalysis*, trans. James Strachey (Harmondsworth: Penguin Books, 1973), pp. 296–312 (Lecture 17, The Sense of Symptoms). All references to Freud in the text are from this lecture.

[19] I have considered how attributing false causal beliefs to others can increase the intelligibility of their actions in *Justificatory Liberalism*, pp. 54–9.

[20] I have defended this dictum in ibid., pp. 47ff.

[21] See Aristotle, *On Memory and Reminsicene (De Memoria et Reminiscentia)*, trans. J. Beare, and *On the Soul (De Anima)* Book III, trans. J. A. Smith, both in *The Basic Works of Aristotle*, ed. Richard McKeon (New York, Random House, 1941).

[22] One would think Nozick must disagree with this; after all, he is offering a theory of symbolic *rationality*. But even he seems to admit that the connections often seem irrational. At one point he simply asks us not to be "too quick" in dismissing symbolic connections (NR, 29).

[23] It thus seems to me much too broad to equate "*A* is rational" with "it makes sense to do *A*." Things can make sense in a crazy sort of way, and there can be insane logics. Cf. Alan Gibbard, *Wise Feelings, Apt Choices: A Theory of Normative Judgment* (Cambridge, Mass.: Harvard University Press, 1990).

[24] See Fetzer, "Signs and Minds."

[25] We may want to distinguish communicating your commitment to V by asserting "I advocate V" from expressing your commitment to V, that is, showing it through your actions. But both are ways to communicate, to induce in others the belief that you value V. See Gibbard, *Wise Feelings, Apt Choices*, p. 84.

[26] See, however, NR, 28, where Nozick suggests an alternative account of expressive actions, according to which "Expressiveness, not utility, is what flows back."

[27] On this point, see Christensen, "Nozick, *The Nature of Rationality*," pp. 263ff.

[28] See Gordon W. Allport, *Pattern and Growth in Personality* (New York: Rinehart and Winston, 1961), pp. 226ff.

[29] H. L. A. Hart, *The Concept of Law* (Oxford: Clarendon Press, 1961), p. 121.

[30] See my "Why All Welfare States are Unreasonable" and "The Limits of *Homo Economicus*" in *Values, Justice, and Economics*, Gerald F. Gaus, Julian Lamont, and Christi Dawn Favor (eds.) (Amsterdam: Rodopi, 2002). See also Frederick Schauer, *Playing by the Rules* (Oxford: Clarendon Press, 1991), pp. 54ff, 72, 77, 113; Benn, *A Theory of Freedom* (Cambridge: Cambridge University Press, 1988), p. 24.

[31] For some reservations about reflective equilibrium as a method of justification in ethics, see my *Justificatory Liberalism*, pp. 101–08.

[32] Emphasis added.

[33] Cf. Rawls's remarks on reflective equilibrium at the top of page 18, *A Theory of Justice*, rev. ed. (Cambridge, Mass.: Belknap Press of Harvard University Press, 1999).

[34] See, for example, Edward F. McClennen, *Rationality and Dynamic Choice* (Cambridge: Cambridge University Press, 1990).

[35] Notation altered.

[36] We would be very much like David Gauthier's constrained maximizers. See his *Morals by Agreement* (Oxford: Clarendon Press, 1986).

[37] For this "solution" to the prisoner's dilemma (PD) to be plausible, it must be the case that the symbolic utility payoff (being a cooperative person) is not reflected in the payoff matrix (otherwise, of course, it is not a PD at all). Nozick tries to argue that this is the case (NR, 55). For doubts, see Christensen, "Nozick's *The Nature of Rationality*," pp. 266–7.

[38] Emphasis added.

[39] Paul K. Moser, "Rationality, Symbolism and Evolution," *International Journal of Philosophical Studies*, vol. 2 (1994), pp. 288ff.

7 Nozick on Knowledge and Skepticism

MICHAEL WILLIAMS

1. KNOWLEDGE AND SKEPTICISM

Two problems have dominated recent Anglo-American epistemology. The first is the analytic or explicative problem: to state, as clearly and precisely as possible, what knowledge is, or what we mean when we say of someone that she knows something. The second is to come to terms with arguments for philosophical skepticism, the thesis that we know nothing whatsoever (or nothing whatsoever of facts belonging to certain very broad types, such as facts about the external world).

Until comparatively recently, it was widely agreed that knowledge is *justified* true belief. Call this "the standard analysis" of knowledge. As long as the standard analysis held sway, the explicative problem was usually treated as a preliminary issue to be briefly dealt with before getting down to epistemology's main task: developing a theory of justification, with a view to showing how skepticism goes wrong. What has made the analytic problem a growth industry is the discovery, originally by Edmund Gettier, of apparent counterexamples to the standard analysis.[1] In a "Gettier example," a situation is described in which, although a person has a very well-justified belief, we are reluctant to count him as knowing. If such counterexamples are genuine, the standard analysis fails to state sufficient conditions for knowledge. Thus, the explicative problem has become the Gettier problem: to state necessary and sufficient conditions for knowledge in the face of Gettier-type "puzzle cases." The upshot has been increasingly complicated analyses of knowledge, met by ever more ingenious counterexamples. The whole project shows signs of collapsing under the weight of the complications it has generated.[2]

This brings me to skepticism. If skepticism is to be a problem of general concern, skeptical arguments had better not depend on the controversial and often arcane details of particular analyses of knowledge (= solutions to Gettier's problem). Skepticism is a serious problem precisely to the extent that arguments for it trade on the sort of lowest-common-denominator ideas about knowledge that any plausible analysis needs to recognize. Furthermore, a particular account of knowledge will yield no insight into skepticism if it is obviously gerrymandered to serve (pro- or anti-) skeptical interests. To be sure, if a certain account of knowledge leads inevitably to skepticism, this may be reason to revise it. But at least initially, the explicative problem can and should be addressed independently of its implications for skepticism.

This is how Nozick proceeds.[3] He develops his solution to the explicative problem intuitively, by exploring how it accounts for the intuitions elicited by certain central puzzle cases. He then connects it with skepticism in an interesting and surprising way.

2. TRACKING THE TRUTH

Knowledge contrasts with ignorance (you can't have knowledge of things you have never even thought about) and with error (your beliefs and opinions do not amount to knowledge unless they are also true). So we can say that S knows that P only if

(1) S believes that P, and
(2) It is true that P.

There is near-universal agreement, however, among philosophers concerned with the explicative problem that knowledge, properly so-called, is more than true belief. Genuinely knowing also contrasts with getting things right purely by luck: by guessing, or as a result of some wildly irrational method that just happens (this time) to hit on the right result. The problem is what to add to (1) and (2) to get conditions that are sufficient for knowledge. Nozick's suggestion is that knowledge is belief that "tracks the truth." The idea of tracking is captured by two conditions, each motivated by a particular type of puzzle case.[4]

Consider first one of Gettier's original counterexamples to the justified true belief account of knowledge:

> Suppose that Smith and Jones have applied for a certain job. And suppose that Smith has strong evidence for the following conjunctive proposition:
> (d) Jones is the man who will get the job, and Jones has ten coins in his pocket.
> Smith's evidence for (d) might be that the president of the company assured him that Jones would in the end be selected, and that he, Smith, had counted the coins in Jones's pocket ten minutes ago. Proposition (d) entails:
> (e) The man who will get the job has ten coins in his pocket.

Let us suppose that Smith sees the entailment from (d) to (e), and accepts (e) on the grounds of (d), for which he has strong evidence. In this case, Smith is clearly justified in believing that (e) is true.

But imagine, further, that unknown to Smith, he himself, not Jones, will get the job. And also unknown to Smith, he himself has ten coins in his pocket. Proposition (e) is then true, though proposition (d), from which Smith inferred (e), is false. In our examples, then, all the following are true: (i) (e) is true, (ii) Smith believes that (e) is true), and (iii) Smith is justified in believing that (e) is true. At the same time, Smith does not know that (e) is true.... [5]

Why does Smith not know that (e) is true? Nozick's suggestion is that, although Smith's belief *coincides* with the facts, it is not *sensitive* to them. Even if (e) had been false, Smith would still have believed it to be true. With this in mind, Nozick stipulates:

(3) If it were not the case that P, S would not believe that P.

This is plausible: a belief that a person would have held irrespective of its truth does not amount to knowledge. His belief is insensitive to the facts.

Now consider the case, much discussed in connection with skepticism, of the person whose brain is removed and kept alive in a vat of nutrients. In the usual version, we imagine that the person's experiences and beliefs are manipulated by direct electrical and chemical stimulation so as to mimic the experiences and beliefs that would result from his living in a "normal" world. But suppose instead that the scientists conducting the experiment decide to let the unfortunate subject in on the secret. By direct electrical and chemical stimulation, they cause the person in the tank to believe that he is in the tank, with his beliefs electrochemically manipulated. Nevertheless, Nozick thinks, he fails to have knowledge, because the scientists could have made him believe whatever they liked, including that he was not in the tank.

This case is unlike the previous one in that the person's belief is caused by the fact that is its content. Accordingly, the person meets (3): if he had not been in the tank, he would never have believed that he was. Still, his connection to the facts seems too roundabout and tenuous for his belief to be properly fact-sensitive. Nozick therefore adds:

(4) If it were the case that P, S would believe that P.

The force of this requirement is not immediately evident. If knowing that P requires that P actually *be* true, what is talk about what would happen if P *were* true supposed to mean? What (4) requires is that if, in slightly different circumstances, it were *still* the case that P, S would still believe that P. A belief tracks the truth, thus amounts to knowledge, if and only if it *covaries* with the facts: if they were different, it would be different; but if they were (in the relevant respects) the same, it would stick with them. Accordingly, Nozick calls (3) a "variation" and (4) an "adherence" condition.

The critical feature of this tracking analysis is that (3) and (4) are both *subjunctive* conditionals: they concern not what *will* be the case if things *are* thus and so, but what *would* be the case if (perhaps contrary to fact) things *were* some way or other. As Nozick acknowledges, he was not the first to analyze knowledge using such conditionals: others had hinted at such an approach. But Nozick develops it in a much more detailed and systematic way than anyone before him does.[6]

NOZICK'S RELIABILISM

Many philosophers think that the lesson to be learned from the Gettier counterexamples is that knowledge requires a *special kind* of justification. A widely accepted idea is that knowledge demands justification that is "indefeasible": that is to say, justification that is proof against being undermined or "defeated" by the acquisition of further correct information. In the example discussed above, Smith's justification for believing that the man who will get the job has ten coins in his pocket does not live up to this standard, since it would be undermined by his learning that he, not Jones, is the successful candidate.

Unlike such theorists, Nozick is not proposing that the traditional analysis be *refined*: He is suggesting that it be *abandoned*. His key clauses (3) and (4), which define the tracking relation, make no mention of justification. They are replacements for, not additions to, the traditional third clause. Nozick's account of knowledge is radically nonjustificational.

In saying this, I am not attributing to Nozick the absurd view that knowledge *never* depends on justification. As Nozick himself points out, sometimes our beliefs track the truth because of the reasoning that leads to them. Discovering mouse droppings, I infer that there are mice in the house. If I had not found the evidence, I would not have believed that there are mice; and if there had been no mice, there would have been no droppings. In this case, my belief tracks my evidence, which in turn tracks the fact for which it is evidence.[7] Nozick's point is rather that knowledge does not depend generally or essentially on justification. We can attribute knowledge to animals (as cognitive ethologists do all the time), though we would hardly credit them with justified beliefs. And even when knowledge does result from justification, what makes the justification appropriate for knowledge will be its implying the satisfaction of the tracking conditions. Truth-tracking is thus fundamental, in a way that justification is not.

All radically nonjustificational analyses of knowledge are versions of "pure reliabilism." The root reliabilist idea is that knowledge is true belief that results from a process that reliably produces true beliefs. Nozick's tracking analysis differs from competing reliabilisms largely by being more abstract. Instead of trying to specify in detail the aetiology in virtue of which a true belief becomes knowledge, Nozick isolates the most general character of the truth-connection that any knowledge-yielding method of belief formation must entail. What is essential to knowledge is not any particular way of coming to track the truth but truth-tracking itself.

An important feature of pure reliabilist accounts of knowledge is that the conditions they lay down are all "external," in the sense that they are not conditions that a person need be aware of meeting. Such theories are thus purely *externalist*, as well as radically nonjustificational. Nozick's analysis – again in its initial presentation – is clearly of this type. Nozick calls attention to this aspect of his view when he insists that knowledge consists in a "real, specific factual relation to the world: tracking it."[8] This relation is real in that it holds (or not) quite independently of whether anyone thinks that it does. Someone knows that P if and only if his belief that P *in fact* tracks the truth: he need not know, have reason to believe, or even have any inkling that his belief is a truth-tracker. Knowing that conditions (1) to (4) are met is relevant, not to knowing that P, but to the quite different matter of knowing that one knows.

Some "internalist" accounts of knowledge, because they make knowledge depend wholly on factors to which the subject has "cognitive access," imply the so-called K-K thesis: that if you know that P, then you know that you know. Like all externalist accounts of knowledge, Nozick's implies that this thesis is false in general. But this is no reason to dismiss his view out of hand. A nervous examinee may know the answers to all the questions, while doubting that he knows the answers to any. He does not even believe that he has correct information, much less know that he does. There is nothing obviously contradictory in the idea of having knowledge that one does not know one has.

While all "nonjustificational" accounts of knowledge are externalist, the converse implication does not hold. It is possible to insist that knowledge always depends on some person's possessing some kind of good evidence but to explain the notion of good evidence in (wholly or partly) externalist terms. Perhaps I can come to know things by way of evidence that is in fact reliable, without evidence of my initial evidence's reliability. Such an account of knowledge, while justificational, also implies that the K-K thesis is false in general. With respect to analyses of knowledge, the internalist/externalist and justificational/nonjustificational distinctions do not line up in any simple way.

POSSIBLE WORLDS

Nozick makes the truth of a knowledge claim depend on the truth of two subjunctive conditionals. But how do we decide whether such conditionals are true? Nozick sometimes appeals to "possible worlds" semantics. On such accounts, the truth-value of "If it were the case that P, it would be the case that Q" depends on the truth value of Q in situations ("possible worlds") in which P is true and which otherwise closely resemble the actual world. Is it true that, if Hitler had invaded Britain after Dunkirk, he would have won the war? In considering this question, we hold as much as we can constant: the strength of the forces available to both combatants, the logistical difficulties of supporting a sea-borne invading army, and so on; if we think that some key factors were variable, we consider a range of scenarios (the invasion takes place very quickly, or is delayed to allow an even stronger force to be assembled); and we determine what seems the most likely outcome in each case. If, according to our best estimates, the Germans win in all the relevant cases, we say it is indeed true that Hitler would have won if he had launched an invasion.

In this spirit, Nozick recommends that, to determine whether P subjunctively implies Q, we "examine those worlds in which P holds true closest to the actual world, and see if Q holds true in all of these."[9] In the case of (3), the key condition in Nozick's analysis of knowledge, we want to know whether S would still believe that P, even if P were false. To decide this, we look at situations like the actual situation, except for the falsity of P: Nozick calls this range of possible situations "the first portion of the not-P neighborhood of the actual world."[10] If we find that these are all situations in which S no longer believes that P, then (3) is satisfied; otherwise not.

We should not take this talk of possible worlds too seriously, for it is in no way *explanatory* of the truth conditions for subjunctive conditionals. Taken literally, Nozick's recommendation is, as Fogelin says, "idle, since nothing counts as *examining* possible worlds to see what is true in them."[11] Possible worlds, in relation to the actual world, are not like planets, which exist at various predetermined distances from Earth and which a space traveler might visit to see what is going on. Talk of what "does" happen in various possible worlds is just a picturesque way of talking about what might or could happen. As Nozick himself says:

> If the possible-worlds formalism is used to represent counterfactuals and subjunctives, the relevant worlds are not those P worlds that are closest or most similar to the actual world, unless the measure of closeness or similarity is: what would obtain if P were true. Clearly, this cannot be used to explain when subjunctives hold true, but it can be used to represent them.[12]

But if the appeal to possible worlds gives no independent way of determining the truth-conditions for Nozick's conditionals, what does? How severe are the constraints on claims to know imposed by the tracking analysis? Nozick says that (3) and (4) are "not easy to satisfy, yet not so powerful as to rule out everything as an instance of knowledge,"[13] prompting Fogelin to remark that Nozick's conditionals "seem to be just strong enough to do the job that epistemologists need done."

In fairness to Nozick, however, conditions (1) to (4) do not represent his final account of knowledge. As is invariably the case with attempts to state precise necessary and sufficient conditions for knowing, further puzzle cases demand complications or "epicycles," as Nozick calls them. Whether, even with all the epicycles in place, Nozick offers a definitive solution to the Gettier problem, one that is proof against all apparent counterexamples, may be doubted. But I do not think that anyone else has come up with such a solution either. As I remarked at the outset, the project of formulating a fine-tuned response to the Gettier problem shows signs of collapsing under the weight of the complications it has generated. The fact remains that, in a general way, Nozick's account of knowledge – particularly his fundamental idea that knowledge demands belief that is sensitive to fact – has a definite plausibility. In my view, then, a much better test of its worth is its capacity to deal with the problem of skepticism.

SKEPTICISM

There are two principal forms of philosophical skepticism, Agrippan and Cartesian.

Agrippan skepticism centers on an apparently fatal trilemma. If I present a claim as something I know to be true, I can be challenged to say how I know. Whatever I say, the challenge can be renewed: is the claim I have put forward to back up my initial claim something that I know, and if so what is my basis to accepting it? And so on indefinitely. I seem to be faced with three options. I can keep trying to think of new things to say, in which case I open up a vicious infinite regress; I can at some point refuse to respond further, in which case I am making an unwarranted assumption; or I can find myself repeating something I have already said, in which case I am reasoning in a circle. According to the skeptic, these options exhaust the alternatives, even though none permits me to claim knowledge.

Nozick is not much interested in Agrippan skepticism. This is not surprising. The Agrippan skeptic takes it for granted that, to know something, I must be able to say how I know. In other words, his argument presupposes a justificationist, indeed fully internalist conception of knowledge. But on Nozick's view, knowing that P is not hostage to being able to say how one knows that P, either by citing evidence or in any other way.

Nozick's principal target is Cartesian skepticism. Cartesian skepticism revolves around "skeptical hypotheses": that I am the victim of Descartes's Evil Deceiver or a brain in a vat. But how exactly do skeptical hypotheses suggest skeptical conclusions?

Consider first a nonskeptical example. You ask me if I know the office telephone number of a colleague in another department. I remember the number well and give it to you. You remind me, however, that the building that houses our colleague's department has just been remodeled and several department members have moved to new offices with new phone numbers. Have I looked into whether our colleague is one of them? I haven't. So do I know his number? It seems not. It may be the same or it may have changed. I am not in a position to say.

The possibility that our colleague has moved to a new office is a "defeater" for my claim to know his number: If I cannot rule out this possibility, my knowledge claim is "defeated" and must be withdrawn. Of course, I may be able to rule it out. Perhaps I visited our colleague in his office yesterday, so I know that he has not moved, in which case my knowledge-claim stands.

Now let us turn to skeptical hypotheses. These too seem to be defeaters for ordinary knowledge-claims. Surely, if I know that I am in Evanston, I know that I am not a brain in a vat somewhere near Alpha Centauri. Conversely, if I cannot rule out the possibility that I am a brain in a vat, how can I be said to know that I am in Evanston. The problem with skeptical defeaters, however, is that they can easily seem to be impossible to rule out. The crucial feature of the brain-in-a-vat example is that the victim enjoys exactly the same perceptual experience as he would in his normal state. But it is evident, the skeptic argues, that when it comes to forming beliefs about the external world, perceptual experience is all that any of us has to go on. Since this evidence fails to discriminate between our ordinary beliefs and bizarre counterpossibilities, those beliefs do not amount to knowledge.

As I have presented it, Cartesian skepticism depends on two key moves, both initially plausible. The first is that, in the end, each person's perceptual experience is her only source of knowledge of the external world. The second is that the evidence provided by this source is epistemically inert. In my view, then, skeptical hypotheses should be understood as posing generalized *underdetermination problems*: Our beliefs about the external world do not amount to knowledge because they cannot be justified; and they cannot be justified because all the evidence we can ever have for them is consistent with their being false. Indeed, it is hard to see why this evidence even makes our ordinary views more likely to be true than various skeptical alternatives: it seems to be neutral.

I said that skeptical hypotheses pose *generalized* underdetermination problems. This is important. The case of my knowing my colleague's telephone number involves at most a local failure of knowledge. The evidence at my disposal right now does not rule out the possibility that he has been relocated, but this gap in my knowledge can easily be repaired by further investigation. In saying this, however, I take it for granted that certain fundamental ways of gathering information about the world are reliable. This is what the skeptic calls in question. His bizarre possibilities force us to wonder what right we have to take the reliability of perceptual experience for granted. But when the reliability of a fundamental cognitive faculty is at issue, it is unclear how "further investigation" could reassure us, for it is not clear that there is any form of investigation that would not rely on the very faculty in question. So in taking for granted the general reliability of perception, are we just making an assumption: an unavoidable assumption perhaps, but an assumption for all that? If we are, then what we like to think of as our "knowledge" of the external world is suddenly cast in a less favorable light.

Nozick does not present the skeptic's case quite this way, or at least he does not do so initially. Again, this is not surprising. Presented my way, skepticism, though typically posed as a problem about knowledge, is really a problem about justification. This problem about justification turns into a problem about knowledge only on the assumption that knowledge depends essentially on justification, which Nozick denies. We might suppose, then, that Nozick would have no more to say about Cartesian skepticism than he does about its Agrippan variant. But this is not so. Nozick is able to formulate a version of Cartesian skepticism using only the resources of his nonjustificational analysis of knowledge.

The skeptic describes various situations – deception by an Evil Deceiver, lifelong dreaming, living as a brain in a vat subjected to electrochemical stimulation – in which most of what we believe is (undetectably) false. Call a typical skeptical possibility "SK." How does SK threaten our knowledge of ordinary matters of fact? Recall Nozick's variation condition:

(3) If P were false, S would not believe that P.

This is false when, if P were false, S would *still* believe that P. But surely this is what SK shows. I believe that I am at home in Evanston. But if I were a brain in a vat, kidnapped by aliens from somewhere near Alpha Centauri, I would still believe that I am in Evanston, even though my belief would be false. The skeptic concludes that I do not know that I am in Evanston. Indeed, since the argument works for any example of ordinary factual knowledge, he concludes that I cannot know anything whatsoever about the external world.

According to Nozick, the skeptic's argument ignores the subjunctive character of (3). If (3) said that my not being in Evanston *logically entails* my not believing that I am, it would indeed be falsified by the mere logical possibility of my believing that I am in Evanston when I am not. But it says nothing of the sort. Rather, (3) concerns the situation that would obtain if P were false. Not every logically possible situation in which P is false is the situation that *would* hold if P were false. If I were not at home now, I would be in my office, or in the city, or perhaps off on a trip: I would not be in Alpha Centauri. And if I were in my office or wherever, I would not believe that I am at home. The mere logical possibility of a situation in which I continue to believe that P, even though P is false, does not falsify (3). Such mere logical possibilities are therefore no obstacle to knowledge.

What about skeptical possibilities, like the possibility that I am a brain in a vat (SK)? Can I know that they are false? Here Nozick's argument takes a surprising turn. My belief that not-SK is not sensitive. If it were the case that SK – that is, if I were a brain in a vat – I would still believe that I am not. We cannot track the truth of a skeptical hypothesis: skeptical hypotheses are *designed* to be untrackable. It follows that, even though I *do* know that I am at home in Evanston, I do *not* know that I am not a brain in a vat.

While this result may seem paradoxical, Nozick regards it as one of the strong points of his view. Suppose that an evil demon was deceiving us, or that we were dreaming, or that we were brains in vats: it seems intuitively obvious that we would not be able to tell what was happening to us. As Nozick says,

> If those things *were* happening to us, everything would seem the same to us. There is no way we can know it is not happening for there is no way we could tell if it were happening; and if it were happening we would believe exactly what we do now – in particular, we still would believe that it was not. For this reason, we feel, and correctly, that we don't know – how could we? – that it is not happening to us. It is a virtue of our account that it yields, and explains, this fact. (201)[14]

Nozick thinks that attempts to show that we do know that we are not the victims of such deception are "bound to fail" and even strike us as "bad faith."[15] His account *insulates* ordinary factual knowledge from skeptical assault, but without trying to beat the skeptic at his own game.

Is Nozick really entitled to claim this insulation? His argument depends critically on his view of the truth conditions for subjunctive conditionals involving ordinary factual beliefs and, as we saw, he does not have much to say about how such truth conditions are determined. This need not be a fatal weakness, however. Knowledge requires belief that is sensitive to fact, not belief that is limitlessly sensitive: sensitive no matter what. But limitless sensitivity is exactly what the skeptic demands. He wants belief that covaries with fact with respect to all logically possible ways of going wrong. This is not sensitivity but supersensitivity. Nozick does not need a precise standard of sensitivity to claim that ordinary knowledge does not require that our beliefs be supersensitive.

EXPLANATION VERSUS PROOF

Nozick's claim that ordinary factual knowledge is not compromised by the insensitivity of beliefs regarding the falsity of skeptical hypotheses *assumes* that the actual world is not a "skeptical" world. It is therefore natural to object that Nozick has made no headway against the skeptic, since the standard skeptical problems reassert themselves one level up. Richard Fumerton makes the point well:

> When Nozick... stresses that his... account allow[s] us to conclude consistently that we know that we see the table, even though we do not know that there is no demon deceiving us, we must surely wonder why he is so confident that the subjunctives that on his view are sufficient for knowledge are true.[16]

Fumerton's point is not just that talk of "examining possible worlds" is not explanatory but that, unless we *already* know that the actual world is not a "skeptical" world, we do not know what worlds to "examine." In a "normal" world, I would not believe that I in Evanston, if I were actually somewhere else (Baltimore, say). Accordingly, (3) is satisfied and I know where I am. But in a "skeptical" world matters are very different. Suppose I were a brain-in-a-vat and that my vat is currently located in Evanston. Even though my program calls for my believing that I am in Evanston, this (true) belief does not amount to knowledge. This is because I would still believe that I am in Evanston even if I were back in the vicinity of Alpha Centauri: The relevant subjunctive conditional is false. Accordingly, if the actual world is a "normal" world, we will know lots of things; but if it is a skeptical world, we will know little or nothing. Since, by Nozick's own account, we cannot know that skeptical hypotheses are false, we cannot know what sort of world we are in. So, for all we know, the relevant conditionals may be false, so that know little or nothing. This meta-skepticism does not seem much of an improvement on straight skepticism.

In fact, as Fumerton recognizes, matters are not so simple. It is true that, for Nozick as for all externalists, knowing that-P does not entail knowing that one knows that-P. But meta-knowledge is not impossible. For me to know that I know that I am at home in Evanston, my belief that my belief tracks the truth must itself track the truth, which it well might do. The same goes for knowing that I know that I know, and so on. Whenever, I know that P, it is always a further question as to whether I know that P. An externalist will say, however, this "regress" is not vicious. Whenever I know anything there will be an infinity of further questions to look into. But my knowing a particular fact about the world does not depend on my having (*per impossible*) settled them all in advance.

As Barry Stroud has remarked, it is not easy to say, in terms that would satisfy an externalist, what is wrong with this line of defense.[17] What he and Fumerton want to say is that externalist defenses of externalist knowledge fail to address the sort of epistemological questions we ought to be interested in *as philosophers*.[18] Thus Fumerton claims that skepticism raises deep questions about the justification of our beliefs about the world; and in so far as externalism tries to address *those* questions, it does so in a blatantly circular manner. In explaining how we obtain ordinary factual knowledge, Nozick assumes that we inhabit a normal world, one in which our cognitive faculties – perception, memory, and so on – are reliable sources of true beliefs. Any explanation of how we know that these faculties are reliable would itself take it for granted that we live in a normal world – that is, a world in which our faculties are reliable.

In evaluating this objection, we must distinguish two questions: whether knowledge is essentially connected with justification; and whether any externalist epistemology begs the question against the skeptic simply by virtue of being externalist. Suppose, for example, Nozick held that our knowledge of the external world depended on some kind of warrant-conferring inference from sensory evidence – how things appear to us. (In fact, as we shall see, he does hold something like this.) Then he would be a justificationist with respect to knowledge of external reality. But suppose he went on to give an external account of the warrant-conferring capacity of sensory evidence, arguing that, the world being what it is, sensory evidence generally tracks the truth: things seem the way they do because, for the most part, they are that way. Of course I make errors. But in general, it would not seem to me that I am in my office, working on a paper unless I were in my office working on a paper, and so on. Arguing this way, Nozick would have told a story about how beliefs about the external world are justified, but it is not a story that would satisfy Fumerton (or Stroud).

What philosophers like Fumerton and Stroud want is not just a story about justification but an answer to a *very special question* about justification. Roughly, they want to know why, in the face of skeptical challenges, we are justified in believing *anything whatsoever* about the external world.[19] This special question demands a special kind of answer. Philosophers who take it seriously want to *convince the skeptic* that we do have knowledge of the world. This means agreeing with the skeptic that sensory evidence is all we have to go on; and it means not just explaining how sensory evidence warrants beliefs about the external world but doing so in terms that presuppose nothing about the external world. As they understand it, the *philosophical* question demands a radically *internalist* answer. This is why Barry Stroud concludes that the philosophical question about our knowledge of the external world, even when answered in externalist terms, requires justifying our claim to knowledge in a sense of "justifying" that no form of externalism can really capture. Perhaps no such justification can be given. But then, according to Stroud, we seem to be left with a perfectly intelligible question that we have no idea how to answer.[20]

Fumerton is surely right that Nozick does not address what he (Fumerton) regards as the philosophical question. Nozick could reply, however, that he and Fumerton have different conceptions of the task of philosophy. Fumerton, Nozick could say, finds externalist responses to skepticism unacceptably circular precisely because he thinks that philosophy should *prove*, in the face of skeptical objections, that we do have knowledge of the external world (and other kinds of knowledge too). For Nozick, however, the task of philosophy is not proof but *explanation*. A philosophical explanation answers a "How possible?" question. Thus, in epistemology, a philosophical explanation will show how knowledge is possible. This project arises because there are arguments purporting to show that knowledge is not possible. Indeed, the only reason philosophers take seriously the thought that we *do* not have knowledge is that there are arguments to the effect that we *cannot* have it.

To see the merit in this reply, let us ask why we take skeptical arguments seriously, in the first place? Clearly, the skeptic's conclusion would not trouble us unless we set some store by knowledge. But we do set store by it, and so the skeptic's conclusion is unacceptable. But this is not all. You can argue for any conclusion, no matter how outrageous, if you are allowed to help yourself to whatever premises you need. We would therefore not have to take the skeptic's conclusion seriously if his arguments relied on what are obviously gratuitous assumptions about knowledge. Skeptical arguments only grip us because they seem to be natural or intuitive. That is, they seem to depend only on the most mundane ideas about knowledge. The skeptic claims to discover a paradox in our ordinary concept of knowledge: reflection on that concept, he claims, leads ineluctably to the conclusion that knowledge is impossible. In sum, skepticism is a problem because it offers natural-seeming arguments for wholly unacceptable conclusions.

If this is why skeptical arguments deserve to be taken seriously, what should we want from a response skepticism? We do not simply want to be shown that skepticism is false, since most of us already believe that. We want also to be shown why skepticism is so appealing: why it *seems* to be correct. We want a response to skepticism that is *diagnostic* and not merely *dialectical*.

A diagnosis of skepticism need not offer a proof, on the skeptic's own terms, that we do have the knowledge the skeptic says we don't have. A good diagnosis may undermine the appeal of skepticism by revealing its source in some less-than-compelling epistemological assumptions. With skepticism's aura of naturalness thus dispelled, we will no longer feel the need for a proof.

We can see Nozick's approach to skepticism as diagnostic in just this way, for it shows that the skeptic, while *ultimately* wrong, is *partly* right. The skeptic is right to insist that we cannot know that his bizarre possibilities do not obtain: they are *constructed* so as to ensure that beliefs involving them will be insensitive-to-fact. But the skeptic is wrong to suppose that this invalidates ordinary claims to knowledge. Nozick's explanation allows us to see that skepticism is *not* the inevitable result of philosophical reflection, while also showing how this can easily seem to be so.

Philosophers like Fumerton and Stroud will probably think that Nozick's idea of philosophical explanation sets the bar too low. But it is not obvious that this is so. Precisely because skeptical arguments seem to be natural, a good diagnosis will not be obvious. Coming up with an analysis of the concept of knowledge that allows for the possibility of knowledge, while providing genuine diagnostic insight into skepticism's appeal, is not a trivial task. Because it offers a diagnosis rather than a proof (on the skeptic's own terms), Nozick's response to skepticism can be defended against the charge of being obviously question-begging. The real issue is how convincing a diagnosis Nozick has offered.

Now philosophers like Fumerton and Stroud will not think much of Nozick's account of knowledge even as an *explanation* of how knowledge is *possible*. If knowledge is possible in normal worlds, but not in skeptical worlds, then unless we know what sort of world we are in, we have a potential explanation of the possibility of knowledge, but not one that is known to be correct. While this response need not be the last word, it does suggest that Nozick's diagnosis is incomplete. To make headway, a diagnosis of skepticism would have to say something more about why the question about how we know anything whatsoever about the external world may be less innocent than it looks, what makes it look like a question that deserves to be taken seriously, and why the apparent impossibility of answering that question reflects unfavorably on everyday knowledge of the world.

Although I cannot explore the matter in depth here, I think that it is clear that there is one fundamental epistemological idea that will figure largely in the answers to all three questions. This is the assumption that, in the last analysis, our epistemic situation is the same in both normal and skeptical worlds. Whether we are embodied persons or brains in vats, in the end, when it comes to knowing about the world around us, our experience – how things perceptually appear to us – is all we have to go on. If an externalist conception of knowledge – not necessarily a pure reliabilist conception, but any conception that involves an externalist component essentially – is to have any hope of appearing satisfactory, it must challenge and undermine this idea of a uniform epistemic situation. If this conception goes unchallenged – or, worse still, if it is endorsed – the sort of question that Fumerton and Stroud see as the philosophical question par excellence will look as though it deserves an answer that no form of externalism will ever yield.

NONCLOSURE

I said that Nozick's response to skepticism looks incomplete. But we have not yet explored that response in full. In fact, we have not yet discussed its most controversial aspect.

If I am in my office, I am not a brain in a vat on Alpha Centauri. This is something that I know. But if, as Nozick says, I know that I am in my office, and if, as just agreed, I also know that my being in my office logically entails my not being a brain in a vat, then I know that I am not a brain in a vat. I reach this knowledge as an elementary logical consequence of something that I know, and surely obviously correct deductive inference preserves knowledge, if any form of argument does. But according to the skeptic – and Nozick agrees – I do not know that I am not a brain in a vat on Alpha Centauri. It is a short step to the skeptic's conclusion that I do not know that I am in my office. The skeptic wins after all.

Nozick thinks that the skeptic's "short step" is longer than it looks. In taking it, the skeptic relies on the principle that knowledge is "closed under known logical implication." As Nozick understands it, closure is itself a subjunctive principle, viz.:

> (C) If S were to know that P entails Q, and were to know that Q, then he would know that Q.[21]

Moving from some item of knowledge to something it is known to entail does not take us outside the (closed) domain of knowledge.

Whether or not (C) is acceptable as it stands, it will seem to many philosophers that something like it must be true. After all, visibly correct deductive inference should preserve knowledge, if any form of argument does. But Nozick thinks that (C) is false, not as a matter of detail, but in principle. Appearances to the contrary, knowledge is not closed under known logical implication.

Although Nozick was not the first to make it – the palm goes to Dretske – this suggestion promises considerable diagnostic insight.[22] Consider G. E. Moore's famous proof of an external world. Moore holds up his hands in good light saying "Here is one hand and here is another."[23] He concludes that, skeptical objections notwithstanding, he knows that two honest-to-goodness external objects exist. This "proof" has struck many philosophers as less-than-satisfactory, although they have not always agreed about what is wrong with it. The Dretske-Nozick denial of closure suggests an answer. While moving in opposite directions, Moore and the skeptic both take the principle of closure for granted. In effect, Moore argues, via the principle, from his knowing that he has hands to his knowing that no skeptical possibility obtains. The skeptic argues, also via the principle, from the impossibility of our knowing that skeptical possibilities do not obtain to our not knowing that we have hands. Seeing that the closure principle is false in general allows us to understand why the skeptic's proof that we do not have knowledge of the external world, and Moore's proof that we do, are equally unsatisfactory.

This promise of diagnostic insight notwithstanding, Nozick's denial of closure is deeply problematic. The example of Moore's proof brings out just how implausible it is. Moore knows that he has two hands, but he does not know that he is not a bodiless brain in a vat. Or: I know that I am not on a planet in the Alpha Centauri system. (I can see that I am not: Alpha Centauri is a three-star system.) But I do not know that I am not on a planet in that system living as a brain in a vat. Given Nozick's account of knowledge, such "abominable conjunctions," as Keith DeRose has called them, can be generated *ad libitum*. Something has gone wrong.[24]

SENSITIVITY RECONSIDERED

Nozick wants to allow that skeptical hypotheses cannot be known not to obtain: they are designed so that their falsity is undetectable. At the same time he wants to insulate ordinary knowledge from skeptical undermining. Given epistemic closure, this attempted insulation must fail. Even disregarding its unpalatable consequences, however, the move of denying closure would be desperate in itself, if it were simply made *ad hoc* to avoid capitulating to the skeptic. Naturally, Nozick thinks his move not *ad hoc* at all but follows naturally from the subjunctive conditional analysis of knowledge. I think he is wrong. His position is theoretically quite unmotivated.

Nonclosure follows from the requirement that knowledge be sensitive to fact, and particularly from

(3) not-P => not-(S believes that P).

To see how (3) leads to nonclosure, consider the statements:

P = I am sitting in my office.
Q = I am not a brain in a vat on Alpha Centauri, electrochemically induced to believe that P.

If P were false, I would be downstairs making coffee, or in class giving a lecture, something comparably familiar. If Q were false, I would be a brain in a vat. These two situations are very different and lead to enormous differences in what I would believe. Because of these differences, my belief that P is sensitive to fact, while my belief that Q is not. So even though I know that P, and know that P entails Q, I do not know that Q.

This argument is correct. But why doesn't it show that there is something wrong with (3)? In fact, Nozick himself has independent reasons for thinking that (3), in its original simple form, rules out clear examples of knowledge and is therefore too strong. Consider the case of a grandmother who comes to believe that her grandson is alive and well because she sees that he is when he visits her. If he had been ill or dead, however, to spare her anxiety the family would have convinced her that he was in good health. According to (3), her belief is insensitive: If her grandson had not been alive and well, she would still have believed that he was. So she does not know that he is alive and well, even though she can see that he is. This seems wrong.

The key feature of the grandmother case is that the grandmother's *way of coming to believe* that her grandson is well itself covaries with his state of health. Nozick therefore modifies his account of knowledge by building in a reference to ways of forming beliefs. S knows, via method M (or way of coming to believe), that P if and only if

(1*) P is true.
(2*) S believes, via method M, that P.
(3*) If P weren't true and S were to use M to arrive at a belief whether (or not) P, then S wouldn't believe, via M, that P.
(4*) If P were true and S were to use M to arrive at a belief whether (or not) P, then S would believe, via M, that P.

With some added details about what it is for one method to outweigh another, Nozick can say that S knows that P (*simpliciter*) if and only if (a) S knows that P via some method M and (b) all other methods not satisfying (1*) to (4*) via which he believes that P are outweighed by M.[25] Thus, in the grandmother case, a belief based on family testimony does not track the truth, since they are committed to telling her the same thing, no matter what. But the method of relying on testimony is outweighed by her actual method: seeing for herself. If she were to *see* her grandson dead, she would not accept her family's assurances. (If she would, it is reasonable to wonder whether she knows anything about his state of health in the first place.)

This modification of the tracking analysis is ingenious. From the standpoint of Nozick's diagnosis of skepticism, however, it is fraught with danger. The problem is that, from an externalist standpoint, standard skeptical puzzle-cases trade on exactly the feature of the grandmother case that inspires Nozick's modification: that in certain cases, when our beliefs are false, our available methods of knowing also change. This threatens to undermine the case for nonclosure. In the actual world, I have various knowledge-yielding methods of belief-formation available to me. One method is ordinary nonmanipulated perception. Another method involves recognizing the logical consequences of knowledge gained by the first method. The second method is obviously supervenient on the first, a possibility Nozick is careful to allow for. If I am a brain in a vat, however, neither method is available to me. The result is that, in a normal world, I know both lots of ordinary facts *and* that skeptical possibilities do not obtain. In a "skeptical world," by contrast, I do not know that skeptical possibilities do not obtain, but then I do not have any ordinary perceptual knowledge either. Closure holds either way.

To put some distance between the grandmother case and skeptical cases, thus to defend nonclosure, Nozick needs to argue that we use the *same* methods in normal and skeptical worlds. This means that he needs to say more about how methods are individuated. But not only does he decline to pursue an issue that he admits raises "large questions," the little he does say is less than helpful. Thus:

> A person can use a method (in my sense) without proceeding methodologically, and without knowledge or awareness of what method he is using. Usually, a method will have a final upshot in experience, and then (a) no method without this upshot is the same method, and (b) any method experientially the same, the same "from the inside", will count as the same method. Basing our beliefs on experiences, you and I and the person floating in the tank are using, for these purposes, the same method.[26]

Here Nozick marches resolutely off in opposite directions. On the one hand, I can use a method without knowing what method I am using: a method's identity does not depend on my being able to identify it. On the other hand, methods cannot be different unless they are experientially distinguishable: so a method's identity does after all depend on my being able to tell what method it is. What is going on?

The answer, I think, is that Nozick is trying to square the circle by incorporating into an externalist analysis of knowledge modifications that make sense only if one has very strong internalist intuitions. Nozick's externalism requires him to hold that a person can use a method without knowing that she is using it. As he is well aware, however, adopting externalism invites an externalist approach to the identity and not merely to the use of methods.

But, in Nozick's eyes, such an approach makes short shrift of the skeptic: too short. This is because:

> you needn't reach to inference to establish your knowledge that you are not floating in the tank on Alpha Centauri. You see that you are not on Alpha Centauri, and via this method, externally specified, you track the fact that you are not – even though if you were it would seem perceptually the same to you as it does now. That perceptual seeming, though indistinguishable internally from your actual current seeing, is distinguishable externally as a distinct method, if such external individuation of methods is allowed to count. Would even Doctor Johnson have said, "How do I know that I am not dreaming? By seeing what is in front of me?"[27]

But what exactly is wrong with the Johnsonian suggestion? Perhaps when I am awake, I know that I am not dreaming; but when I am dreaming, I am not is a position to know anything. This thought is not evidently absurd. Unless, that is, that externalism is itself a nonstarter, for it is characteristic of externalist epistemologies to open up just such possibilities.

If the suggestion that we know things in normal worlds that we do not know in skeptical worlds seems unsatisfactory as a response to skepticism, it can only be for the sort of reasons given by Fumerton: that, as philosophers, we need to be able to *prove to the satisfaction* of the skeptic what kind of world we are in. This will mean showing how knowledge of how things appear, which we retain in both normal and skeptical worlds, points to our being in a normal world, and to do so without at any point assuming that our world is normal. Certainly, if the philosophical task is to answer Fumerton's question, we need to individuate methods by experiential criteria. But if the task is only explanation, and not proof, there is no obvious reason for going down this road. Nozick's argument consists in helping himself to rhetorical questions he is not entitled to.

As we have seen, Nozick thinks that attempts to do what Fumerton wants done are "bound to fail." Nozick thinks that it is obvious that we cannot know that we are not brains in vats, because we cannot "tell" that we are not. But this claim depends on a strongly internalist conception of "telling": telling by Fumerton's standards. What Nozick fails to see is that Fumerton's conception of the philosophical task, and his (Nozick's) own insistence that methods be individuated by purely experiential criteria, are part of the same philosophical package; and that it is this philosophical package that underwrites the feeling that we cannot know that skeptical possibilities do not obtain. But Fumerton's internalist conception of what it would be to rule out skeptical possibilities and Nozick's basically externalist approach to everyday knowledge are oil and water. They don't mix and the result of trying to mix them is an endless round of abominable conjunctions.

In fact, it is not clear that building in reference to methods even saves nonclosure. There is some indication that the result ought to be skepticism. In its original form, Nozick suggests that the worlds with respect to which ordinary factual beliefs must track the truth, are those that are factually close to the actual world. When he introduces reference to methods into his analysis of knowledge, however, things change drastically. The introduction of reference to methods suggests that beliefs must track over all worlds that are close (i.e., relevantly similar) *epistemically*. Given his internalist criterion for individuating methods, it looks as though skeptical worlds ought to be included. As Nozick remarks, although it is my belief that is connected to the facts via the tracking relation, "when a method shows an inner face, tracking via the method depends on what would happen in other situations identical in inner cues."[28] But the whole point of skeptical hypotheses is to describe situations that are "identical in inner cues." If internalism wins the day, beliefs never track and that knowledge is generally impossible, as the skeptic says.

Nozick will say, that with respect to ordinary factual beliefs, the inner cues are connected, in worlds "close" to the actual world, with mechanisms that reliably link us with external reality. In other words, the evidential link between the inner cues and external reality is itself conceived in an externalist manner. But this just takes us back to the question of why methods should ever be identified by their inner aspect alone. This reply brings out just how *ad hoc* Nozick's position is: It is tailored to protect nonclosure, but has no deeper theoretical motivation.

If Nozick's denial of closure, or collapse into skepticism, reflects lingering internalist intuitions, maybe he should drop it in favor of a more thoroughgoing externalism. Doing so, however, would leave very little that is distinctively Nozick's. A more thoroughgoing externalism may allow that, in normal worlds, we know that a skeptical possibility does not obtain. But since our belief that it does not will still not be sensitive by Nozick's standards, such a version of externalism will raise the question of whether sensitivity – the centerpiece of Nozick's epistemology – is really necessary for knowledge after all. More significantly still, Nozick's argument for the skeptic's being partly right is essential to the diagnostic-explanatory aspect of his position. Take this away, and the skeptic is merely confronted with a rather generic epistemic externalism. Nozick's position may have its problems, but it offers more than that.

CONCLUSION

The problems that emerge in Nozick's discussion of skepticism reflect deep problems in his conception of knowledge. The deepest concern pure reliabilism itself.

There are many ways in which (I would argue) pure reliabilism goes wrong and I cannot discuss them all here. But let me mention one, which is perhaps the most fundamental. Pure reliabilism treats "knowledge" as if it were some kind of purely factual concept. Nozick is clearly thinking along these lines when he insists that knowledge involves "a specific, real factual relation to the world: tracking it."[29] But knowledge is an evaluative or normative concept. We know when we meet certain standards of excellence or good performance in the way of belief. The question is not just how reliable we are, but how reliable we *ought to be*. The claim that knowledge involves tracking the truth does not settle the question: With respect to what range of possible situations?

The conceit of "examining possible worlds" to see what we believe in them plays a role in obscuring this crucial issue. It suggests that we can read epistemic standards off metaphysical facts. All that examining nearby worlds, however, worlds in the "Not-P neighborhood" of the actual world, really amounts to is considering situations in which P is false but that are otherwise *similar* to our actual circumstances. Anything is similar to anything else, however, one way or another: the similarity in question must be *significant* or *relevant* similarity. Thus, on the tracking analysis, a belief amounts to knowledge if it covaries with the facts over some range of significantly or relevantly similar situations. But what makes for relevant similarity? Some evidence of the deceptive appeal of possible worlds talk is given by the fact that Nozick thinks that the tracking analysis, especially condition (3), explains what it is for an alternative possibility to be relevant.[30] This strikes me as getting things exactly backwards. Standards of relevance determine what is involved in tracking.

So what does make for relevant similarity? The skeptic – and critics of externalism like Fumerton and Stroud – take it that, at least for the purposes of answering the fundamental philosophical question, the relevant similarity is epistemic, and that the identity of methods is fixed by "internal" criteria. This implies that we are stuck with the same methods of belief formation in normal and skeptical worlds. Thus, we are only justified in claiming knowledge of the world – indeed we can only really understand how such knowledge is possible – if we can show how those experience warrants our believing that our world is normal. As Nozick sees, if this is what understanding the possibility of knowledge requires, it is doubtful that we shall ever understand it. Either way, we are confronted with the issue of underdetermination that, I argued, was always at the heart of Cartesian skepticism.

Nozick's discussion of knowledge and skepticism is exceptionally ingenious and full of intriguing details that I have not been able to discuss. Nevertheless, I believe that, if we are to get to the bottom of skepticism, we need a much more detailed investigation of the central ideas of traditional epistemology than Nozick gives us. In the end – in his concession that the skeptic is straightforwardly right to claim that we do not know that skeptical possibilities do not obtain, and in his adoption of a strongly internalist criterion for the identity of methods – Nozick remains himself too much under the spell of the very ideas that call for our diagnostic attention.

Notes

[1] Edmund Gettier, "Is Justified True Belief Knowledge?" *Analysis*, 26 (1963), pp. 144–6.

[2] For an excellent critical account of the ups and downs of Gettierology, see Robert Fogelin, *Pyrrhonian Reflection on Knowledge and Justification* (Oxford: Oxford University Press, 1994), Part 1. Fogelin's book also contains some of the sharpest criticisms of Nozick to have yet appeared.

[3] Robert Nozick, *Philosophical Explanations* (Oxford: Oxford University Press, 1981). Cited below as PE. Nozick's chapter is reprinted in Steven Luper-Foy (ed.), *The Possibility of Knowledge* (Totowa, N.J.: Rowman and Littlefield, 1987). This volume, which contains a number of interesting critical essays, is perhaps the best place to start for further study of Nozick's epistemological ideas.

[4] PE, p. 172ff.

[5] Gettier, op. cit., p. 144.

[6] For anticipation of Nozick's approach, see Fred Dretske, "Conclusive Reasons," *Australasian Journal of Philosophy*, 47 (1971), pp. 1–22; also Alvin Goldman, "Discrimination and Perceptual Knowledge," *Journal of Philosophy*, 78 (1976), pp. 771–91. Nozick takes note of Dretske and Goldman: *Explanations*, p. 689, n. 53.

[7] PE, p. 248ff.

[8] PE, p. 178.

[9] PE, p. 173.

[10] PE, p. 176.

[11] Fogelin, op. cit.

[12] PE, p. 174. See also p. 680, n. 8.

[13] PE, p. 173.

[14] PE, p. 201.

[15] PE, p. 201.

[16] Richard Fumerton, "Externalism and Skepticism," in R. Fumerton, *Metaepistemology and Skepticism* (Lanham, Mass.: Rowman and Littlefield, 1995), pp. 159–81. Reprinted in E. Sosa and J. Kim (eds.), *Epistemology: An Anthology* (Oxford: Blackwell, 2000), pp. 401–12. Quotation, Sosa and Kim, p. 408.

[17] Barry Stroud, "Understanding Human Knowledge in General," in M. Clay, and K. Lehrer (eds.), *Knowledge and Skepticism* (Boulder, Col.: Westview, 1989). Quotation, p. 47.

[18] Fumerton, op. cit., p. 410.

[19] According to Stroud (op. cit., p. 32), a philosophical theory of knowledge aims at "an account that is completely general in several respects. We want to understand how any knowledge at all is possible – how anything we currently accept amounts to knowledge. Or less ambitiously, we want to understand with complete generality how we come to know anything in certain specified domains" (e.g., the external world).

[20] Stroud, op. cit., p. 47.

[21] PE, p. 204. Nozick calls the principle "P". I have changed this to (C) to avoid confusing the principle with the proposition P.

[22] Fred Dretske, "Epistemic Operators," *Journal of Philosophy*, 67 (1970), pp. 107–1023. Nozick acknowledges Dretske's priority: *Explanations*, p. 689, n. 53.

[23] G. E. Moore, "Proof of an External World," in Moore, *Philosophical Papers* (London: Allen and Unwin, 1959).

[24] Keith DeRose, "Solving the Skeptical Problem," *Philosophical Review*, 104 (1995), pp. 17–52. Reprinted in Sosa and Kim, op. cit., pp. 482–502. DeRose shows how to incorporate some of Nozick's ideas, particularly the importance of sensitivity, into a version of contextualism: the idea suggested by David Lewis and developed by Stewart Cohen, that standards for claiming and attributing knowledge are not fixed but go up and down with the course of conversation. I think that DeRose's approach is the best hope for salvaging something from Nozick's diagnosis of skepticism. For Lewis's version of contextualism, see his "Elusive Knowledge," *Australasian Journal of Philosophy*, 74 (1996), pp. 549–67; reprinted in Sosa and Kim, op. cit., pp. 503–16. For Cohen's approach, see his "How to Be a Fallibilist," *Philosophical Perspectives*, 2 (1988), pp. 91–123. I examine Lewis's contextualism in "Contextualism, Externalism and Epistemic Standards," *Philosophical Studies* (forthcoming). The criticisms I develop are readily adapted to DeRose's ideas.

[25] PE, pp. 179–80.

[26] PE, pp. 184–5.

[27] PE, p. 233.

[28] PE, p. 281.

[29] PE, p. 178.

[30] PE, p. 175.

8 Nozick on Free Will

MICHAEL E. BRATMAN

Robert Nozick's *Philosophical Explanations*[1] is a rich and wide-ranging exploration of some of the deepest issues in philosophy. Nozick examines fundamental questions about, among other things, personal identity, knowledge, free will, value, and the meaning of life. In this chapter, my primary concern will be with Nozick's discussion of free will: What is it, might we have it, and why should we want it? Nozick says much about free will that is fascinating, suggestive, and worth our further reflection.[2] His discussions of free will also are linked with many of his other views in this book – especially about personal identity and value. This presents both an opportunity and a problem. The opportunity is to see a sketch of one way we might profitably conceptualize some of the interrelations among these issues.[3] The problem is that Nozick's views about personal identity and value themselves raise a host of difficult questions; yet in each case the examination of those questions would require an essay of its own. My strategy will be to try to take advantage of the opportunity while avoiding the temptations to write yet another paper.

1. FREE WILL AND DIGNITY

What is free will and why do we want it? As Nozick notes, many have been interested in free will because they believe that some form of free will is necessary for a person to be an appropriate target of moral praise or blame, or of forms of criminal punishment. While recognizing the importance of such matters (indeed, there is an extended discussion of punishment in PE, pp. 363–97), however, Nozick's primary concern lies elsewhere. Nozick believes that the absence of free will would "undercut human dignity" (291). So he seeks to "formulate a conception of human action" that sees us as having a kind of free will sufficient to ground human dignity (291). And here Nozick grapples with a familiar, traditional puzzle.

155

Ignoring some subtleties, we can put the puzzle this way: An event, E, is causally determined if conditions prior to that event, together with causal laws of nature, ensure that E occur. Determinism is the view, roughly, that every event is causally determined by prior conditions. Suppose that determinism is true and so that every choice, decision, action is determined by prior conditions that were causally sufficient for its occurrence. In this case, it seems that when one acts one is not free to act otherwise, and so there is no free will.[4]

Suppose, in contrast, that determinism is false and that some choice, decision, or action is not determined by prior conditions. Given all prior conditions and all relevant causal laws that choice, decision, or action might not have happened. But then it seems that the occurrence of that choice, decision, or action was a matter of chance – a random, unexplainable event. Such a random event is not a ground for human dignity. But, given any choice, decision, or action either it is determined by prior conditions or it is not. In either case it does not involve a kind of free will that could ground human dignity. So there is no such free will.

That is the traditional puzzle. There are, of course, traditional lines of response. Libertarians agree that the causal determination of a decision is incompatible with its being free. They then try to construct a model of free, nondetermined choice or decision, a model that shows how choice, decision, or action can be nondetermined and free, and yet not happen at random, as a matter of chance.[5] Note that a libertarian need not deny that free choices and decisions have causes; she need only deny that these causes, if such there be, function deterministically.[6]

Compatibilists try instead to answer by constructing a model of free choice and action such that a choice or action can be both free (in the relevant sense) and causally determined by prior conditions.

Nozick's response is complex, and does not fit neatly into either of these categories (though he would very much like to be a libertarian). Nozick presents three different models of human action. The first is offered as a form of libertarianism; the other two are seen by Nozick as the best we could do in a deterministic world. Nozick is not confident that the first successfully answers worries about randomness; but he also doubts that the latter two – which he sees as "second best" (293) – even taken together, fully capture what we want when we want free will.

I turn first to Nozick's proposed libertarian model of human agency.

2. MODEL #1: SELF-SUBSUMING DECISIONS TO BESTOW WEIGHTS

We are frequently faced with conflicting considerations that favor conflicting options. In an effort to decide what to do we need to weigh these conflicting considerations. One model of such weighing is that we consult "previously given precisely specified weights" (294). But on Nozick's first model of human agency, we sometimes instead *decide* what the relative weights of these considerations are to be in our deliberation. Such a deliberative process "not only weighs reasons, it (also) weights them" (294). Our decision bestows weights for our deliberation, weights that thereby settle the decision problem with which we were faced. Furthermore, the decision to bestow these weights is normally in part about itself: It is a decision to give these weights to these considerations in this very decision. In this sense the decision is "self-subsuming." Such a decision also can set up a framework of weights to be used in future deliberation. Later decisions may then stand to such an earlier decision in something like the way a later court decision stands to an earlier, precedent-setting decision: "The decision represents a tentative commitment to make future decisions in accordance with the weights it establishes" (297). Sometimes the earlier weight-bestowing decision is a decision in favor of a general principle concerning such weights.[7] In especially reflective cases the decision is a decision to be a certain kind of person, one who lives a life that involves bestowing such weights. In these cases, the "self-subsuming" decision to bestow certain weights is a decision in favor of a certain "conception of oneself" (300).

Now, suppose one acts on the basis of such a self-subsuming, weight-bestowing decision in favor of a conception of oneself. Suppose such a decision were not itself determined by prior conditions. Given the kind of decision that it is, it seems it nevertheless need not thereby be a random decision, one that is a matter of chance. The decision is a decision to bestow weights in a way that makes that very decision reasonable and understandable: "Such a self-subsuming decision will not be a random brute fact; it will be explained as an instance of the very conception and weights chosen" (300–01). So Nozick conjectures that this model of self-subsuming decisions can serve as a model of libertarian free agency: it is a model of a kind of agency that can at the same time be both nondetermined, free, and nonrandom.[8] And that is what the libertarian wants.

An important question here is whether Nozick's claim is that such a self-subsuming, weight-bestowing decision cannot be determined by prior conditions, or only that it need not be determined. Nozick does toy with the idea that such a self-subsuming decision could not be determined (308–09). But in the end, so far as I can tell, he does not endorse this claim. He grants the possibility of a weight-bestowing self-subsuming decision – even one involving a decision in favor of a conception of oneself – in a deterministic world.[9] And this seems right: If we suppose, as Nozick does, that thought and action might, in general, be embedded in a deterministic web, it is not clear why self-subsuming, weight-bestowing decisions could not be. But then we need to reflect on the significance of the issue of whether such a self-subsuming weight-bestowing decision is determined by prior conditions.

Suppose for the moment that we agree that such a weight-bestowing decision, given its self-subsuming structure, would be intelligible and non-random even if nondetermined. And now consider such a self-subsuming decision in a deterministic world. It would seem that a determined, but self-subsuming decision would also be intelligible in just the way (whatever that is) a nondetermined self-subsuming decision would be. But then, if a nondetermined self-subsuming decision is a source of dignity, why isn't a determined self-subsuming decision also a source of dignity? But if we say that a determined self-subsuming decision is also a source of dignity then we have left the libertarian, incompatibilist framework.[10]

This is a version of one traditional worry about Libertarian theories. Most such theories agree that a mere absence of prior causal determination is not yet enough for the kind of free will we want. After all, it may be that the disintegration of a uranium atom is nondetermined; but that is not a promising model for a source of human dignity. Libertarians standardly respond with a further, positive condition on free will. (In Nozick's case, the positive condition is the role played by a self-subsuming weight-bestowing decision.) But then one may ask whether this positive condition might not by itself be enough for free will, even in a deterministic world.[11]

Now, it is common to hold that moral responsibility and accountability for doing something requires the ability to do otherwise. This is a view that is standardly called the principle of alternate possibilities. It is also common, although controversial, to hold that the relevant ability to do otherwise, properly understood, is itself incompatible with causal determinism. Someone who held both these views would see the absence of causal determinism as a necessary condition for moral responsibility and accountability.[12] On such a view, no positive condition that was itself compatible with causal determination could by itself be sufficient for moral responsibility.

It is important to see, though, that this cannot be Nozick's primary response to the present challenge. Nozick has made it clear that his interest is not primarily in the claim that the absence of causal determinism is necessary for moral responsibility and accountability; he is instead interested in the claim that the absence of causal determinism is necessary for the kind of free will that grounds human dignity.[13] We must look elsewhere, then, for Nozick's response to this challenge.

3. ORIGINATIVE VALUE

The place to look is Nozick's appeal to what he calls originative (or, sometimes, originatory) value. Here is what Nozick says:

> something's originative value . . . is a function of the value it newly introduces into the world, the new instrumental or intrinsic value it introduces that was not presaged by or already fully counted in previous instrumental value. (311)
> What causal determinism does not allow is originatory value. (313)
> [I]t is originatory value that is crucial to the problem of free will. (315)

The idea, I take it, is that we can see that our human dignity depends on our having a special kind of value – originatory value – and that we also can see, on reflection, that we would not have this value in a deterministic world. In particular, agency in which the weight-bestowing self-subsuming decision was causally determined by prior conditions would not have originatory value. And that is why such agency in a deterministic world would not ground special human dignity.

But what exactly is originative value? Nozick expresses one of the intuitive ideas here in this way:

> A being with originative value, one whose acts have originative value, can make a difference. (312)

What does it mean to make a difference? One natural understanding is this: for x to make a difference is for x to be a cause of some effect such that, in the absence of x, that effect would not have occurred. But a decision can, in this sense, make a causal difference even if it is determined by prior conditions; for a decision, even if determined, can be a cause of downstream effects, and it can be true that those effects would not have occurred in the absence of the decision.

Nozick's response would be that if the decision is determined by prior causes then the good downstream deterministic consequences of that decision are also deterministic consequences of the prior causes. So those good consequences are "already fully counted in previous instrumental value," namely, the instrumental value of those prior, upstream causes. This is true even though the decision itself makes a causal difference in the sense that the downstream good consequences depend causally on that decision. The decision would have what Nozick calls "contributory value," but not originatory value.[14]

But does our human dignity really depend on the idea that the good we cause is not also a deterministically causal effect of yet earlier conditions? A random disintegration of a uranium atom in a nondeterministic world would, it seems, have originative value if it results in something of value. How could a feature we would share with such a nondeterministic system be so central to an account of our distinctive dignity? Why shouldn't we instead see our special dignity as grounded in the very special role we play (but the uranium atom does not) in the causal route to downstream good consequences? And once we see the matter this way, it will be an open question whether this role can be played in a deterministic world.

To be sure, we would need a story about that role, a story that helps us understand its special, distinctive features. But such a story might well defuse the temptation to think that in a deterministic world we simply would be like puppets manipulated by the past.[15] (Indeed, I think that much of what Nozick says about human agency can be seen as a contribution to such a project – a point to which I will return.)

We can put the point as a challenge: Why must our dignity depend on the failure of conditions prior to our choices and actions also to have related forms of instrumental value? Why should we care so much about that? We don't care, I take it, that our parents and background social institutions are recognized as having instrumental value for helping us to lead good lives. Indeed, it would be a mistake – a kind of hubris – to refuse to ascribe such instrumental value. So why should we care, in general, that prior determining causes also turn out to have instrumental value when we do good things?[16] (Of course, if the prior causes do not involve persons in the right way this will not amount to assigning moral credit to those prior causes.) Granted, we might well care that certain kinds of causes not be operative – for example, forms of coercion, brainwashing, and the like.[17] But we may care about that without thinking that our dignity is undermined simply by the existence of prior determining causes that get credited with instrumental value when we do good things.

There may be other reasons to hope that our world is not deterministic. Perhaps we think that this is needed if we are fairly to hold people morally accountable and subject to retributive punishment.[18] But, as we have seen,

Nozick is not arguing in this way.[19] Nozick is, rather, seeking to articulate conditions of our human dignity. And it is not clear that we think, or should think, our dignity really does depend on our having, in Nozick's technical sense, originative value. So it is not clear that Nozick's appeals to originative value can play the role he wants them to play in his views about free will.

This may be one of those fundamental matters on which reasonable people will, in the end, disagree.[20] But, however we decide this issue, we also will be faced with a further challenge to Nozick's libertarian conception. This further challenge echoes a second common objection to libertarian theories. Is it true that a nondetermined self-subsuming, weight-bestowing decision would not be, at bottom, random and unexplained? After all, an alternative self-subsuming decision to bestow weights in an alternative way would also, if it occurred, make itself intelligible in this reflexive way. And we are supposing that it is fully compatible with the past and the causal laws of nature that this alternative decision occur instead. So does not the occurrence of the actual decision remain, at bottom, random and unexplained?

Nozick himself expresses some uncertainty on this point (301, 305), though he thinks this is the best chance for a libertarian model of free will. To arrive at a considered view on this matter, though, it will be helpful first to turn to other elements of Nozick's overall view of our agency.

4. MODELS #2 AND #3: TRACKING BESTNESS AND EQUILIBRIUM

Nozick sees his first model as a libertarian model of free will in the absence of determinism. But he also wants a model of action that is the best we can do in a deterministic world; for he fears that determinism may well be true (317). He believes that in a deterministic world we would not have all we want: we would not have originative value, and so, he claims, would not have the special dignity that goes along with that value. But we still might have an important and distinctive value.

Nozick sketches two distinctive kinds of agency possible in a deterministic world. First, our actions might, as he says, track bestness or rightness in roughly the sense that if one intentionally does A then A is right or best, and if A weren't right or best one would not intentionally have done it.[21] This is not yet to say what makes an act right or best. It is only to say that there is, in such agency, this systematic interdependence between such deontic or axiological features and what one intentionally does.

One's decision and action might track bestness in a deterministic world. Furthermore, there seems no necessary connection, in either direction, between tracking bestness and acting on the basis of self-subsuming, weight-bestowing decisions. The latter involves a certain process of choice, one that might issue in wrong choices; the former is a condition of subjunctive dependency between choice and bestness/rightness (327, 352), a dependency that, it seems, may arise from a process that did not involve self-subsuming, weight-bestowing decisions. Nevertheless, there may in some cases be a mesh of these two conditions; one might, for example, arrive at and successfully execute a self-subsuming decision in favor of a policy of tracking bestness (300).

Nozick's third model focuses on how we would see our actions if we knew their causes. Many times we are ignorant of causes of our actions, but if we had known them at the time of action would have wanted to act differently. If, for example, I had known that my chastizing you was grounded in an old resentment, not – as I think – my present assessment of your work, I wouldn't have done it. But sometimes an act may be in "equilibrium" in the sense that even if one fully knew its causes one would not want any less to do it than one did want to do it when one did it. "An act in equilibrium withstands knowledge of its own causes."[22]

Nozick's second and third models are models of agency possible in a deterministic world. Nozick does not, in the end, offer these as models of free will. As I understand him, he remains, in the end, an incompatibilist about free will and causal determinism.[23] But he does suggest that we can combine these two models, and arrive at a model of the best agency available to us in a deterministic world: "We would want our causally determined acts to be in (unfrozen) equilibria, tracking bestness."[24]

These two conditions might come apart. Perhaps my mode of thinking does support agency that tracks bestness, but I would want to change it if I knew what its causes were. But Nozick can simply grant this possibility and insist that what we most want, in a deterministic world, is agency in which these conditions do not come apart but are jointly realized.

5. A THREE-PRONGED, COMPATIBILIST MODEL?

Why not combine all three models into a compatibilist model of agency that is possible in a deterministic world? Why not consider agency in a deterministic world, agency that involves self-subsuming, weight-bestowing decisions in favor of self-conceptions, that thereby tracks bestness, and that is in equilibrium? The need to track bestness would limit which self-conceptions are available. And we have noted that the second and third prongs might come apart, but need not. The idea that agency in a deterministic world might exhibit all three features depends on the possibility of self-subsuming, weight-bestowing decisions in a deterministic world. But we have seen that, in the end, Nozick appears to grant this possibility.

The idea need not be that all three prongs are necessary for free will, self-determination, or the like. We may want to allow that there can be self-determined but evil agents who do not track bestness. The idea is, rather, that the three prongs, taken together, give us a sketch of a compatibilist story about sufficient grounds for human dignity. An agent whose motivation is in equilibrium, whose actions are grounded in self-subsuming weight-bestowing decisions,[25] and who thereby tracks bestness is a very special kind of agent. Many purposive agents – including, probably, the non-human animals with whom we are familiar – do not instantiate this three-pronged model.

So we can ask: Would such a three-pronged model of agency in a deterministic world capture grounds sufficient for human dignity in the absence of Nozickian originatory value?[26] One advantage to a positive, compatibilist answer is that we would then be protected from the worries about randomness that challenge the libertarian project.[27] Although Nozick does not consider such a three-pronged model of agency in a deterministic world, however, it is clear he would answer in the negative; for such agency would still not have originatory value, in Nozick's technical sense. So this returns us both to the issue of the significance of such originatory value, and to the issue of Nozick's success, in his first model, in responding to worries about randomness.

To make further progress with these matters, it will be useful first to turn to Nozick's views about personal identity and value.

6. NOZICK ON PERSONAL IDENTITY AND VALUE

Begin with a question brought powerfully to our attention by John Locke: What is it for one and the same person to persist over time? In Locke's famous case of the prince and the cobbler, one person at a later time has the cobbler's body but seems to remember the prince's earlier experiences.[28] We can also suppose that the person at the later time with the prince's body seems to remember the cobbler's earlier experiences. Which of the two later persons is the prince and which the cobbler? To answer we seem to need to say what is more important to the identity of a person over time: bodily continuity or (as Locke concluded, in his so-called memory theory of personal identity) the kind of psychological continuity involved in (at least, apparent) memory.

Nozick would approach this example with the idea that the later prince-body person and the later cobbler-body person are each a "continuer" of the earlier cobbler person (35). They each have certain qualitative similarities with the earlier cobbler person: in one case (the case of the later cobbler-body person) the similarities are physical, in the other (the case of the later prince-body person) psychological. And in each case, some properties of the later person are causally connected to those of the earlier cobbler person.

Nozick's idea (which he calls the "closest continuer theory") is that if the earlier cobbler person persists to the later time,[29] the later person who is identical to the earlier cobbler person is the *closest* continuer of that earlier person. But who is the closest continuer? To answer we need a way of measuring closeness, a way that would assign relevant weights to such physical and psychological continuities. We can see Locke's memory theory as assigning all weight to certain psychological continuities: Thus, Locke concludes that the prince persists with the cobbler's body. But, according to Nozick, other metrics are theoretically possible:

> Does psychological continuity come lexically first; is there no tradeoff between the slightest loss of psychological continuity and the greatest gain in bodily continuity; is bodily continuity (to a certain degree) a necessary component of identity through time; . . . what are the relevant subcomponents of psychological continuity or similarity (for example, plans, ambitions, hobbies, preferences in flavors of ice cream, moral principles). (69)

Nozick does not try to provide a single, objective story about "closeness" for personal identity. Instead, he claims that there is no such single story:

> What is special about people, about selves, is that what constitutes their identity through time is partially determined by their own conception of themselves, a conception which may vary, perhaps appropriately does vary, from person to person. (69)

Nozick later puts this idea as follows:

> The self's conception of itself will be, in the terms of the closest continuer theory, a listing and weighting of dimensions. This provides, implicitly, a measure of closeness. . . . (105)

The metric of closeness needed for a closest continuer theory of personal identity is partially provided by the person herself, in her "self-conception."[30]

We are not free to adopt just any such self-conception and thereby individuate selves in radical ways. I cannot successfully "synthesize" myself as including both Moses Mendelsohn and Michael Jordan.[31] There are objective constraints on "self-synthesis." But there is also some latitude, some room for personal decision:

> there is not simply one correct measure of closeness for persons. Each person's own selection and weighting of dimensions enter into determining his own actual identity, not merely his view of it. (106)

Let me stop here to emphasize a structural feature of this view of the person. Persons persist through time; the conditions of their actual persistence involve a metric of closeness; this metric has objective constraints; but its details are also to some extent a matter of decision for the person, a decision of how to weigh "dimensions [that] enter into determining [one's] own actual identity." Personal identity is, in this sense, a *hybrid* phenomenon.

Turn now to Nozick's approach to value, to what it is that an action tracks when it tracks bestness. Here Nozick's views come in three stages. Nozick begins not with the question of whether there are "objective values" but, rather, with the question how objective values are "even possible": "the project is to sketch what an objective ethics might look like, to understand how there (so much as) could be such a thing" (400). Here Nozick arrives at the view that if there are things that have intrinsic value, their degree of value is determined by what Nozick calls "degree of organic unity" (418). The idea of degree of organic unity is drawn from concerns in aesthetics with "the virtues of unifying diverse and apparently unrelated . . . material" (415).

> Holding fixed the degree of unifiedness of material, the degree of organic unity varies directly with the degree of diversity of that material being unified. Holding fixed the degree of diversity of the material, the degree of organic unity varies directly with the degree of unifiedness. . . . (416)

Nozick's conjecture is that a generalized notion of organic unity captures "the basic dimension of intrinsic value" (418). "[S]omething is intrinsically valuable in accordance with its degree of organic unity."[32]

Nozick then notes that this view about intrinsic value allows for an "ineradicable plurality of values" (446). Many things have intrinsic value, and there is no reason to think that they can all be realized in a single life. Indeed, Nozick believes that "these diverse values cannot be (tightly) unified, that there are ineradicable conflicts, tensions, needs for tradeoffs, and so on" (447). So an agent who is trying to respond to value will need to make choices among the plurality of values, will need "to formulate her own package of value realization" (447).

This has, for Nozick, two important implications. First, it blocks "the threat that the objectivity of values might appear to pose to individuality" (448). We need not worry that a world of objective values dictates a single way to live to all agents. Instead, "[i]ndividuality is expressed in the interstices of the objective rankings of value, in the particular unified patterning chosen and lived" (448).

Second, the plurality of values means that one *must* make decisions about which values to weigh in one's deliberation, and how to weigh them:

> each person must (within the objective limits) arrive at her own weighting. That giving of weights is not something we happen to do, it is necessitated by the pluralist nature of the realm of values. (448)

The weights that one invokes in one's deliberations will, then, have a hybrid structure. On the one hand, they will be accountable to "objective limits." On the other hand, they will be shaped partially by the agent's own decisions.[33]

So far, Nozick's discussion has "bracketed the ontological question about the existence of value" (562). Nozick returns to this ontological question toward the end of PE. He suggests there that once we see what value would be like and how it would fit into our agency, if there were value, we can just choose to live as if there is value. And if we make such a choice then there is value. Or so Nozick avers. Here is how he puts the view:

> We know what value would be; we have only to bring it to life, to value it, to seek and pursue it, contouring our lives in accordance with it. We have only to choose that there be value. What is needed to bring value to our universe is our reflexive choice that there be value. . . . (563)

What is it to "choose that there be value"? It is to value things in the way described by Nozick's theory: "The choice that there be value is made in valuing things" (558). The deliberative process of bestowing weights, within objective constraints provided by the significance of organic unity in any world in which there is value, is enough to "bring value to our universe."

I am not sure how best to interpret Nozick's talk here of "bring[ing] value to our universe" simply by "valuing things." For present purposes, however, we can limit our attention to the question of how these hybrid approaches to valuing and personal identity can help buttress Nozick's defense of his libertarian model in response to a concern about randomness.

7. WEIGHT-BESTOWING DECISIONS REVISITED

The concern, recall, is that if a self-subsuming, weight-bestowing decision were nondetermined then, even given the kind of decision that it is, it would remain, at bottom, arbitrary or random. After all, "there are different and conflicting self-subsuming decisions that could be made." So we may wonder: "Is it not arbitrary then that one-self-subsuming decision is made rather than another" (301)?

Nozick's response, we have seen, is that a self-subsuming, weight-bestowing decision provides a kind of explanation of itself: for it is intelligible in light of the weights it itself bestows (304). The point to note now is that Nozick's hybrid accounts of personal identity and valuing allow him to deepen this response.

First, in the most basic case the self-subsuming, weight-bestowing decision is a decision in favor of a "self-conception." Nozick's view is that such a self-conception helps in part to structure who one in fact is, by providing, to some extent, weights for the metric of closeness of continuer (306). Given the hybrid nature of personal identity, the provision of such weights, by way of a self-subsuming decision, is an essential element in what is involved in the persistence of the person over time.

Second, such self-subsuming, weight-bestowing decisions are a needed response to value pluralism, a response that is to respect "the objective limits." And the bestowal of such weights itself has objective value, for a "life based upon such weightings will be unified by them, and so more valuable than one that exhibits no weighting or ignores value altogether" (449).

So, the theory is that a self-subsuming, weight-bestowing decision that favors a self-conception helps to some extent both to determine who the agent is and, in a way that is responsive to "the objective limits" and is itself needed and valuable, what the agent does. Of course, it remains true that if the decision is not determined then it is consistent with the past and the causal laws that a (to some extent) different agent, and different weightings, instead emerge. But the tight connections provided by the theory between the (partially self-constituted) agent, her (partially self-constituted) weightings, and the action performed may provide as strong a form of intelligibility and nonarbitrariness for a nondetermined decision as a libertarian can aspire to.

There is a possible problem here, as Nozick notes (306). In the case of a fundamental decision in favor of a self-conception – say, in Sartre's famous case, a decision to fight with the Free French rather than stay with one's mother[34] – it seems that the decision may, on the theory, be so tightly connected to who the agent is that it will not be true that *that very agent* could have decided otherwise. I am not sure what to say here; perhaps we can simply see this as an insight of the theory.[35]

Another point is that the connection between weight-bestowing decisions and personal identity has a further dimension that Nozick does not highlight but that may be useful to note. Recall Nozick's idea that some weight-bestowing decisions set a framework for later decisions, much as precedent-setting decisions do in the courts. One function of such weight-bestowing decisions may be, then, to create associated continuities over time. And these are kinds of psychological continuities that will be, on many versions of the closest continuer theory, partly constitutive of the person's persistence over time. To have this role in creating continuities a weight-bestowing decision need not itself be a decision about a metric of closeness of continuer. Instead, a function of such weight-bestowing decisions can be to create the very continuities that are frequently a concern of such a metric.[36] The resulting action will be an issue of a decision whose function it is to induce continuities that are, on most relevant metrics, partly constitutive of the persistence of the person.

We have now arrived at a full Nozickian response to worries about randomness for the libertarian model. A self-subsuming, weight-bestowing decision provides an explanation of itself and its ensuing action as intelligible in light of the weights it itself bestows. Furthermore, this source of intelligibility, in ways noted, both partly constitutes basic features of the agent and is a needed, valuable response to the pluralism of value. So there is significant intelligibility of action despite the absence of prior determining conditions.

Is the response adequate? I am unsure. Here, again, we may have arrived at one of those fundamental matters on which reasonable people will disagree. What I would like to emphasize at this point, however, is that nothing about the story just told about how such decisions make actions intelligible, nonarbitrary, or the like, depends on the condition that the decision is not determined by prior conditions. If this story of intelligibility of decision and action works for the case of such self-subsuming decisions when they are not determined it will work also for the case in which the decision is determined.

This is to return to the general worry that libertarianism is unstable: It needs a positive condition on free will in order to avoid seeing free will as merely the absence of causal determination; but then we can ask why that positive condition is not sufficient, on its own, for the kind of agency we seek. In the present case, we can ask why it is not sufficient for human dignity that we have the capacity to act on the basis of a self-subsuming, weight-bestowing decision that is a decision in favor of a self-conception. This concern is made more pressing when we see that the features of such decisions that are needed to provide the best answer to concerns about randomness are equally available to a compatibilist theory.

We can deepen the point. We have just noted that the explanatory, intelligibility-bestowing role provided by self-subsuming decisions within Nozick's first model is one that may be played by such decisions in a deterministic world. We can add to this the idea, broached earlier, that this model may be wedded to Nozick's other two models: that of tracking bestness, and that of equilibrium in light of knowledge of causes. We can then offer such a three-pronged model as the beginnings of a compatibilist model of the grounds of human dignity.[37]

In his thoughtful survey of the literature on free will, Gary Watson observes that "the structure of an adequate libertarian account of freedom must be such that the condition of self-determination itself entails indeterminism."[38] Nozick's model of self-subsuming, weight-bestowing decisions is his version of a libertarian account of self-determination. So far as I can see, however, it is not true that this model of self-determination "itself entails indeterminism."

Nozick's response, I believe, would be that Watson's requirement is misguided; for there is independent reason to ask that the most basic decisions of an agent with dignity not be determined. After all, only then would the agent have originative value. This returns us to the fundamental question of whether we really think, or should think, that our special human dignity is a hostage to a concern with this special value. An agent who tracks bestness, whose motivation is in equilibrium, and whose actions are grounded in self-subsuming weight-bestowing decisions and (as I would say) policies is a distinctive kind of agent. If we are, sometimes, such agents, is that a sufficient ground for human dignity? Or does our dignity really depend, further, on whether or not our world is deterministic? Nozick would answer this last question in the affirmative. Even if, on reflection, we are not convinced by Nozick on this matter, we are in his debt for his suggestive discussions of forms of agency that even a compatibilist will value.[39]

Notes

[1] (Cambridge, Mass.: Harvard University Press, 1981). Parenthetical page references in the text are to this book.

[2] See esp. PE, pp. 291–362.

[3] Recently, a number of theorists have explored ways of understanding connections between forms of free will, autonomy, or self-determination, on the one hand, and personal identity, on the other. This makes Nozick's early discussion of such connections of particular interest. For recent discussions of different versions of such connections see Christine Korsgaard, *The Sources of Normativity* (Cambridge: Cambridge University Press, 1996); Harry Frankfurt, "On the Necessity of Ideals," in his *Necessity, Volition and Love* (New York: Cambridge University Press, 1999): 108–116; Gideon Yaffe, *Liberty Worth the Name: Locke on Free Agency* (Princeton, N.J.: Princeton University Press, 2000); J. David Velleman, "Identification and Identity," in S. Buss and L. Overton, eds., *Contours of Agency: Essays on the Philosophy of Harry Frankfurt* (Cambridge, Mass.: MIT Press, forthcoming); and my own "Reflection, Planning, and Temporally Extended Agency," *Philosophical Review* 109 (2000): 35–61.

[4] See Peter van Inwagen, "The Incompatibility of Free Will and Determinism," *Philosophical Studies* 27 (1975): 185–99.

[5] For recent defenses of a libertarian conception, see Robert Kane, *The Significance of Free Will* (New York: Oxford University Press, 1998), and Timothy O'Conner, *Persons and Causes: The Metaphysics of Free Will* (New York: Oxford University Press, 2000).

[6] PE, 295. And see G. E. M. Anscombe, *Causality and Determination* (Cambridge: Cambridge University Press, 1971).

[7] In a later work [*The Nature of Rationality* (Princeton, N.J.: Princeton University Press, 1993), Ch. 2], Nozick considers principles of decision that confer different weights to expected causal utility, expected epistemic utility, and what Nozick calls symbolic utility. Nozick suggests that there is a range of possible weight-bestowing principles here, and we are in effect faced with a choice. As Elijah Millgram suggested to me, we can see the choice of one such weight-bestowing principle as an example of the kind of weight-bestowing decision highlighted in PE.

[8] Nozick briefly suggests an analogy between such a weight-bestowing decision and measurement in quantum mechanics, as understood in "the currently orthodox interpretation of quantum mechanics" (298).

[9] "Suppose that in certain types of situations, we did reconsider our weighting of reasons, our self-conception, and our lives, but the new position we arrived at was causally determined – we always would arrive at precisely that position in precisely those circumstances.... How significant is the difference between this deterministic situation and its indeterministic mate?" (PE, 310). There are, however, places in the text where Nozick seems to be thinking that such a process is of necessity not determined by prior conditions. See, for example, p. 448, where he labels his view of "weighting values" "indeterminist."

[10]Indeed, we might then be moving in the direction of the sort of view I sketch in "Reflection, Planning, and Temporally Extended Agency." I appeal there to "self-governing policies" of treating certain desired ends as reasons to a certain extent. Such policies may be the upshot of a decision. So these self-governing policies share important similarities with Nozick's self-subsuming, weight-bestowing decisions. My understanding of such policies is grounded in the planning theory of intention I develop in *Intention, Plans, and Practical Reason* (Cambridge, Mass.: Harvard University Press, 1987; reissued by CSLI Publications, 1999). And it is no part of my understanding of such self-governing policies that they cannot be determined by prior conditions.

[11]See Gary Watson's "Introduction" to his *Free Will* (New York: Oxford University Press, 1982), at p. 11.

[12]Nozick thinks justified retributive punishment is compatible with the causal determination of action (393–7). And he seems in general to understand the ability to do otherwise in an incompatibilist way. So he probably does not accept the principle of alternate possibilities. This interpretation is also supported by Harry Frankfurt's reference to Nozick's lectures in Frankfurt's "Alternate Possibilities and Moral Responsibility," in *The Importance of What We Care About* (New York: Cambridge University Press, 1988), p. 6 n. 2.

[13]Gary Watson distinguishes between concerns about "accountability" and concerns about "attributability." Watson suggests that the former are the main source of pressure for a demand for alternate possibilities. [Gary Watson, "Two Faces of Responsibility," *Philosophical Topics*, 24 (1996): 227–48, esp. p. 237]. Nozick's concerns, in contrast, are in the spirit of a concern with attributability.

[14]PE, p. 313. This raises the question of whether Nozick's concern with originatory value should lead him to want not merely that decisions not be determined but, further, that they not be caused. After all, if there are prior causes of a decision which in fact leads to later good consequences, won't those prior causes get credited with the instrumental value of causing (although not determining) those later consequences? In the main text, though, I focus on the idea that our dignity requires the absence of deterministic causation.

[15]Nozick invokes the metaphor of puppethood on pp. 310 and 313. See also Susan Wolf, "The Importance of Free Will," *Mind*, 90 (1981): 386–405, at 404–05.

[16]Cf. Harry Frankfurt's remark, about a related matter, that "[t]here is a difference between being *fully* responsible and being *solely* responsible." "Freedom of the Will and the Concept of a Person," in *The Importance of What We Care About* (New York: Cambridge University Press, 1988), at p. 25n.

[17]Cf. Nozick's remarks about coercion on pp. 49, 520. There are hard questions about cases involving some such untoward form of causation – the work of a nefarious neurosurgeon, perhaps. See the discussion of related issues about moral responsibility in John Martin Fischer and Mark Ravizza, S.J., *Responsibility and Control* (New York: Cambridge University Press, 1998), pp. 194–201.

[18]See the critical discussion of this idea in R. Jay Wallace, *Responsibility and the Moral Sentiments* (Cambridge, Mass.: Harvard University Press, 1994), esp. Chs. 4 and 7.

[19]Indeed, as noted earlier, he thinks justified retributive punishment is compatible with determinism (393–7).

[20]See PE, p. 21.

[21]PE, pp. 317–20. There are complexities here about cases in which several conflicting options are each permissible; but we can put these matters aside for now.

[22]PE, p. 349. Nozick returns to this idea of equilibrium in his discussion of symbolic meaning in NR, at p. 31.

[23]Nozick writes:

> . . . we are left with the feeling that the notion of 'tracking bestness or rightness' has not gotten to the heart of the free will problem. . . .
> Though it leaves the issues of free will dark, nevertheless, the situation of tracking bestness or rightness may be a very desirable and valuable mode of action, the best we can hope to achieve. (332)

See also pp. 328–9.

[24]PE, p. 352. Nozick explains the idea of "frozen" as follows: "an action is frozen if no possible knowledge of its causes can lead a person not to (want to) do it or to want (to want) it less." (716, n. 62).

[25]And policies. See note 10.

[26]Gideon Yaffe discusses a way of putting together our concerns with forms of agency roughly along the lines of the first two prongs in his "Free Will and Agency at its Best," in *Philosophical Perspectives: Action and Freedom* 14 (2000): 203–29. Yaffe calls a concern (roughly) with the first prong a concern with "self-expression" and a concern with the second prong a concern with "self-transcendence."

[27]Recall that Nozick himself is unsure abut the success of his libertarian response to worries about randomness.

I don't mean to say, by the way, that a compatiblist theorist can simply borrow these models from Nozick without further ado. In particular, there will be questions about why such self-subsuming decisions count as fully the agent's own, in contrast with other psychological elements – for example, a desire for revenge that one does not reflectively endorse – that seem not to have authority to speak for the agent. The philosopher who has contributed the most to our understanding of these issues is Harry Frankfurt. See esp. his *The Importance of What We Care About*. I discuss related matters in my "Reflection, Planning, and Temporally Extended Agency."

[28]*An Essay Concerning Human Understanding*, Book II, Ch. XXVII, Section 15.

[29]This condition serves to leave room for cases in which the closest continuer is not close enough for the earlier person to survive at all.

[30]Nozick arrives at this idea by reflection on the special knowledge we seem to have in identifying ourselves. When I think or say "I am tall," I might be wrong about my height, but it seems I can't be wrong about the reference of "I": the reference of "I" is, of course, me. But why is it that I am, as Shoemaker puts it, "immune to error through misidentification" (quoted in PE, 90)? Nozick's answer is that I am

immune to such error because the use of "I" in my thought in a way individuates its referent:

> I know that when I say "I", the reference is to myself, because myself is synthesized as the thing which that act refers to, as the tightest and greatest organic unity including the act, and referred to by the act because including it (90).

Nozick call this "the theory of the self as reflexively synthesized" (91). Nozick then extends this view about the referent of "I" at the present time to the persistence of the self, or person, over time. This leads him to the idea that "The I's self-synthesis includes a self-conception which projects itself into the future" (105).

For a different approach to such self-knowledge, see John Perry's discussion of what he calls "self-attached knowledge" in his "Myself and I" in Marcelo Stamm, ed., *Philosophie in Synthetisher Absicht* (Stuttgart: Klett-Cotta, 1998), pp. 83–103.

[31] Nozick suggests, boldly, that these limits may be, at bottom, social (107–08).

[32] PE, p. 446. Note that this is a claim about *intrinsic* value and so, I take it, is not offered directly as an account of originatory value.

In a later work, Nozick notes that principles can function in a person's life in ways such that "[t]hrough them, one's actions and one's life may have greater coherence, greater organic unity. That may be valuable in itself" [NR, 13]. I would want to make a similar claim about the role of intentions, plans, and policies in our lives. See my *Intention, Plans, and Practical Reason*.

[33] As I understand him (although I am unsure about this), Nozick does not claim that in giving weights within "the objective limits" one thereby makes it the case that it is objectively best to act in accord with those weights.

[34] "Existentialism is a Humanism," in W. Kaufmann, ed., *Existentialism from Dostoevsky to Sartre*, rev. and expanded (New York: Meridian/Penguin, 1975), pp. 345–69; at 354–6.

[35] Nozick's discussion of this possible problem on pp. 306–07 does not seem to provide a direct response.

[36] This distinction between two ways such decisions can shape conditions of personal identity parallels a distinction Nozick suggests in his later discussion of principles in NR. He says there that "[p]rinciples may be one way a person can define her *identity*. . . . Further, principles followed over an extended period are a way a person can integrate her life over time and give it more coherence" (NR, 13–14). It is this second, integrating role that I want to emphasize here. To play this role a weight-bestowing decision need not itself be a decision about a "metric" of closeness.

In my "Reflection, Planning, and Temporally Extended Agency," I make the related point that (what I call) self-governing policies organize our lives in part by creating psychological continuities and connections that are partly constitutive of the identity of a person over time. And self-governing policies can play this role without themselves being "self-conceptions."

[37] As Nozick remarks (p. 448), we need to interpret tracking bestness in a way that is compatible with his value pluralism. I take it that this means that to track bestness is to track "the objective limits." And this three-pronged model will also continue to face issues about authority noted above (note 27).

[38] "Free Action and Free Will," at p. 165.

[39] Thanks to John Fischer, Elijah Millgram, David Schmidtz, Manuel Vargas, and Gideon Yaffe for helpful comments.

9 How to Make Something of Yourself[*]

ELIJAH MILLGRAM

In the philosophical practice that is dominant today, the product of philosophizing is understood to be a *theory*: a set of statements, in the ideal case carefully articulated and supported by arguments, about matters philosophical. The theoretical mode of philosophy boasts a distinguished ancestry, one going all the way back to Plato, whom Bernard Williams has recently called its inventor. There is, however, an alternative tradition, which begins with Socrates, and so has an even more distinguished ancestry, and in which philosophizing aims to produce not a theory but a philosophical *persona*. Besides Socrates, the tradition includes Nietzsche, Kierkegaard, Montaigne, and, probably, the later Wittgenstein; Michel Foucault and Alexander Nehamas are nominees about whom I have my doubts; Stanley Cavell is a well-known contemporary representative, and Robert Nozick's *The Examined Life*, which I will discuss here, is an exercise in this genre as well.[1]

Academic philosophy has not known quite what to make of Nozick's book. By contemporary professional standards, it is badly underargued, and when philosophical exposition of the familiar kind does appear, it is, for instance, relegated to an appendix, which the reader is advised he may want to skip.[2] A well-known twentieth-century figure is introduced as "the English philosopher J. L. Austin" – a strong signal that the intended audience does not consist of philosophers, for whom such an introduction would be unnecessary.[3] Many of the topics that it takes up – among

[*] I'm grateful to Lanier Anderson, Jon Bendor, Sarah Buss, Alice Clapman, Alice Crary, Rachana Kamtekar, Alexander Nehamas, Robert Nozick, Arlene Saxonhouse, David Schmidtz, Amy Schmitter, Rachel Shuh, and Candace Vogler for comments on earlier drafts, and to Margaret Battin, Alyssa Bernstein, Michael Bratman, Steve Downes, Christoph Fehige, Amy Johnson, Mitzi Lee, Maria Merritt, Klara Starr, Ulla Wessels, and Nick White for helpful conversation. The paper was improved by responses from audiences at Washington University, Bowling Green State University, the University of Wisconsin-Milwaukee, and Northwestern University. Work on this paper was supported by fellowships from the National Endowment for the Humanities and the Center for Advanced Study in the Behavioral Sciences; financial support was provided through the Center by the Andrew W. Mellon Foundation.

175

the chapter headings one will find "Sexuality," "The Holiness of Everyday Life," "Parents and Children," and "Enlightenment" – are at the margins of the discipline, or beyond. The prose is too personal for scholarly respectability, and Nozick acknowledges that it is likely to sound overblown and precious. Unsurprisingly, philosophers have for the most part decided that this book was not meant for them, and it seems to have fallen, as Hume said of his *Treatise*, stillborn from the presses.

But contemporary professional standards presuppose that what is being assessed is the exposition of a theory, not the presentation of a philosophical self. That is, the reception accorded *The Examined Life* is in the first place a consequence of failing to place it in the genre to which it belongs, and the first section of this chapter will be concerned to document its membership, as well as to make some preliminary points about works of this kind. I will then argue that, as a member of its genre, it is worth careful attention, because it shows how to solve a problem that has turned some of the best-known philosophical lives into spectacular failures. I will describe a way in which attempts to fabricate a philosophical persona are liable to backfire, and then lay out Nozick's solution; I will conclude by very briefly considering an alternative to it.

1

At one point in *The Examined Life*, Nozick asks his readers not to summarize or sloganize it (EL, 284f). I am going to have to do a certain amount of the former, but I will try to respect his wishes by rehearsing what the book says only to the extent necessary to explain what it is doing.

If its readers have for the most part not recognized *The Examined Life* as belonging to the personal tradition, that is probably best chalked up to expectation determining perception; Nozick himself is entirely up front about his agenda. His announced purpose is to "present a *portrait*, not a theory" (EL, 12), one that, like a certain kind of painting, will piece together fragments of his past and present personality into something more than a snapshot of what happens to be there at any particular moment:

> During the extended hours a painting is sat for . . . its subject shows a range of traits, emotions, and thoughts, all revealed in different lights. Combining different glimpses of the person, choosing an aspect here, a tightening of muscle there, a glint of light, a deepening of line, the painter interweaves these different portions of surface, never before simultaneously exhibited, to produce a fuller portrait and a deeper one.[4]

Nozick means the result of the process to be especially *real* – for the moment, in the way that some literary characters are especially real. (But only for the moment, because Nozick later glosses the notion with a discussion of the nature of reality, extending over several chapters.[5])

Because this mode of philosophizing has a relatively low profile these days, there are a number of issues concerning its mechanics that I need to address before proceeding to my main problem; let me turn to these now. First, one must be careful, while approaching the genre, not simply to assume that the person constructing a philosophical persona and the philosophical persona he is constructing are identical, and in fact Candace Vogler has characterized *The Examined Life* "as an undergraduate text . . . written in a kind of philosophical persona which probably has little to do with the man himself."[6] Caution, however, has recently become a pervasive and entrenched disposition to enforce some such distinction a priori, that is, to insist that person and persona *must* be distinct. I think that is a mistake, and let me explain why.

In favor of the identification here are the benefits for the sake of which philosophical self-portraiture is to be undertaken. Becoming more real involves both literally and literarily constituting oneself. That is, by finding in one's life "a new overall pattern that alters how each part of life is understood" (EL, 15), one is taking possession of the bits and pieces that make up one's life, in a way that is continuous with, and an extension of, the way the self is assembled in the first place. "Thinking about life is . . . mulling it over, and the more complete understanding this brings . . . feels like growing up more."[7] Now, if it is not your *own* life you are rendering, those benefits do not accrue to you, and this is a reason to think that the author is very much putting himself on the line.[8]

The a priori insistence on distinguishing person from persona has two main motivations. The first is a widespread nervousness about committing the intentional fallacy, which translates into resistance to just about any way of taking authors to be relevant to the interpretation of their writings. (Call this *Intentional Fallacy Dread*.) The second is the worry that identifying an author as the subject of his self-representation would open up the issue of the accuracy of the representation, but since all we ever see, after all, is one or another text in front of us (and never the author himself), we had better come up with a spin on the representation that preempts the question.[9] (Call this stance *French Verificationism*.) To take Nozick's announcement that this is a self-portrait at face value – so goes the objection – would be to commit the fallacy of taking an author's intentions as relevant, and in any case, that announcement is just another snippet of text, not the real voice of the author.

But both of these motivations take too much for granted. Intentional Fallacy Dread presupposes that we already know the medium in which the artifact we are considering has been executed: (literary) text, with respect to which its author's thoughts and actions are external. A stand-alone text, however, is not the only pertinent option; think of performance art, and specifically of pieces in which writing, and the texts it generates, are part of the performance.[10] In a persona-as-life, authorial intentions are components of (and not external to) the object being produced.[11] French Verificationism, for its part, takes for granted the related idea that, if a portrait is really a self-portrait of its author, then the relation between them is that of (attempted) correspondence between two independently existing objects. (That is, French Verificationism, oddly enough, takes for granted the correspondence model of truth.[12]) But that understanding of representation is inappropriate here; when the medium in which a persona is executed is the life, its written account of itself is, like its thoughts, intentions and so on, part of the life. It is a further especially visible episode within it, rather than a more or less accurate *copy*.[13]

So, because my use of "persona" means to be neutral as to what the medium can be, it is also neutral as to whether the persona and the person are one and the same. I see no reason to insist that they have to be distinct, and no reason to insist that they have always to be identical. In Nozick's case, I think that the best reading does identify them, since, as we have noted, the project's aims will not be attained if Nozick is not actually representing himself.

Second, Nozick's use of painted and literary portraits as models or analogs might suggest that the exercise is primarily aesthetic, and that its point is to produce a work of art. Today especially that is likely to be the default reading, since Nehamas, whose discussions of this genre of philosophy are largely responsible for the revival of interest in it, has influentially argued that Nietzsche's philosophical persona was so intended; his more recent book, *The Art of Living*, develops similar treatments of several other figures. But taking this to be true of all instances of the tradition would be once again to mistake an optional spin on the enterprise of persona construction for one of its ground rules, and would be an unhelpful way of approaching *The Examined Life*. One might try to make out of one's life a work of art that was not particularly philosophical, Oscar Wilde being a notorious instance.[14] And conversely, one might construct a philosophical persona that was neither meant, nor plausibly understood as, a work of art, and the self-portrait we have on hand is an example of that. While Nozick is aware that constructed figures can have "artistic impact" and be "artistically interesting" (EL, 255), becoming more real is not primarily an aesthetic process, because aesthetic qualities like beauty are, on his view, only some dimensions of the many along which one's reality can be augmented.[15] The philosophical persona *can* be a work of art – but it doesn't *have* to be one.

Third, his persona will, Nozick tells us, be "made up of theoretical pieces – questions, distinctions, explanations . . . the concatenation of [which] constitutes a portrait . . ." (EL, 12). This is typical of the genre, and it confronts us with the following question: If the point of philosophizing, in this tradition, is to produce a persona rather than a theory, why is it that the personae produced are so characteristically engaged in philosophical theorizing? (Even when they produce no theories themselves, their work is oriented *toward* theory, in the case of Socrates, by demanding theories of others, but more usually by addressing themselves to the theoretical work of their predecessors.)

Nehamas seems to think that failure to engage the theoretical tradition would entail not counting as a *philosophical* persona. There is something to this, and saying what that is would mean spelling out how constructing a persona can be a specifically philosophical undertaking; this is an issue I will not try to resolve now.[16] In Nehamas's understanding of the point, however, it is merely taxonomy; those who do not respond to philosophical theory are not *classified* as philosophers. A second reason for being dissatisfied with Nehamas's explanation is that it gives the theoretical tradition a priority that makes the competing personal tradition out as derivative or parasitic on it, and I doubt very much that this is how those working in the personal tradition see it themselves.[17]

Philosophical theory could be used to underwrite the design of a persona by providing arguments for one or another blueprint of a life. But why then should the theorizing appear as part of the life, rather than remaining discreetly offstage? Or theory might, as Plato thought, make virtue teachable, and presumably less corruptible.[18] But both of these accounts of the relation between theory and practice get not only the priorities but the direction of persuasion backwards: As Nozick realizes, the personae's

> lives play a crucial role in convincing us of what they say. It is not that we derive their doctrine, or their being right, from some other body of preformulated statements. If we accept their views upon their authority . . . that authority is derived only from what they are and show in their lives. . . .[19]

The persona-to-theory direction of persuasion is a central (and I am inclined to think of it as a defining) feature of the tradition; I will have further use for it later on. In the meantime, bear in mind that the genre we are considering is not to be confused with the application of an ethical theory within a life, or with the drawing of practical conclusions from one's arguments. (Think of the utilitarian philosopher impersonally applying his moral theory to his own actions.) Using the direction of persuasion as a distinguishing mark helps forestall that confusion.

The point of engaging in theory must be, rather, that the *activity* of theorizing is a component of the well-lived life: that the unexamined life really is not worth living (or at least that, whatever the merits of the unexamined life, the examined life has a lot to be said for it). And we should not expect to be convinced of that so much by argument for it as by lives on display.

Allow that the importance of philosophical theory, within a project of this kind, is that it enriches a life. How the activity of theorizing enhances a life may properly vary with the style of the life overall, and (the fourth, and last, of the preliminary points I want to make) this variability must be taken into account when we critically assess the theories that accompany or constitute philosophical personae. Consider logical consistency, one of the standard virtues of theory. If the persona is committed to consistency and logical rigor (as was, say, Socrates), detecting an inconsistency in its theoretical views may count as an objection to it. But if, to take an extreme case, theory functions merely as fashion accessory, to a character such as Oscar Wilde, whose trademark is being arch and perverse, then to complain of paradox and contradiction is just to miss the boat.[20] We should not allow the presence of theoretical elements in a persona to trigger our standard methods of inspecting theories, and then conflate assessment of the theory with assessment of the persona. Our methods for handling the theoretical dimension of a philosophical persona will normally have to be more self-aware, and less straightforward, than that. So if *The Examined Life* lacks some of the theoretical virtues, for example, tight argumentation, we ought nonetheless to suspend judgment until we are in a position to say how theoretical activity is supposed to figure into the character being assembled.

2

Philosophy in the personal mode has its undeniable attractions. The question, Socrates insisted, was: How should one live? And this is a question to which a life seems like a much better answer than a theory: As Kierkegaard emphasized, the palace of philosophical theory, however grand, should not impress us if the philosopher himself cannot occupy it. Again, most of us are inclined to think that there is more than one right answer to Socrates' question;[21] philosophizing that proceeds by constructing a life well-lived easily allows that there might be other lives just as well-lived, whereas philosophical theories that cover the same territory are normally mutually exclusive. Or again, if one does regard oneself as composing (oneself as) a work of art, one will be working in the most challenging possible medium, and producing an object of perhaps great aesthetic value. A philosophical persona may have therapeutic uses, the most familiar (but also the most rarefied) being a cure for the distraction of philosophy-as-theory.[22] There are the benefits that we saw Nozick using to justify his own self-portrait. And finally for now, philosophers have been teachers; what more appropriate teaching than a life that is philosophically exemplary?[23]

Now, given how talented the genre's most famous practitioners have been, we would expect to find its highlights to be lives we would ourselves wish to live, people we would want to be, or to have as our friends, or invite into our homes, or, especially, teachers we would want to be taught by. But in fact the genre has a surprisingly dismal track record. I won't try to review that record here; in the space I have, I could not possibly avoid caricaturing these rich, complicated philosophical figures, and treatments that are both cursory and overdrawn will be unconvincing. So let me instead put on the table for your consideration a sweeping and, for now, unsupported claim: that the most visible philosophers of the personal tradition are, almost uniformly, very hard to take: not people you would want for friends, or in your home, and especially, not people that you would want to be like. I would go so far as to say that many of them are positively – to use an ordinary but vivid word – *creepy*.

Let me add to that a subsidiary – equally sweeping and equally unsupported – claim. It is evidently a very central feature of the tradition that the personae in it are meant as pedagogical devices. But, with occasional and sometimes quite remarkable exceptions, apprenticeship to philosophers in this lineup works out rather badly. The students typically prove to be the very opposite of independent thinkers living admirable lives. Sometimes the discipleship seems to make them morally corrupt (or that anyway was the complaint brought against Socrates, and one could work up a related complaint having to do with the way Nietzsche tends to go down in one's undergraduate classes); sometimes it seems to be philosophically crippling

(think of Wittgenstein's effect on many of those close enough to the construct to be called Wittgensteinians); and sometimes they seem to turn into
what look like, well, groupies. It is typical for practitioners in the genre to
supply a disclaimer, to the effect that they do not want imitators, disciples,
and so forth; these disclaimers get repeated by camp-followers as though
they absolved the persona from responsibility for its imitators, and the gestures at the disclaimers have become almost a reflex. But on this count I
agree with Nozick:

> if time after time an ideal gets institutionalized and operates in the world
> a certain way, then *that* is what it comes to in the world. It is not allowed
> then simply to disclaim responsibility for what repeatedly occurs under its
> banner. (EL, 279)

A pedagogical device has to be judged by how it works, not by how
it *says* it should work. So the motif of the groupie cannot simply be
shrugged off.

Grant me for the sake of the argument that I am right about the genre's
track record, and overlook the tactlessness of my disrespectful-sounding
claim about figures who are by consensus – a consensus from which I am
not dissenting – among the great philosophers. Still, you may want to object,
what legitimate use could I have for the track record? It is evidently meant
as the starting point for some sort of *ad hominem* argument, and *ad hominem*
arguments are, as we all know, a kind of fallacy. So if that is where we are
going, we can stop the proceedings right now.

Let us remind ourselves why *ad hominem* arguments are illegitimate.
When the product of philosophical activity is a theory, *ad hominem* arguments are fallacious because the facts they adduce are irrelevant. But what
they are irrelevant to is the truth or falsity of the philosophical theory or
claim at issue. When the products of philosophizing, however, are taken to
be, not theories or claims, but *homines*, then it is the argument *ad hominem*
that is the appropriate form of criticism; as we have already seen, it is criticism directed to the theory that is indirectly relevant at best.

What the logic of the enterprise requires, its practice bears out. Socrates
was trying to expose a personal failing in his interlocutors, their pretence to
know something they did not.[24] Nietzsche's objection to morality was that
the moral are spiteful, bitter, weak, resentful, and secretly eating their hearts
out.[25] Cavell's objection to skepticism is that the skeptic is someone who
needs to believe that the world, or other people, are not really there, in more
or less the way that Othello needed to believe that Desdemona was unfaith-
ful to him.[26] Kierkegaard's objection to systematic philosophy – by which

he meant Hegelian philosophy, the most prominent theoretical school of his day – was that the philosophers who engage in it exhibit a peculiar kind of absent-mindedness. (Kierkegaard mentions the local bookseller who was so absent-minded that when he died one night, he simply didn't notice; Hegelian philosophy is no good, because the people who do it are like *that*.[27]) If we are going to take the tradition we are considering on its own terms, we will have to swallow our reflex objections to *ad hominem* arguments, and concentrate instead on developing and deploying them.

Now, there would be much more to launching the *ad hominem* argument at which I have been gesturing – the one whose conclusion is that something must be very wrong with this way of doing philosophy – than establishing that the philosophers in this tradition often turn out, say, creepy. We would have first to convince ourselves that the group we are considering has more in common than not being very likeable. (In particular, if the common property were merely being *not nice*, where that is the term used by the conventional to express discomfort at having the conventions challenged, we would be begging questions against those practitioners of the genre who mean to be challenging convention.) We would need to show that the common feature arises out of the enterprise of persona construction, and is not, as far as that is concerned, accidental or a coincidence. And, finally for now, we would need to do this in a way that is sensitive to whether a persona under consideration is identical with the person composing it. If the persona is the philosopher himself, pointing out that it is less than admirable has bite that it lacks when the persona is a freestanding construct, one which might be meant precisely as an example of a less than admirable character.

These are issues I will in a moment address; but I will not proceed with the *ad hominem* argument. To anticipate, the reason is that the results I have been reminding you of are not inevitable; *The Examined Life* has its problems (some of which we'll get to), but, I will suggest, not the usual problem.

3

I now want to sketch a pattern that naturally appears in the course of a philosophical persona's development. I don't want to claim that the pattern precisely matches any of the genre's instances; each of these philosophers has an agenda of his own, and not infrequently idiosyncrasy heads the agenda. I am instead hoping that the template will give us a way of organizing and explaining what we see case by case. Sometimes it will help us notice conformity to the pattern; sometimes it will help us see steps taken to avoid conformity.

It is natural, when going into the business of fabricating a persona, to be ambitious about it. Why bother, after all, if the persona is going to look just like everyone else, or if it is easy, or sloppy? Especially when one identifies oneself with one's persona, one wants to do one's very best. (You have only one life to live; make the most of it!) So the persona under construction will normally be constituted by most or all of one's literary corpus, or of one's life; the performance will be difficult, roughly to the degree that the blueprint is unusual; and we can expect a perfectionist approach to getting the details to line up with the blueprint. Everything will have to fit, because what one is committing oneself to is staying in character.

To the extent that the undertaking is ambitious, it also will be strenuous. For it to be motivationally possible to sustain such an effort over the course of (most of) a life, the persona must be *compelling*. It must be compelling first of all to the philosopher who is constructing it. But there are also reasons to have it be compelling to others, and I want to take a look at those before getting back to the way in which the personal philosopher has to see himself.

When one's commitments are as elaborate and offbeat as an ambitious persona's are, it is very difficult to do without external sources of correction, and this is where disciples come in handy. For these purposes, a disciple is someone who is paying full and continuous attention to the persona, who has internalized the pattern of commitments and so will notice (and perhaps even call one on) lapses in stylistic integrity, but who is not *critical* of the design for the persona. The disciple, that is, exerts pressure to conform to the blueprint for the persona, not pressure to change the blueprint.[28]

For a disciple to play this role, the persona must be compelling to him. And perhaps in any case one wants the product of one's philosophizing to be compelling, in something like the way that a philosophical theory can be. But recall what I labeled the direction of persuasion at work in the genre: from the persona to the opinions, rather than the other way around. So where the theoretician looks for arguments that compel, the philosopher constructing a persona falls back on making himself *fascinating*. (I will return later to the question of whether there are other ways to make a persona compelling.) It is tempting to describe this authorial strategy as an attempt at eroticizing the relationship between oneself and one's pupil or audience; because I do not have a theory of the erotic on hand, I will pursue the point only sporadically. Be that as it may, the followings that these personae often acquire, as well as their typical emotional coloration, can be made sense of as a kind of external conscience developed in order to keep projects of this kind on track.

To sustain his commitment, I claimed, the philosopher's persona must be compelling *to himself*. But there is a kind of parity of privilege, with respect to justification, between oneself and others. It is not as though the personal philosopher is withholding from his audience his arguments for being precisely who he is; what they do not have, he does not have either. So if such a philosopher is going to make his persona compelling to others by making it fascinating, he will make his persona compelling to himself in the same way: by being, or becoming, fascinating to himself. If we think of the relation between such personae and their audiences as eroticized, we can analogously think of their relation to themselves as narcissistic.

This account goes some way toward explaining the worrisome effects of personae in this tradition on their disciples. Because argumentation cannot be mustered to anchor the persona itself, it often functions in a kind of ground-clearing capacity. (Think of the Socratic elenchus, or Nietzsche's genealogies, or the dialectical moves that are Wittgenstein's analogs of genealogies.) Students appropriate the visible slash-and-burn technique, but cannot appropriate what is tying together the positive features of the persona. (For instance, his students could not see why Socrates himself was courageous, temperate, and so on: he had no plausible arguments for being virtuous, or even a satisfactory account of what being virtuous was.) Because the characteristic direction of persuasion has justification bottoming out, not only for others, but for oneself, in one's persona, there is nothing for one's disciples to see that would translate well into a justification for personae they might adopt for themselves.

If the outline I have just presented is a satisfactory first approximation, then there is a shape that constructed personae will tend to assume as the result of a series of quite natural tactical and strategic choices. The vices it predicts are not of course unique to this tradition; philosophers of the theoretical persuasion, not to mention popular musicians, can be found indulging in them as well. But we have seen that in this genre they have a different significance. If the students of a theoretical philosopher turn out to be unimaginative copies of their teacher, or if the teacher seems to have too much, or the wrong kind, of a stake in himself, that is neither here nor there as far as the philosophical work goes. But it is fully relevant to the assessment of the work when the personality is not just a means to the philosophical product, but is, rather, the philosophical product itself.

4

There were a number of choice points along the route into the trap, and so there is evidently a menu of preemptive moves. One would be to refuse to take on the project of producing a persona that is compelling, and I am going to suggest that this is Nozick's way out of the problem we have been looking over. I will move our focus back to *The Examined Life* in stages, beginning with a bit of framing from its author's previous book:

> The terminology of philosophical art is coercive: arguments are *powerful* and best when they are *knockdown*, arguments *force* you to a conclusion, if you believe the premises you *have to* or *must* believe the conclusion, some arguments do not carry much *punch*, and so forth. A philosophical argument is an attempt to get someone to believe something, whether he wants to believe it or not. A successful philosophical argument, a strong argument, *forces* someone to a belief. . . . A "perfect" philosophical argument would leave no choice.

> Why are philosophers intent on forcing others to believe things? Is that a nice way to behave toward someone? I think we cannot improve people that way – the means frustrate the end. Just as dependence is not eliminated by treating a person dependently . . . a person is not most improved by being forced to believe something against his will. . . . (PE, 4f)

On the assumption that what he is calling "coercive" is what I have been calling "compelling," Nozick is going into the construction of his philosophical persona already unwilling to compel his philosophical audience on matters of theory.[29] Now recall that theoretical philosophy is the paint out of which Nozick's portrait is built up. While the paint's not being compelling doesn't entail that the painting itself is not, something like narrative consistency (which is to be distinguished from logical consistency) suggests that the two ought to go hand in hand. To see how, I want to take up Candace Vogler's "Sex and Talk," which remains one of the few philosophical engagements with *The Examined Life* so far in print.[30]

Vogler's paper develops a disconcerting analogy between, on the one hand, the way an erotic relationship can grind to a deadening halt and, on the other, the professional routine of the theoretical genre of philosophy. If you flip through the marriage manuals in the self-help section of your local bookstore, you will find, she tells us, a recurring scenario. The couple is in the marriage counselor's office; he says she won't have sex with him; she says he won't talk; the counselor says they should both get to know each other better. Vogler points out that this is not very helpful advice, because it is obvious, if you take a closer look, that the couple being counseled know each other rather too well. They have, she says, "so profound a knowledge of their spouses' selves that they can silence or push them to the breaking point with the simplest of gestures." This knowledge, and the insistence on it, is a source of marital misery: " 'I'm like this,' 'you're like that,' 'you never,' 'I always,' 'you always,' 'I never,' that sort of thing . . . the problem is [one of] being too much in the grip of an artificially solid sense of one's self (and its history and interests) and too attached to one's view of one's spouse's (equally solid, equally trackable) self " (ST, 329f, 365). Vogler's suggestion is that what each of the "case-study spouses" really wants is the very opposite of that: activities in which they are not held responsible to their self-definitions, which the men stereotypically look for in sex, and the women in talk.

Talk in the theoretical genre of philosophy can, Vogler further suggests, take either of these forms:

> Think about the difference between the sort of intellectual conversation where interlocutors lay out positions, deploy their stock of argumentative tactics in defending themselves, attempt to act as though they already have thought about what anyone has to say on some subject, and, unsurprisingly, even if things go splendidly, leave with no more than something new to say on behalf of the view they held from the start.

This is, on Vogler's view, a lot like the joyless, deadlocked marriages we find in the self-help books, and notice what is going on: a philosophical self that is overly invested in the opinions that make it up has become artificially solid by having opinions that are too rigidly tied down.

> Contrast this with the sort of intellectual conversation where instead you pose questions that none of you knows how to answer, or discuss hunches without already knowing how to develop and defend them, where you might be surprised by what gets said and where you sometimes even lose track of who said what. (ST, 341)

This would be philosophy that looks like a playful erotic relationship, the kind that doesn't need first aid from a marriage counselor because the participants are so preoccupied with insisting on who they are.

The business of constructing philosophical personae can take both of these forms as well, and I am proposing that we see Nozick as trying to produce a persona that stands to the exemplars of the tradition roughly as the intellectual conversation that Vogler admires stands to a public lecture by the entrenched defender of a position. His strategy for producing a persona that is not artificially solid is one that the comparison cases we have just glanced at might have suggested: to avoid tying down the theoretical elements that are the constituents of the representation we have in front of us. Vogler casts Nozick as "the villain of [her] piece" (ST, 331), largely because of the way the solid self figures in his account of sexuality. But while Nozick may have what Vogler regards as all the wrong views when the topic is sex, he should count as one of her saints when the topic is talk.[31]

5

Let's upgrade Vogler's notion of solidity from metaphorical to literal by distinguishing the *articulation* of a self from the *commitment* to a self. To articulate a self is merely to present it, for instance by describing it; commitment makes it possible to be *held* to the description. Now, arguments and opinions are, in the normal run of things, commitment-laden: to believe that p is to have assumed a set of commitments, most familiarly, to the consequences of p, but also to having arrived at p in an appropriate way.[32] Philosophers often treat having a belief as having to defend it, perhaps because a belief gives you a very special kind of stake in its propositional object: if you believe that p, then if p is true, you are *right*, and if p is false, you are *wrong*.[33] All in all, this normally means that a character made up for the most part of beliefs and arguments for them is adopting a defensive posture (though widespread allegiance to the dictum that the best defence is a good offence can sometimes make that hard to see). Its arguments must be defended, the reliability of its modes of acquiring beliefs more generally must be defended, and the beliefs themselves must be defended. A persona made up primarily of beliefs and arguments will be not just articulated, but heavily committed.

However, while the materials out of which Nozick constructs his persona are indeed theoretical (that is, they have their first home in the activity of theorizing), they are for the most part "questions, distinctions, [and] explanations" (EL, 12). There are hardly any arguments, and there are not nearly as many beliefs as one might expect. Where other philosophers go in for insisting on the truth of their claims, Nozick is happy simply to *entertain* one thought or another, and here is a sampling of his characteristic substitutes for the more usual Fregean assertion sign: "My guess – no better than anyone else's…" (EL, 23); "I tend to one-quarter think…"; "I sometimes wonder if…" (EL, 24); "I want to say…" (EL, 132); "Perhaps…Or perhaps…" (EL, 36); "This does not get the concept exactly right, yet I don't know how important it is to get this right" (EL, 46); "While this strikes me as so, it is less clear why it is so" (EL, 92).

Nozick is not just damping down the assertoric force of his thoughts; he is restricting their range:

> I used to think it important, when I was younger, to have an opinion on just about every topic: euthanasia, minimum-wage legislation, who would win the next American League pennant, whether Sacco and/or Vanzetti were guilty – you name it. … Now I find it very easy to say I don't have an opinion on something and don't need one either. … (EL, 17)

So it is not surprising that *The Examined Life* does not give us as much in the way of the author's beliefs as most of us have become accustomed to. By saying that, I do not mean that the author is being insincere, or disingenuous, or cagey, nor do I mean that there are no (or even only a few) assertions to be found in the book. Rather, there is again a kind of parity between others and oneself: if one has not tied down one's opinions with arguments suitable for defending them to others, one is not forced to continue to believe those opinions against one's own will, either. A persona composed primarily of ideas entertained can keep its commitments to the barest minimum, and this is how Nozick manages to articulate a persona without assuming much in the way of commitment to it.

The strategy I am attributing to Nozick dictates the departure from the norms of scholarly writing that I remarked on at the outset. Adopting the academic prose style generates a large and complicated set of commitments: not to retract the claims one is making, but to support them if they are challenged, using the moves and methods accepted in one's discipline; to ensure that one's claims are jointly consistent; not simply to try ideas on for size but instead to marshal evidence for one's theses; and so on. Writing in the academic style also implies a commitment to staying in it; because the academic prose style is above all *controlled*, and because the implicit disciplinary strictures to which one thereby subjects oneself are nothing if not elaborate, this means maintaining a state of high tension over the course of one's published output. Sloughing off the style avoids all of this, and in particular makes it practically possible to mull over claims about which one is unabashedly tentative.

What I called the genre's characteristic direction of persuasion is still in place – it is the thoughtful tone of voice, for instance, that is supposed to get Nozick's ideas a hearing – but the tentativeness with which the views are advanced means that Nozick is not insisting that the reader end up endorsing those ideas himself. *The Examined Life*'s intentions with regard to its audience are not primarily *persuasive*. To make something else more real can be a way of becoming more real oneself, in roughly the way that being involved in an important historical event can make one derivatively more important.[34] So bringing others to do what *The Examined Life* shows Nozick doing would, by making them more real, make Nozick himself still more real (and I take it that this is the account that *The Examined Life* is providing of its own publication).[35] However, while getting others to mull over their lives may mean getting them to think about roughly the range of issues that Nozick is taking up, it does not mean getting them to think the same things about those issues. On the contrary, one should expect properly done self-portraits of different people to end up looking *different*. Evidently, the pedagogical point of the work is not to impart Nozick's beliefs to his audience (or more generally, to convey information of any kind) but, rather, to prod the audience into (what will start out as) a certain kind of theoretical activity. The incentive (and here is the characteristic direction of persuasion once again) is given by exhibiting someone who in doing it is clearly having a lot of *fun*.

I earlier claimed that one has to hold off on criticism of the theoretical elements of a philosophical persona until one knows how they function in it. Lack of tight argumentation, which I remarked on at the outset, has turned out to be an asset rather than a liability, and so has the writing style that made it so hard for professional philosophers to swallow. Not having to have arguments for one's views, and more generally not having to discipline one's written self-presentation in the way demanded by scholarly convention, is continuous with a more relaxed attitude toward oneself and toward one's autobiographical project, in roughly the way that one personality trait can be continuous with another.[36]

Character continuity can be more or less tight, and just as a persona may, for one reason or another, forgo consistency in its views, so it may forgo various degrees of narrative or character consistency. The more usual stance in the personal tradition is that of maximal commitment, as in Nietzsche's criterion of "eternal recurrence": be so absolutely committed to every detail of your life that you would be willing to relive it without change infinitely many times. It is worth noting, however, that Nozick is not the first to adopt the opposing posture; most notably, Montaigne similarly circumscribes his commitment to the personality he presents, and perhaps this is why, early on in *The Examined Life*, Nozick puts Montaigne's *Essays* among "the very few books that set out what a mature person can believe" (EL, 15).

I earlier suggested that personae need to be compelling because they are overextended; the protagonist of *The Examined Life* sidesteps the problem by keeping the undertaking manageable.[37] First, Nozick distances himself from the perfectionists who

> give the impression that they would give up their lives to avoid the *slightest* falling short from their very highest ideals. I . . . would choose to give up my life to avoid sinking to the very *lowest* level – I certainly hope I would – perhaps also to avoid falling some considerable distance, but I would not, I think, do this simply to avoid the slightest falling from the very highest ideals. (EL, 255f)

Second, even though the persona we are being shown is not distinct from the philosopher who is constructing it, it is a one-book project, rather than a whole life or literary output, and here is how.

There are two ways to understand what Nozick is doing. First, when one is constructing a persona out of beliefs in which one is fully invested, to change one's mind about something is, literally, to change one's mind. But Nozick's less brittle persona can leave its old thoughts, and move on to entertain new and different ones, without falling out of character. The demands the persona makes on its author are much less exacting than usual, and for that reason the author need not find the persona he is constructing compelling. The second way to see its lack of rigidity is as producing a character that it's easy to leave behind. A character that is easy to leave behind is one that doesn't compel you, and since others can leave it behind in the just same way – by going on to entertain different thoughts – it will not be compelling to others, either. The looseness in the composition we are considering is not just a way out of *having* to be compelling; it is a way of not *being* compelling as well.

6

Because there is so little to which Nozick is willing to be held, he does not need to be monitored by an enchanted audience, and he does not need to maintain an ongoing motivational state of emergency. He can, that is, afford not to be compelling, and this allows him to sidestep the problem we saw dogging the tradition. *The Examined Life* does not need (or have) groupies, and it does not need to be propelled by narcissistic motivations. Nozick's alternative is worth careful attention from those who are in the course of getting their own philosophical personae up and running.

Nozick's solution, however, comes at a price, that of being uncompelling. While I am not myself inclined to undertake a philosophical project of this kind (I prefer theory, thank you very much), I like my philosophy, of whatever sort, compelling or, if you like, "coercive." So I want to wrap up by considering whether there is a way to have a persona that is compelling but does not take on the cluster of unappealing traits that we identified as the problem. Since I also have very little patience for philosophers' attempts to eroticize their relations to their audiences, the question I would most like to see addressed is whether we can have a character that compels without relying on fascination.

Philosophy at its inception positioned itself over against rhetoric by distinguishing logical from merely psychological persuasion. One aspect of the contrast is where responsibility for failure is located: if I am a rhetorician, and my flowery language fails to persuade my audience, the failure is mine; but if I am a philosopher presenting a good argument, and I fail to persuade my audience, the failure is theirs. The turn to fascination is a mistake because it settles for being *psychologically* compelling, where only being *logically* compelling will do; in surrendering the distinction between the two forms of persuasion, it surrenders the original high ground of philosophy. So the issue the personal tradition needs to face is whether there is a way in which a persona can be compelling that is something like the way a good argument can be.

I think there have been occasional experiments along these lines. For instance, Kierkegaard sets up the pseudonymous author of the *Concluding Unscientific Postscript* for ridicule; as you read along, laughing at how silly he is, you are suddenly supposed to realize that *you* are like *that*; the realization is supposed to be accompanied by a cringe; and the cringe is supposed to propel you into the next of Kierkegaard's "stages." The point here is that if, on coming to the realization, you fail to experience the cringe, you are (supposed to be) making a *mistake*: the failure will be yours, analogously to the way that, when you fail to draw the conclusion from a sound and valid argument, the failure is yours. I am not sure what I think about Kierkegaard's attempts at personae that are not merely psychologically compelling; so instead, let me return to the more straightforward case that we have in front of us.

One way that a persona can be compelling without necessarily being fascinating comes in for mention in *The Examined Life*: A philosophical life may succeed in "prov[ing] that a certain way of being really is possible" (EL, 255). For instance, a Stoic might, by his actions and demeanor, make it completely convincing – but not by *argument* – that one can bring oneself to care only about those things under one's control, and that a life so lived has something to recommend it. Now, if I am right, *The Examined Life* can be treated as a demonstration of this kind: that it is possible to compose a philosophical persona that does not work by fascinating either its own author or its audience. And if that is correct, then perhaps the Robert Nozick that it presents us with is a compelling character, after all.

Notes

[1] New York: Simon and Schuster / Touchstone, 1989; I'll cite it by EL and page number. I'll also give abbreviated citations for two other books by Nozick: PE for *Philosophical Explanations* (Cambridge, Mass.: Harvard University Press, 1981), and SP for *Socratic Puzzles* (Cambridge, Mass.: Harvard University Press, 1997).

See Bernard Williams, *Plato: The Invention of Philosophy* (New York: Routledge, 1999). For this way of reading Nietzsche, see Alexander Nehamas, *Nietzsche: Life as Literature* (Cambridge, Mass.: Harvard University Press, 1985). For Socrates, Montaigne, and Foucault, see Nehamas, *The Art of Living: Socratic Reflections from Plato to Foucault* (Berkeley: University of California Press, 1998), cited as AL, below. For Nehamas, see Lanier Anderson and Joshua Landy, "Philosophy as Self-Fashioning: Alexander Nehamas's Art of Living" (unpublished manuscript); they attribute to Nehamas a view, which they also endorse, that Plato belongs to this tradition as well. For Cavell, see Stanley Cavell, *A Pitch of Philosophy: Autobiographical Exercises* (Cambridge, Mass.: Harvard University Press, 1994).

I do not, of course, mean to suggest that every philosopher falls neatly into one tradition or the other. Some philosophers work to one degree or another in both, and some philosophy goes in other directions entirely.

[2] EL, p. 96; see also similar remarks on pp. 144, 157, 158, 184, 185 and 264n.

[3] EL, p. 192; compare "a kind of value philosophers call 'intrinsic value' " at EL, p. 91, and similar gestures on pp. 80, 92 and 96.

[4] EL, p. 13; the portrait is explicitly claimed as a self-portrait at EL, p. 12.

[5] EL, pp. 129–131; chs. 12–18. Nozick remarks of the latter discussion that it "contains strange and sometimes bewildering pieces of theorizing, very much against the grain of contemporary philosophy. Omitting it would save me much

grief from the current philosophical community – writing it has already cost me uneasiness" (EL, 184). Nozick's treatment of the topic does indeed occasion squeamishness on the part of members of the trade; however, it might help to think of it not, in the first place, as metaphysics in the usual sense, but as the specification of an end or ideal (EL, 210).

[6] "Sex and Talk," *Critical Inquiry*, 24, Winter 1998, pp. 328–65, note 41; cited henceforth as ST. For a short piece that makes the distinction between an actual author and a distinct implied author of the same name, see "Fiction" (SP, 313–16). There the actual author is distinguished, not in a very principled manner, from the implied author and from the narrator as "the Robert Nozick . . . who attended P.S. 165."

[7] EL, p. 12; see also Nozick's discussion, at pp. 39f, of the ways in which a creative work is a surrogate for its creator. For "constitution," see EL, p. 128; Nozick gives a supporting account of how the self is constituted at EL, pp. 144–50. He remarks that "when we guide our lives by our own pondered thoughts, then it is *our* life that we are living, not someone else's" (EL, 15); on the supporting account, that could be strengthened to: our life, rather than hardly anybody's.

[8] Nozick's is not the only project that needs personae that are identical with persons. The tradition we are considering has had the ambition of providing models or exemplars; these are meant to be models for one's *life*. If the result of engaging in such a project were inevitably to produce a *representation* of a life, rather than an actual life, the most-touted point of providing such models would be lost. For an overview of the relevant ambitions in an earlier period of the tradition, see Pierre Hadot, *Philosophy as a Way of Life*, trans. Michael Chase (Malden, Mass.: Blackwell, 1995).

These considerations also speak against interposing Nehamas's distinction between the "postulated author" and the "writer". For the distinction, see Nehamas, "Writer, Text, Work, Author," in J. Cascardi (ed.), *Literature and the Question of Philosophy* (Baltimore, Md.: Johns Hopkins, 1987), pp. 267–91; "The Postulated Author: Critical Monism as a Regulative Ideal," *Critical Inquiry*, 8, Autumn 1981, pp. 133–49.

[9] I find it very interesting that this objection has come up repeatedly in the case of a living author, whom we can presumably compare to the texts. But this is not the occasion to engage the broader questions the objection raises.

[10] Compare the way in which one can make the mistake of thinking of photographs as the artworks to be assessed, when in fact they are only elements of a space installation. (For an example, in an installation which is itself meant as background for further activities, see Gabriele Juvan's Five Cities Project, described in "Die grosse Welt ein kleines Zuhause," *Weiner Zeitung*, 149, August 4/5, 2000.)

[11] I'll briefly discuss an indication of what Nozick takes his own medium to be in note 19, below.

[12] *The Examined Life* does not endorse this model; see EL, pp. 187ff.

[13] The relevant notion of representation is much closer to one that crops up in the ideology of European royalty, where portraits of the monarch were sometimes understood to be manifestations and extensions of the royal presence. For a careful

and detailed account of how one such representation worked, see Amy Schmitter, "Picturing Power: Representation and *Las Meninas*," *Journal of Aesthetics and Art Criticism*, 54(3), Summer 1996, pp. 255–68. Spaulding Grey's well-known monologues are an interesting variation on the theme: one wants to say that, rather than the representation being part of the life, the life, used as background and stage prop, has been incorporated into the representation. (I'm grateful to Lanier Anderson for pointing out this example.)

[14] For two very different biographical treatments, see Richard Ellmann, *Oscar Wilde* (New York: Vintage, 1988), and Neil Bartlett, *Who Was That Man? A Present for Mr Oscar Wilde* (Baltimore, Md.: Serpent's Tail, 1989). The claim that Wilde's project was unphilosophical needs qualification. There are points at which Wilde's project does take on a philosophical tone: for example, his criterion for being a successful work of art, which invokes the secondary qualities it makes perceptually available. For the most part, however, the characterization stands; although Wilde is perhaps the best case we have of someone living out the ethical views that Nehamas has attributed to Nietzsche, he himself was neither philosophically trained nor interested in philosophical questions.

[15] EL, p. 137; cf. pp. 130, 132. By way of preempting the response that the overall organization of the different qualities must be an aesthetic matter, note that Nozick is explicit as to what that organization is: a 4 by 4 by 3 matrix (EL, 193–7). While he does allow that matrices can serve aesthetic functions (EL, 184), it would be uncharitable to take the primary point of the project to be aesthetic.

[16] AL, pp. 3, 6. Nehamas does not take up the issue himself because he does not think it is one: "the essence of philosophy . . . ," he tells us, "does not, in any case, exist" (AL, 4).

[17] If Hadot, *Philosophy*, can be relied on, during the Hellenistic period the priority relations between the two genres were very much the other way around.

[18] On this point, see Williams, *Plato*, pp. 18f.

[19] EL, p. 254; compare EL, p. 16. Nozick is discussing what he calls "spiritual teachers," and his list of examples, variants on which appear throughout the book, includes Buddha, Socrates, Jesus, and Gandhi, but not Nietzsche, Wittgenstein, and so on. I think the right explanation for the fact that Nozick's list does not include the other philosophers that I have mentioned is that he takes living an exemplary life and constructing a merely literary persona to be very different projects. Wrapping up a paper called "Socratic Puzzles," Nozick says: "Socrates teaches with his person. Buddha and Jesus did as well. Socrates is unique among philosophers in doing this" (SP, 154). And elsewhere he provides a roughly Gricean account of what it is to teach with one's life, but does not extend the account to cover literary constructs (PE, 574–8). We have here a further reason for identifying the author of *The Examined Life* with the character it presents.

[20] Presenting oneself as inconsistent is not that unusual in the tradition: "A foolish consistency is the hobgoblin of little minds" ("Self-Reliance," in *Selections from Ralph Waldo Emerson*, ed. Stephen Whicher [Boston: Houghton Mifflin, 1960], p. 153); "This is a record of . . . irresolute and, when it so befalls,

contradictory ideas. . . . So, all in all, I may indeed contradict myself now and then" (Donald Frame, trans., *The Complete Essays of Montaigne* [Stanford: Stanford University Press, 1958], III:2, p. 611).

[21] As does Nozick: EL, pp. 15, 24, 28.

[22] See Ludwig Wittgenstein, *Philosophical Investigations*, 3rd ed., trans. G. E. M. Anscombe (Oxford: Blackwell, 1958), §§133, 254f, 309. There also have been attempts to cure ailments one might reasonably think were far more urgent than this one; see Martha Nussbaum's discussion of Hellenistic philosophy in *The Therapy of Desire* (Princeton, N.J.: Princeton University Press, 1994). (Her scathing review of Nehamas suggests, however, that Nussbaum would object to being linked in any way to the tradition we're discussing: "The Cult of the Personality," *New Republic*, Jan. 4/11, 1999, pp. 32–7.)

[23] Here is Nehamas: "The self presented by the[se] philosophers . . . can function as an example that others, depending on their own views and preferences, can either imitate or avoid . . . follow, ignore or deny as they form their own selves" (AL, 3).

For another version of the idea that persons make better instruction than impersonally presented theories, see Søren Kierkegaard, *The Point of View for My Work as An Author*, trans. Walter Lowrie, ed. Benjamin Nelson (New York: Harper and Row, 1962), pp. 40, 44f.

[24] There is a standard puzzle in the literature regarding the Socratic technique, and one on which Nozick has elsewhere made an attempt: what guarantees that applying the elenchus will bring you around to the truth (SP, 145–55)? If I am right, however, Socrates was not particularly interested in having such a guarantee, because his concern was not so much the impersonal truth as whether his interlocutors could live up to what a Brandomian might nowadays call their inferential commitments. And if this was his primary interest, the elenchus was an entirely appropriate method.

[25] Nietzsche insists that his inquiry is into the value of values, and so you might expect him to tell you just what is so bad about *ressentiment*, anyway. (It is not something he should just be taking for granted.) The answer he puts on the table is yet another piece of personal criticism: that it is caused by, or part of, being *sick*. That answer has come in for criticism on the part of one of Nietzsche's most famous followers, Michel Foucault, who in *Madness and Civilization* (New York: Vintage, 1988) sketches a genealogy of mental illness, that is, of the idea that a psychological condition could be a medical problem.

[26] *The Claim of Reason* (New York: Oxford University Press, 1999).

[27] Søren Kierkegaard, *Concluding Unscientific Postscript to Philosophical Fragments*, trans. and ed. David Swenson and Walter Lowrie (Princeton, N.J.: Princeton University Press/American-Scandinavian Foundation, 1944), p. 149.

[28] Those who work in the genre vary in how effectively they are able to develop and use this kind of resource. One problem is that followers may lack the temerity to correct their exemplar, and that the hierarchical relationship is not conducive to the exemplar's heeding corrections. Here we will see a selection effect at work: The more a practitioner is able to respond to feedback from his disciples, the tighter, more elaborate, and more memorable the resulting persona will be.

Even when actual corrections are not being offered or used, the sense of performing before an audience may be invaluable, and while many of the practitioners of this mode of philosophy develop followings in their lifetimes, for some an entirely imaginary audience of future disciples seems to suffice. (For an early variation on the device of the imaginary audience, see Hadot, *Philosophy*, p. 135.)

[29] One might well be uncomfortable here; on the usual way of thinking, presenting someone with arguments is giving them an opportunity to make up their minds on the basis of reasons rather than rhetoric. That is, what to Nozick looks like coercion can also look like a way of respecting the rational autonomy of one's interlocutors. (I'm grateful to Alice Crary for suggesting this version of the worry.) I will touch on this issue again toward the end of this chapter, but note in the meantime that the turn to persona construction is not infrequently the consequence of disillusionment with theory and argument – as in the case of Wittgenstein, whose mode of engaging theory is to try to expunge it.

[30] Op. cit.; see note 6, above.

[31] I earlier suggested characterizing relations between philosophical personae and their audiences as often eroticized; we can ask whether something like that is going on in *The Examined Life*. Determining whether a relationship is erotic might seem to require having a theory of the erotic, and as I have remarked, this is one subject on which I do not have a theory to hand. There is, however, a way around the requirement. The Nozick persona is, to borrow a term from Vogler, heteronormative, and in the ideology of heteronormativity, eros is identified with heterosexual romantic love. *The Examined Life* spends two chapters on that subject; it is as much as anything Nozick's willingness to announce to his reader what he thinks about sex and romantic love that explains the discomfort *The Examined Life* causes many of its readers. So we ought to be able to use Nozick's treatment of it to arrive at a view as to whether, by his own lights, the presentation of his persona counts as an erotic endeavor.

In the course of his discussion, Nozick runs through a longish list of characteristic features of romantic love, and it would be counterproductive to survey them all. One of these, however, receives the greatest emphasis: a defining feature of romantic love is, on Nozick's view, the desire to form a "we" – a sort of joint person whose interests, scope for decision making and mode of agency differ from those of its human components. But forming a "we" with the reader is quite clearly not part of the project; there is no invitation to do anything that looks like merging biographies or selves; and while considering models for his project, he makes a point of reminding the reader that "[t]he author's voice is never our own, exactly; the author's life is never our own" (EL, 15). Nozick does use the authorial "we" (or "our," in the quote above), discussing, for example, what we would care about. But he moves to preempt the joint-person reading of the pronoun: "When I use 'we' in this way, I am inviting you to examine whether or not you agree. If you do, then I am elaborating and exploring our common view, but if . . . you do not . . . , then I am traveling alone for a while" (EL, 100).

[32] For the first kind of commitment, see Robert Brandom, *Making It Explicit* (Cambridge, Mass.: Harvard University Press, 1994). For the second, see my *Practical Induction* (Cambridge, Mass.: Harvard University Press, 1997), ch. 2.

[33] For this last point, presented as an analysis of belief, see Arthur Collins, *The Nature of Mental Things* (Notre Dame, Ind.: University of Notre Dame Press, 1987).

[34] EL, p. 173ff; cf. also EL, p. 155.

[35] Notice that what matters here is, again, the *actual* effect on his readers. If *The Examined Life* were to acquire a following whose members were thereby *less* real than they had been (perhaps because they were simply parroting what they thought were its doctrines), Nozick would not be in a position to write such results off as collateral damage.

[36] That is not meant as a stab at necessary or sufficient conditions. The tradition provides examples both of characters who claim to have no philosophical views, but who are as overcommitted as it gets (the later Wittgenstein, for instance), and of characters (such as Montaigne) who deploy arguments and announce beliefs without being committed to much at all.

[37] There may be other ways off the beaten path. The motivational burden taken up in the standard case by absorption with oneself might be replaced by the focus on some external locus of concern; Kierkegaard's rather picturesque version of this was a sense that God was looking over his shoulder as he wrote (*Point of View*, pp. 67f).

10 The Meanings of Life

*DAVID SCHMIDTZ**

APOLOGY

I remember being a child, wondering where I would be – wondering *who* I would be – when the year 2000 arrived. I hoped I would live that long. I hoped I would be in reasonable health.

I would not have guessed I would have a white collar job, or that I would live in the United States. I would have laughed if you had told me the new millennium would find me giving a public lecture on the meaning of life. But that is life, unfolding as it does, meaning whatever it means. I am grateful to be here. I also am simply amazed.

I am forty-four. Not old, but old enough that friends and family are beginning to provide more occasions for funerals than for weddings. Old enough to love life for what it is. Old enough to see that it has meaning, even while seeing that it has less than I might wish.

I am an analytic philosopher. Analytic philosophers are trained to spot weaknesses in arguments. Unfortunately, that sort of training does not prepare us for questions about life's meaning. A perfect argument, Robert Nozick suggests in jest, would leave readers with no choice but to agree

* Professor of Philosophy and joint Professor of Economics, University of Arizona, Tucson, AZ 85721–0027, schmidtz@u.arizona.edu (http://w3.arizona.edu/~phil/faculty/dschmidtz.htm).

This paper was first presented at the Boston University Institute for Philosophy and Religion in December 1999, and later at the universities of Arizona, British Columbia, Cape Town, and North Carolina (Chapel Hill). A transcript of the talk appears in Boston University Studies in Philosophy and Religion, vol. 22, *If I Should Die*, edited by Leroy S. Rouner (South Bend, Ind.: University of Notre Dame Press, 2001).

I thank the University of Arizona, the Social Philosophy and Policy Center at Bowling Green State University, and the Centre for Applied Ethics at the University of British Columbia for supporting my research. Thank also to Daniel Amoni, Julia Annas, Dorit Bar-On, Carrie-Ann Biondi, Pamela J. Brett, David Chalmers, Dan Dahlstrom, Peter Danielson, Walter Glannon, Kristen Hessler, Tom Hill, Keith Lehrer, Chris Malony, Wayne Norman, Lee Rouner, Paul Russell, Geoff Sayre-McCord, Holly Smith, Kyle Swan, and Teresa Yu for generous and thoughtful reflections on the topic. And I thank Elizabeth Willott, not so much for the paper as for the life that enabled me to write it.

with the conclusion.[1] When we think about life's meaning, though, we are not trying to win a debate. Success in grappling with the question is less like articulating and defending a position and more like growing up.[2] Perhaps that is why academics have written so little on the meaning of life, despite it being arguably the central topic of philosophy.[3] Speaking to analytic philosophers about life's meaning would be like stepping into a boxing ring in search of a dance partner. Or so we fear.

Perhaps there is no excuse for venturing into an area where we cannot meet our usual standards. More likely, one way of respecting philosophical standards is by not trying to apply them when they are not apt, thus refusing to let them become a straitjacket – a caricature of intellectual rigor. So, I do not here seek the kind of argumentative closure that we normally think of as the hallmark of success in analytic philosophy. This chapter is simply an invitation to reflect. I try to get closer to some real (even if inarticulate) sense of life's meaning by reflecting on what it has been like to live one.

WHAT THE SAGE KNEW ABOUT THE LIMITS OF MEANING

In *Philosophical Explanations*, Nozick says the question of life's meaning is so important to us and leaves us feeling so vulnerable that,

> we camouflage our vulnerability with jokes about seeking for the meaning or purpose of life: A person travels for many days to the Himalayas to seek the word of an Indian holy man meditating in an isolated cave. Tired from his journey, but eager and expectant that his quest is about to reach fulfillment, he asks the sage, "What is the meaning of life?" After a long pause, the sage opens his eyes and says, "Life is a fountain." "What do you mean life is a fountain?" barks the questioner. "I have just traveled thousands of miles to hear your words, and all you have to tell me is that? That's ridiculous." The sage then looks up from the floor of the cave and says, "You mean it's not a fountain?" In a variant of the story, he replies, "So it's not a fountain."[4]

The sage feels none of the angst that led the seeker to the cave. So, who's missing something: sage or seeker? The story suggests a contrast of attitudes. I'll call them Existentialist and Zen, meaning only to gesture at the traditions these names evoke. The Existentialist attitude is that life's meaning, or lack thereof, is of momentous import. We seek meaning. If we don't get it, we choose between stoicism and despair. The Zen attitude is that meaning isn't something to be sought. Meaning comes to us, or not. If it comes, we accept it. If not, we accept that too. To some degree, we choose how much meaning we need. Perhaps the sage achieves peace by learning not to need meaning. Perhaps that's what we're meant to learn from the sage's seemingly meaningless remark that life is a fountain.

The Existentialist insight, in part, is that meaning is something we give to life. We do not find meaning so much as throw ourselves at it. The Zen insight, in part, is that worrying about meaning may itself make life less meaningful than it might have been. Part of the virtue of the Zen attitude lies in learning to not need to be busy: learning there is joy and meaning and peace in simply being mindful, not needing to change or be changed.[5] Let the moment mean what it will.

Nozick concludes the section with another story.

A man goes to India, consults a sage in a cave and asks him the meaning of life. In three sentences, the sage tells him, the man thanks him and leaves. There are several variants of this story also: In the first, the man lives meaningfully ever after; in the second he makes the sentences public so that everyone then knows the meaning of life; in the third, he sets the sentences to rock music, making his fortune and enabling everyone to whistle the meaning of life; and in the fourth variant, his plane crashes as he is flying off from his meeting with the sage. In the fifth version, the person listening to me tell this story eagerly asks what sentences the sage spoke. And in the sixth version, I tell him.[6]

Another joke? What are we meant to imagine happening next? What does Nozick the fictional character say? Nozick the author never tells us, unless we read the book's final seventy pages as Nozick's effort to imagine what we might extract from the sage's three sentences. The story leads us to expect some sort of joke, but it would not be a joke if an analytically trained sage were to say:[7]

"Your ambiguity is a form of self-indulgence. Figure out your real question; then you will have the beginnings of an answer. The ambiguity of the word 'life' is a problem. If you ask for the meaning of all 'Life' then your question is like asking for the (singular) meaning of all words. There is no such thing. It is particular words and particular lives that have or can have meanings.

"If you seek the meaning of a particular life (yours, say) then I will not tell you life is a fountain. Instead, I will invite you to reflect on what it has been like to live your life, and on what it will be like to carry on from here. You may conclude that meaning comes from spending time with your family rather than at the office.[8] (On their deathbeds, people often wish they had spent less time at the office; they never wish they had spent more.) Or, you may conclude that if you are to find meaning when you go back to your suburban life, it will be because you create it there – not only in virtue of what you choose but also in virtue of how you attend to what you choose – and no lifestyle ensures you will successfully undertake such creation.

"As with the ambiguity of 'life,' the ambiguity of 'meaning' is a problem. Questions about life's meaning often are synonymous with questions about life's value. Not always. By analogy, if the subject were an abstract painting, its meaning and its value would be different (though probably related) topics. Or, when you ask about life's meaning, your question may be less about what makes life good and more about what makes life significant – what purpose is served by living it. You may even feel a need for such purpose to be granted to you by some outside agency. If so, you may want to reconsider, for the life of a cow on a factory farm has that kind of purpose. An externally given purpose is neither necessary nor sufficient for the kind of meaning you appear to want.[9] What you really want is a purpose you can embrace as your own, but also one that will be recognizable as a real purpose independently of the fact that you embraced it as such.

"You would not be satisfied to learn merely that your life serves some outside purpose, so the answer to your question about life's purpose becomes: What purpose do you want? If there is a certain purpose you want your life to have, then consider whether you can live in a way that serves that purpose. If you can and if you do, then your life's intended purpose will be the purpose (or at least one of the purposes) your life actually serves. Of course, purpose intended and purpose actually served are different things. Part of what makes life interesting is the ongoing challenge of keeping the two in line.

"Finally, if your question about life's meaning is really an oblique request for advice on what to do with the rest of your life, so as to make it as worthwhile as possible, then the answer is to identify your most fundamental values and dedicate your life to living in a way that tracks (respects, promotes, etc.) those values. There is no key that unlocks the simple secret of how to do that. There is no recipe. There is no guarantee. It is hard work."

The thing to expect from a sage is sagacity, not revelation. A sage knows how to live well. That is not the same thing as knowing a recipe for living well. The fulfillment we are seeking when we ask about life's meaning cannot be handed to us in the form of a jingle.

I have achieved the age of mid-life crisis, an age when many begin to feel trapped in a way of life that threatens to waste their remaining years.

Although I have no sense of crisis, I still need to make an adjustment, for the struggle of youth is over and something else is taking its place. When I was fifteen, the game was to figure out what I could do with my life that I would be proud of thirty years later. Today, the game somehow is not about the future anymore. It (sometimes) feels as if the world has grown still, as if time is slowing down, and now the point is no longer to prove myself and make my place in the world but to understand the place I've made, respect the meanings it can have, and just live.

I no longer identify with the seeker, and it would be comical if I said I now identify with the sage. Yet, here I am, having agreed to speak on this topic. So, I need to think of something, knowing that if I try too hard to find the answer that will mark me as a true sage, I will look less like a sage and more like a person who is trying too hard to look like a sage.

LIMITS

There is such a thing as limited meaning. Some lives mean more than others, but the most meaningful lives are limited in their meaning. Consider a few of the ways in which life's meaning might be limited. First, meanings need not last. A life may have a meaning that truly matters but that nevertheless does not matter forever. Or we might say a particular episode – getting the highest grade in high school calculus – truly had meaning, but the meaning did not last.[10] We might accurately say, "It meant a lot at the time." Why would that not be enough? *When* would that not be enough?

Second, meanings change. Even when meaning lasts a lifetime, it is not constant. Short though life may be, it lasts long enough for its meaning to evolve. To look for meaning that does not change is to look, I suspect, for something that is at best purely formal, and at worst a mirage.

Third, meanings need not be deep. As some people use the word, a meaning is deep when it leaves no question unanswered, no longing unfulfilled. (We are tempted to scoff at ideas like "deep." Sometimes, smugness is a mask, a way of coping with fear of uncharted conceptual and emotional terrain. I do not mean to scoff.) If that is what people are longing for when they long for deep meaning, what should they do? Some longings are best handled by getting over them rather than by trying to fulfill them, and this may be an example. I do not know.

Or if deep meaning is possible, maybe life per se is not the kind of thing that can have it. Life is a cosmic accident. It is not here for a purpose. It is simply here, and that is all there is to it. A deeply worthwhile life is simply a series of mostly worthwhile – sometimes deeply worthwhile – episodes. There is meaning in life, we might say, but a life per se is just an allowance of time. Its meaning resides in how we spend it. We might wish we had more to spend, but meaning emerges from how we spend, not how much we spend.

Fourth, and finally, life is short. Would it mean more if it lasted longer? Quite possibly. By contrast, if life truly lacked meaning, making it longer would not help. Nozick asks, "If life were to go on forever, would there then be no problem about its meaning?"[11] There would still be a problem, as Richard Taylor shows in his recounting of the myth of Sisyphus.[12] Sisyphus was condemned by the gods to live forever, spending each day pushing the same stone to the top of the same hill only to see it roll back down to the bottom. The life is paradigmatically pointless, and no less so in virtue of lasting forever.

Unlike Sisyphus, of course, we are mortal. We achieve immortality of a kind by having children to carry on after we die, but Taylor says that only makes things worse. Life still "resembles one of Sisyphus' climbs to the summit of his hill, and each day of it one of his steps; the difference is that whereas Sisyphus himself returns to push the stone up again, we leave this to our children."[13] Having children is as pointless as anything if all we accomplish is to pass the same dreary struggle – the rock of Sisyphus – down through generations.

Ultimately, any impact we have is ephemeral. "Our achievements, even though they are often beautiful, are mostly bubbles; and those that do last, like the sand-swept pyramids, soon become mere curiosities, while around them the rest of Mankind continues its perpetual toting of rocks."[14] And if we did have a lasting impact? So what? As Woody Allen quips, what he wants is immortality not in the sense of having a lasting impact but rather in the sense of not dying.

So, death and the prospect of death can limit how much a life can mean. Yet, limiting life's meaning is a long way from making it altogether meaningless. As Kurt Baier observes, "If life can be worthwhile at all, then it can be so even though it is short. . . . It may be sad that we have to leave this beautiful world, but it is only so if and because it is beautiful. And it is no less beautiful for coming to an end."[15] Moreover, if looming death can affect us in ways that make life mean less, it also can affect us in ways that make life mean more, at least on a per diem basis, for if we are going to die, time becomes precious.[16] People who know they are terminally ill often seem to live more meaningfully. Though dying, they somehow are more alive. They cherish each morning, and are vividly aware of each day's passing. They see despair as a self-indulgent waste, and they have no time to waste.

I do not know why we are not all like that. I suppose something changes when the doctor actually delivers the prognosis. Our daily schedules are the result of an ongoing war between what is truly important and what is merely urgent, and that latter normally wins. Even rudimentary self-preservation often is lost in the daily blur. Before my brother was diagnosed with lung cancer, a part of him was gripped by a fantasy that the world would give fair warning: The day would come when a doctor would see a small lump on an x-ray, and Jim would have to quit smoking that very day or else the lump would turn out to be terminal cancer. Jim did quit that very day, too, but the lump was not a warning.

Commentators have treated Taylor's article as a definitive philosophical counsel of despair regarding life's meaning, but near the end of the article, Taylor offers a lovely counterpoint that seems to have gone unnoticed. Taylor says people's lives do resemble that of Sisyphus, and yet, "The things to which they bent their backs day after day, realizing one by one their ephemeral plans, were precisely the things in which their wills were deeply involved, precisely the things in which their interests lay, and there was no need then to ask questions. There is no more need of them now – the day was sufficient to itself, and so was the life."[17]

Perhaps therein lies an idea that is as close as we reasonably can come to specifying the nature of a life's meanings. There is more than one sense in which even short lives can have meaning, but for people's lives to have meaning in the sense that concerns us most is for people's wills to be fully engaged in activities that make up their lives.[18]

Taylor observes, "On a country road one sometimes comes upon the ruined hulks of a house and once extensive buildings, all in collapse and spread over with weeds. A curious eye can in imagination reconstruct from what is left a once warm and thriving life, filled with purpose.... Every small piece of junk fills the mind with what once, not long ago, was utterly real, with children's voices, plans made, and enterprises embarked upon."[19]

Where did those families go? Day after day, they bent their backs to the building of lives that appear as mere bubbles in retrospect. Yet, as Taylor goes on to say, it would be no "salvation to the birds who span the globe every year, back and forth, to have a home made for them in a cage with plenty of food and protection, so that they would not have to migrate any more. It would be their condemnation, for it is the doing that counts for them, and not what they hope to win by it. Flying these prodigious distances, never ending, is what it is in their veins to do...."[20] The point of human life likewise is to do what it is in our veins to do, knowing we have choices that migratory birds do not. The special glory of being human is precisely that we have choices. The special sadness lies in knowing there is a limit to how right our choices can be, and a limit to how much the rightness of our choices can matter.

MEDITATIONS ON MEANING

There is something wrong with lists. Lists are boring. They fail to make us stop and think. They fail to illuminate underlying structure. With misgivings, then, this section lists things that tend to go with living a meaningful life. As far as I can tell, there need be no particular feature that all meaningful lives share. Given the term's ambiguity, there probably is no such thing as the very essence of meaning. Different lives exhibit different features, and the features I discuss need not be compatible. Even features that are in some sense contraries may come together to endow a life with meanings, for a life is not a logically pristine sort of thing. To give a simple example, some things mean what they mean to me partly because of the price I paid for them. Other things mean what they do partly because they are gifts.

The first feature I will mention, though, does seem just about essential, namely that meaningful lives, in one way or another, have an impact. Most crucially, the counsel of despair typically is grounded in an observation that our lives are not of cosmic importance. Therein lies the beginning of a fundamental error. The question is not whether we can identify something (e.g., the cosmos) on which your life has no discernible impact. The question is whether there is anything (e.g., your family) on which your life *does* have a discernible impact. The counsel of despair typically is grounded in a determination to find some arena in which nothing is happening and to generalize from that to a conclusion that nothing is happening anywhere. This fundamental error seems ubiquitous in the more pessimistic contributions to the literature on life's meaning.

There are innumerable impacts your life could have but does not, and there is nothing very interesting about that. It makes no sense to stipulate that a particular impact is the kind you need to have so as to be living a meaningful life, when other kinds of impact are on their own terms worth having. If you honestly wish to find meaning, don't look where the impact isn't. Look where the impact is. Life's meaning, when it has one, is going to be as big as life, but it cannot be much bigger than that. It will not be of cosmic scope.[21]

Nozick says, "A significant life is, in some sense, permanent; it makes a permanent difference to the world – it leaves traces."[22] I wonder why. Why must the traces we leave be permanent? More generally, is it possible to try too hard to leave traces? One thing you notice about philosophers, at least the productive ones, is that hunger for leaving traces. It must be a good thing, that hunger. It makes people productive, and in producing, they leave traces. And yet, the hunger is insatiable so far as I can tell. No amount of attention is enough. We all know the kind of person – many of us *are* the kind of person – who gets upset because our reputations do not match Robert Nozick's. The few who attain that stature immediately proceed to get upset about Bertrand Russell. And so just as surely as there is something good about the hunger to leave traces, there is something bad too. Even while that hunger fuels our efforts to leave valuable traces, it leads us to overlook the value of the (impermanent) traces we actually leave.

Here are some of the other features meanings can have. Again, think of these as independent meditations. As I was writing, I had to make a choice, and it seemed more important simply to express the thought, not letting it be twisted by an overarching goal of making different thoughts fit neatly together.

1. MEANINGS ARE SYMBOLIC. Taylor recalls his experience seeing Glow Worms in New Zealand. There are caves "whose walls and ceilings are covered with soft light. As one gazes in wonder in the stillness of these caves it seems that the Creator has reproduced there in microcosm the heavens themselves, until one scarcely remembers the enclosing presence of the walls. As one looks more closely, however, the scene is explained. Each dot of light identifies an ugly worm, whose luminous tail is meant to attract insects from the surrounding darkness."[23] The worms are carnivorous, even cannibalistic. To Taylor, it epitomizes pointlessness.

I was intrigued when I read this because, by coincidence, my wife and I have been to New Zealand's Glow Worm Grotto. I cherish the memory. We got up at four in the morning so we could get there before the sun came up. We got there in time, and we were the only ones there. The cliff wraps around in a horseshoe and the walls nearly meet overhead, creating the impression of being in a cave. We knew what we were looking at, but still they were a beautiful sight – hundreds of glowing blue dots all around us, alive! Of course we find no meaning in the bare phenomenon. That's not how meaning works. Meaning is what the phenomenon symbolizes to a viewer. Elizabeth and I were there to celebrate our lives together, and that purpose gave the occasion its meaning. That we could be in New Zealand at all, that we could get up long before dawn to see something together, unlike anything we had ever seen before, and that we could be together, alone, in this grotto, thoroughly and peacefully in love, sharing this silent spectacle of glowing blue life, blown away once again by the thought of the wonders we've seen together – that's meaning. No one needed glow worms to be intrinsically meaningful (any more than ink on a page needs intrinsic meaning to be meaningful to readers). No one needed glow worm life to be meaningful to glow worms, not even glow worms themselves. That was never the point. The point was, we were capable of attributing meaning to them and to their home and to our fleeting chance to share it with them.

But perhaps you would have had to be there, or at least have had similar experiences, to understand. That, too, is meaning. Meaning isn't some measurable quantity. There is something perspectival and contextual and symbolic about it. (How could meaning be otherwise?) Taylor and I could be standing in the same place seeing the same phenomenon and the experience could be meaningful to me but not to him. That's how it works.

Had I been there by myself rather than with Elizabeth, I would have seen the same thing but it would have meant so much less. The experience meant what it did partly because I shared it with her. The day was sufficient to itself, partly because it was a symbolic microcosm of a sufficient life, but neither the day nor the life would have been sufficient without her.

2. MEANINGS AS CHOICES.   Life's meaning is contingent on how we live. As life takes one direction rather than another, so does its meaning. Does life have enough meaning? Enough for what? No fact of the matter determines whether the meaning a life has is enough. We decide. Is it worth striving to make life mean as much as it turns out lives can mean? We decide. Is it worth getting what is there to be gotten? We decide. We inevitably make up our own minds about how to measure the meanings of our lives.

What is a person? Among other things, persons are beings who choose whether to see their experiences as meaningful. By extension – I do see it as an extension – persons choose whether to see their *lives* as meaningful. The less inspiring corollary is, persons also are capable of seeing their lives, and other lives, as meaningless. We choose whether to exercise this capacity. If we do exercise it, though, we can imagine being told we have made a mistake. If it is meaningless, then so is being hung up about its meaninglessness. We may as well enjoy it.

An incurable pessimist might say that misses the point, because it is not possible to enjoy that which is pointless. But a Zen optimist rightly could respond: That's not quite true. Closer to the truth: we can't enjoy what we *insist* on *seeing* as pointless. Part of what makes life meaningful is that we are able to treat it as meaningful. We are able and willing, if all goes well, to make that Existentialist leap. (Or we simply let it be meaningful, which would be a sort of Zen leap.)

Singer John Cougar Mellencamp once titled a record album, "Nothin' matters, and what if it did?" A funny title, and it is interesting that it is funny. You see the paradox. Someone who was sufficiently depressed would not. Having acknowledged that something matters, the incurable pessimist is the one who would fail to appreciate the paradox in going on to say, "So what?"

3. MEANINGS TRACK RELATIONSHIPS.   Meaning ordinarily is not solipsistic. Typically, when our life means something to people around us, it comes to mean something to us as well, in virtue of meaning something to others. Our lives become intrinsically valuable to us by becoming intrinsically valuable to others.

Our lives also become intrinsically valuable to us by becoming *instrumentally* valuable to others. A few years ago, I joined thousands of others in trying to save a small community in Kansas from rising floodwaters, as we surrounded it with dikes made of sandbags. We failed. Had we known our efforts would have no instrumental value, it would have been pointless to proceed as we did. But so long as we thought we might succeed, the effort had an intrinsic value predicated on its hoped-for instrumental value. The effort meant something – it made a statement – because of what we were trying to accomplish.

The idea that meaning tracks the making of statements suggests we might be able to connect the rather metaphorical idea of life's meaning to meaning in a more literal sense. When we talk about meanings of words, we normally are talking about how they function in an act of communication.[24] Maybe life's meaning likewise is tied to what it communicates, to themes people read into it. If so, it seems worth noting that not all communication is intentional. Even if there's nothing we intend our life to symbolize – no statement we intend our life to make – it still can mean something, communicate something, to other people, with or without our knowledge.

The meaning that can emerge from our relationships often is something like an exchange of gifts. If my life means something to people around me, then it means something, period. What if their lives are not meaningful, though? Don't their lives need to have meaning before their lives can have the power to confer meaning on ours? If so, are we not looking at an infinite regress?

No. Not at all. We need not get the meanings of *words* from something bigger than us. Neither must we look to something bigger for meaning in our lives. We get it partly from communion with each other, just as we get the meanings of words. Meaning can be our gift to each other.[25] Or, it may be a consequence of living in a way that does justice to the gift. (No one can simply give us a meaning worth having; there has to be uptake on our part.) In any case, we need not seek meaning in some outside source. Even if our lives have meaning only because of what we mean to each other, that is still something.

4. MEANINGS TRACK ACTIVITY. The Experience Machine, described in Nozick's *Anarchy, State, and Utopia*, lets us plug our brains into a computer programmed to make us think we are living whatever we take to be the best possible life. The life we think we are living is a computer-induced dream, but we do not know that.[26] Whatever would be part of the best possible life for us (the optimal mix of wins and losses, adversities triumphantly overcome, lectures on the meaning of life – anything at all) will in fact be part of our felt experience. "Would you plug in? What else can matter to us, other than how our lives feel from the inside?"[27]

And yet, most people say they would not plug in, even though by hypothesis their felt experience would be as good as felt experience can be. The lesson appears to be that when we have all we want in terms of felt experience, we may not yet have all we want. Something is missing, and it seems fair to describe the missing something as life's meaning. Meaning is missing because activity is missing. As Nozick puts it, "we want to do certain things, and not just have the experience of doing them."[28] Nozick says we also want to be a certain kind of person, and "there is no answer to the question of what a person is like who has long been in the tank. Is he courageous, kind, intelligent, witty, loving? It's not merely that it's difficult to tell; there is no way he is."[29]

A further thought on life in the machine: The Experience Machine provides us with experiences, but not with judgments about what those experiences mean. If you plugged in, would you judge that life had meaning? That would still be up to you. Which raises a question: What experiences would you need to have in order to have *no doubts* about life's meaning? Would the best possible life leave you with time to think? If so, then by that very fact, it would leave room for doubt. Accordingly, while there is an obvious gap between subjective experience and objective meaning, there also is a more subtle gap between subjective experience and subjective judgment that experience has meaning. Plugging in creates a gap of the former kind; less obviously, it fails to close a gap of the latter kind.

Meaning also may track something related to activity, namely the making of contact with an external reality. Several years ago, my sister visited me in Tucson. I took her to the Sonoran Desert Museum just outside Tucson. At the museum is a cave. As we descended into the cave, my sister marveled at how beautiful it was. After a few minutes, though, her eyes became accustomed to the dark. She took a closer look, and reached out to touch the wall. "It isn't real. It's just concrete," she said, deflated.

Why was she disappointed? Because she thought the cave was a magically wild "other" when in fact it was an Experience Machine. If what we experience is a human artifact, intended to produce a certain experience rather than being some independent miracle of nature, that somehow cheapens the experience, at least in some contexts. Maybe the problem with the Experience Machine is not only that the experience it provides is a mere dream. It is also a dream deliberately scripted.

If you go to zoos, you have probably witnessed little kids ignoring the tigers and zebras and squealing with excitement about a ground squirrel running down the path beside them. The kids know: The squirrel is real in a way zoo animals are not. Somehow, there is more meaning, more reality, in the wild – in experiences that have not been scripted, especially by someone else.

Complications: First, if we were to plug in, we would be deluded about the nature and meaning of our real lives. We would have the subjective feel that goes with what our fantasy life *would* mean, if only it were real. Is that what we want? When people say they would not plug in, we may hesitate to take their reports at face value, because here and now, lacking the option of plugging in, we *need* to say the subjective feel is not what we are after. Why? Because if we are not convinced that our objective goals are what really matter, then why have any deep feeling of accomplishment when we achieve them? If we allow ourselves to concede that the subjective feel is what matters, we undercut the very source of the subjective feel.

Second, we may intuitively see something wrong with letting the Experience Machine cut us off from reality. As Nozick observes in a later book, however, the optimal degree of contact with reality need not be 100 percent.[30] A concentration camp prisoner who sometimes imagines he is at a concert is doing something apt for the circumstances. Evidently, the bare fact of taking a trip into the Experience Machine is not the problem. The problem arises when we fail to return. We would not be troubled to learn that a friend watches television for half an hour per day, but learning that she watches for five hours a day would tell us something has gone wrong.

MEANING AS A PERSONAL TOUCH

Nozick finds it "a puzzle how so many people, including intellectuals and academics, devote enormous energy to work in which nothing of themselves or their important goals shines forth, not even in the way their work is presented. If they were struck down, their children upon growing up and examining their work would never know why they had done it, would never know *who* it was that did it."[31]

Life is a house. Meaning is what you do to make it home. Giving life meaning is like interior decorating. It is easy to overdo it, so that the walls become too "busy." But if our walls are bare, the solution is not to spend our days stoically staring at bare walls, or philosophizing about their meaning, or lack thereof, but to put up a few photographs, making the walls reflect what we do, or care about, or making them reflect our judgment about what is beautiful or worth remembering. We need not fear bare walls. We need not deceive ourselves about their bareness. We need not dwell on the "fundamental underlying" bareness of walls we have filled with pictures. If we do that, we are not being deep. We are pig-headedly ignoring the fact that the walls are *not bare*. We are failing to take our pictures seriously, which is metaphorically to say we are failing to take seriously what we do with our lives. We are saying, what would be the meaning of this life (the wall) if the activities that make it up (the pictures) were not real? But they *are* real.

There are questions we are not good at answering. Or maybe we are not good at accepting answers for what they are. We do what we do. It means what it means. Thomas Nagel says, "justifications come to an end when we are content to have them end.... What seems to us to confer meaning, justification, significance, does so in virtue of the fact that we need no more reasons after a certain point."[32] After a point, further questions betray something like the willful incomprehension of a child who has no purpose in mind to help him see when it is time to stop asking "Why?" Meaning is in the things we do that make us who we are, the things we remember – not the wall but the pictures that adorn it over the years.

METAMORPHOSIS

Nozick's *The Examined Life* begins with an observation that we fly through life on a trajectory mostly determined before we reached adulthood. With only minor adjustments, we are directed by a picture of life formed in adolescence or young adulthood.[33] Nozick concludes that book by wondering what the fifteen-year-old Nozick would think of the person he grew up to become.[34] Interesting question. Why might we want an answer? Consider what Nozick says in an earlier book. "The young live in each of the futures open to them. The poignancy of growing older does not lie in one's particular path being less satisfying or good than it promised earlier to be – the path may turn out to be all one thought. It lies in traveling only one (or two, or three) of those paths."[35]

I believe I understand. Every day, doors click shut behind us, on paths we might have taken, on meanings life might have had. No matter. The Zen insight, in part, is that meaning emerges not from picking the right door so much as from paying attention – the right kind of attention – to whatever path we happen to be on.

Maybe it is easier for me, because the paths I envisioned when I was young were all pretty grim compared to the path I ended up on. In one of the possible worlds closest to this one, the end of the millennium finds me delivering mail in Prince Albert, Saskatchewan. The turning point in this actual world occurred almost exactly twenty years ago, when I had been a full-time mailman for nearly five years, and as I was waiting for the Post Office to transfer me from Calgary to Prince Albert. I already had bought a house. While I was waiting, though, I signed up for a night school course on Hume's *Treatise*. (After nine years of taking courses, I was near a science degree. I hoped to finish before leaving town, so as to have something to show for all those years. I needed a humanities elective, and Hume was the only option on the night school schedule.) By the time the transfer came through, later that semester, I knew I could no longer be a mailman. Had the transfer come through a couple of months earlier, or had that time slot been occupied by some other course, then as far as I know I would still be a mailman today. I would not have gone to night school; Prince Albert had none.

Being a mailman was my "dream job" as I was growing up. It was not a bad life. The only nightmarish thing about that possible world is that, from time to time, that version of me would have woken up in the middle of the night to the realization that there comes a time to be seeker, not sage, a moment not for Zen acquiescence but for hurling oneself at an unknown future. The Zen way is partly an appreciation of the danger in wanting too much, but this world's mailman saw, just in time, what a terrible thing it can be to want too little. Had I not learned that lesson when I did, I would have let the moment pass, growing old mourning for worlds that might have been, trying to love life for what it is, but not fully succeeding. So, when I contemplate versions of me that might have been, versions quite a bit more probable than the me who actually came to be, to this day there is a fifteen year old inside me that just about faints with gratitude and relief: it so easily could have been me. For a time, it *was* me. Yet, through a series of miracles, I now find myself in that barely possible world where the mailman gives a public lecture on the meaning of life.

On some philosophical topics, we reflect so as to reach a conclusion. On this topic, the reflection itself is the objective. There is no conclusion that would count as stating the meaning of life. The point of the exercise is not to articulate a proposition but to mull things over – the relations and activities and choices that make up a particular life. Peace comes from the process, not from reaching conclusions. On this topic, then, our reflections can never be more than work in progress.

One of the best things I ever did was to coach little league flag football. But if I had to explain how something so mundane could mean so much, I would not know where to begin. I could have told my players they were accidents of natural selection in a quite possibly godless world, but that bit of information was not germane to our shared task of living that part of our lives to the hilt. Year after year, four years altogether, we had a mission, my players and me, a mission that left no void needing to be filled by talk of meaning. On the contrary, life was, however fleetingly, a riot of meaning. It was as Taylor says. There was no need for questions. The day was sufficient to itself, and so was the life.

Notes

[1] Robert Nozick, *Philosophical Explanations* (Cambridge, Mass.: Belknap Press, 1981), p. 4.

[2] In Robert Nozick's words, "Give us specific problems to solve or paradoxes to resolve, sharp questions with enough angle or spin, an elaborate intellectual structure to move within or modify, and we can sharply etch a theory. . . . However, thinking about life is more like mulling it over, and the more complete understanding this brings does not feel like crossing a finishing line while still managing to hold onto the baton; it feels like growing up more." See Nozick, *The Examined Life: Philosophical Meditations* (New York: Simon and Schuster, 1989), p. 12.

[3] As a vague indication of how intimidating a topic this is, consider that the September 1999 *Philosophers Index* on CD-ROM lists only 102 entries under the topic of "meaning of life" since 1940. By way of comparison, the Index lists 3,339 works under the topic of "justice."

[4] PE, p. 571.

[5] I have learned much of what I know about the practice of meditation from Marvin Belzer. I thank him for sharing his experience and insights.

[6] PE, pp. 573–4.

⁷I thank Wayne Norman and Dorit Bar-On for conversations that led me to write this passage.

⁸Nozick (PE, 572) wonders whether this is what we think the seeker expects to hear.

⁹If Iris Murdoch is correct, "There are properly many patterns and purposes within life, but there is no general and as it were externally guaranteed pattern or purpose of the kind for which philosophers and theologians used to search. We are what we seem to be, transient mortal creatures subject to necessity and chance." See *The Sovereignty of Good* (New York: Routledge & Kegan Paul, 1970), p. 79.

¹⁰Months after writing this, not intending the example to be read autobiographically but also thinking it best not to make something up, it suddenly dawns on me what that episode actually meant to me. It was how I met my wife. Everyone expected Elizabeth to get the highest grade, and so to my adolescent mind, getting the highest grade was my best chance of attracting her attention. A silly idea, but it gave me the courage to ask her for a date.

¹¹PE, p. 579.

¹²Richard Taylor, "The Meaning of Life," *The Meaning of Life*, ed. E. D. Klemke, 2nd ed. (New York: Oxford University Press, 1999), pp. 167–75.

¹³Taylor, p. 172.

¹⁴Taylor, p. 172.

¹⁵Kurt Baier, "The Meaning of Life," *The Meaning of Life*, ed. Steven Sanders and David Cheney (Englewood Cliffs, N.J.: Prentice Hall, 1980), pp. 47–63, here p. 61.

¹⁶Nozick (PE, 579) touches on this theme, attributing the idea to Victor Frankl. Nozick cautions against making too much of this point, though, and more generally against trying too hard to "disarm the fact of death" (PE, 580).

¹⁷Taylor, p. 174.

¹⁸One way in which our lives engage us is by virtue of fitting into a larger design. But the Existentialist and Zen attitudes both presuppose that a life's meaning cannot simply derive from how it fits into a larger plan. The Existentialist attitude is that the plan must be of our own devising, and must be one in which we play an active role. The Zen attitude is that no plan is needed. The Zen way involves learning that there is no deep self that has or needs to have any particular meaning in the grand scheme of things.

In the closing essay of *Socratic Puzzles* (Cambridge, Mass.: Harvard University Press, 1997), Nozick wonders whether God's existences could acquire meaning in virtue of His creating (for no larger purpose?) the larger plan that gives meaning to the lives of His creatures.

¹⁹Taylor, p. 172.

²⁰Taylor, p. 174.

²¹Admittedly, we can imagine the following: Light streaming from here into space will one day fall upon the super-telescopes of civilizations in far-off galaxies and (via a physics unknown to us today) will be used to reconstruct pictures of life

on Earth in minute detail, such that in the discussion following this paper, the person who asks the best question will one day be revered as a god in one or more such galaxies. That might confer cosmic significance on that person's life, but such cosmic meaning would be of no consequence here.

[22] PE, p. 582.

[23] Taylor, p. 170.

[24] Not all meanings can be put into words. (I won't try to settle whether this is a limit of meanings or of words.) And philosophical arguments are only one vehicle within which words convey meanings. Poetry, for example, will not articulate a sense of life's meaning, but the function of poetry is to evoke rather than articulate. Poetry gives us a feel for life's meaning, not a description of it.

[25] Do we need a common understanding of the meanings of life? I suppose not. Givers and receivers often have differing understandings of a particular gift's meaning. It may or may not cause a problem.

[26] Nozick, *Anarchy, State, and Utopia* (New York: Basic Books, 1974), pp. 42–5.

[27] ASU, p. 43.

[28] ASU, p. 43.

[29] ASU, p. 43.

[30] EL, p. 121.

[31] PE, p. 578.

[32] Thomas Nagel, "The Absurd," *The Meaning of Life*, ed. E. D. Klemke, 2nd ed. (New York: Oxford University Press, 1999), pp. 176–85, here p. 180.

[33] EL, p. 11.

[34] EL, p. 303.

[35] PE, p. 596.

Bibliography

BOOKS BY NOZICK

Anarchy, State, and Utopia (New York: Basic Books, 1974).

Philosophical Explanations (Cambridge, Mass.: Belknap Press, 1981).

The Examined Life: Philosophical Meditations (New York: Simon and Schuster, 1989).

The Nature of Rationality (Princeton, N.J.: Princeton University Press, 1993).

Socratic Puzzles (Cambridge, Mass.: Harvard University Press, 1997). This volume collects Nozick's articles.

SELECTED COMMENTARY ON NOZICK

Barry, Norman P. *On Classical Liberalism and Libertarianism* (New York: St. Martin's Press, 1987).

Brueckner, Anthony. "Unfair to Nozick," *Analysis* 51 (1991): 61–4.

Capaldi, Nicholas. "Exploring the Limits of Analytic Philosophy: A Critique of Nozick's *Philosophical Explanations*," *Interpretation* 12 (1984): 107–25.

Cohen, G. A. *Self-ownership, Freedom, and Equality* (New York: Cambridge University Press, 1995).

Den Uyl, Douglas, and Douglas B. Rasmussen. "Nozick on the Randian Argument," *The Personalist* 59 (1978): 184–205.

Garrett, Brian J. "A Sceptical Tension," *Analysis* 59 (1999): 205–06.

Keller, Simon. "How Do I Love Thee? Let Me Count the Properties," *American Philosophical Quarterly* 37 (2000): 163–73.

LaFollette, Hugh. "Why Libertarianism Is Mistaken," in J. Arthur and W. Shaw (eds.), *Justice & Economic Distribution* (Englewood Cliffs, N.J.: Prentice Hall, 1978), pp. 194–206.

Lipson, Morris. "Nozick and the Sceptic," *Australasian Journal of Philosophy* 65 (1987): 327–34.

Luper-Foy, Steven (ed.). *The Possibility of Knowledge: Nozick and His Critics* (Totowa, N.J.: Rowman and Littlefield, 1987).

Machan, Tibor. "Nozick and Rand on Property Rights," *The Personalist* 58 (1977): 192–5.

Mack, Eric. "Nozick's Anarchism," in *Anarchism*, J. R. Pennock and J. W. Chapman (eds.) (New York: New York University Press, 1978), pp. 43–62.

Mack, Eric. "The Self-Ownership Proviso: A New and Improved Lockean Proviso," *Social Philosophy and Policy* 12 (1995): 186–218.

Megone, Christopher. "Reasoning about Rationality: Robert Nozick, *The Nature of Rationality*," *Utilitas* 11 (1999): 359–74.

Meyer, Leroy N. "Wisdom and the Well-Being of Humanity," *Contemporary Philosophy* 20 (1998): 15–18.

Miller, Fred D. "The Natural Right to Private Property," in *The Libertarian Reader*, Tibor Machan (ed.) (Totowa, N.J.: Rowman and Littlefield, 1982), pp. 275–87.

Narveson, Jan. *The Libertarian Idea* (Philadelphia: Temple University Press, 1988).

Narveson, Jan. "Libertarianism vs. Marxism: Reflections on G. A. Cohen's 'Self-Ownership, Freedom and Equality,'" *Journal of Ethics* 2 (1998): 1–26.

Narveson, Jan. "Property Rights: Original Acquisition and Lockean Provisos," *Public Affairs Quarterly* 13 (1999): 205–27.

Paul, Jeffrey (ed.). *Reading Nozick* (Oxford: Basil Blackwell, 1982).

Paul, Jeffrey. "Property, Entitlement, and Remedy," *Monist* 73 (1990): 564–77.

Smith, Tara. "Intrinsic Value: Look-Say Ethics," *Journal of Value Inquiry* 32 (1998): 539–53.

Spector, Horacio. *Autonomy and Rights: The Moral Foundations of Liberalism* (New York: Oxford University Press, 1992).

Wolff, Jonathan. *Robert Nozick: Property, Justice, and the Minimal State* (Stanford: Stanford University Press, 1991).

Index